POCKET

GUIDES

CHARLES MACLEAN

Scotch
Whisky

This book is dedicated to those who first developed in me a fondness for whisky: my father, the late A Bruce MacLean, and Charles Grant, Glenlivet (1952–73)

Scotch Whisky
Charles MacLean

First published in Great Britain in 1993 as *The Mitchell Beazley Pocket Whisky Book* by Charles MacLean. This edition, revised, updated and expanded, published in 2004 by Mitchell Beazley, an imprint of Octopus Publishing Group Limited, 2-4 Heron Quays, London E14 4JP.

A CIP catalogue record for this book is available from the British Library.

ISBN 1 84000 990 X

The author and publishers will be grateful for any information that will assist them in keeping future editions up to date. Please send such information to MacLean Dubois (Writers & Agents), Hillend House, Edinburgh EH10 7DX.

Although all reasonable care has been taken in the preparation of this book, neither the author nor the publishers can accept liability for any consequences arising from the information contained herein, or from the use thereof.

Commissioning Editor: Hilary Lumsden
Executive Art Editor: Yasia Williams
Managing Editor: Juanne Branquinho
Production: Seyhan Esen

Typeset by Intype Libra in Helvetica and Versailles

Printed and bound by Toppan Printing Company, China

Contents

Preface

Soon after the first edition of *Scotch Whisky* was published in 1993, I was approached at a book launch in Edinburgh by a distinguished-looking gentleman, who, having ascertained that I was its author, asked me bluntly if it was accurate.

I told him that it was as accurate as I could make it, taking into account marketing hyperbole and the industry's penchant for reinventing its history.

"Oh, good," he said. "I have just been appointed Director General of the Scotch Whisky Association [the industry's governing body] . . . I rely on your book utterly as I meet companies and visit distilleries, so I hope it will not cause me to shoot myself in the foot."

I was flattered by Hugh Morison's faith, although somewhat daunted by the responsibility it placed upon my text.

What I should have said was that the book was as accurate as my knowledge of the whisky industry allowed at that time. Since the first publication, I have continued to research and write about Scotch whisky. I have published eight books on the subject, talked about it on television and radio, delivered lectures, and led hundreds of tastings. This edition embodies the fruits of my increased knowledge.

My research has been aided greatly by the publication, since 1993, of two sourcebooks that have proved invaluable for checking dates and wild claims: *The Scotch Whisky Industry Record* by H. Charles Craig, and *The History of the Distillers Company 1877–1929* by Dr R.B. Wier.

I have also been lucky enough to have been asked by several whisky companies and magazines to research and write historical and promotional materials or articles, or to provide consultancy. This has allowed me to keep body and soul together while continuing my research. In this connection I should particularly like to thank Diageo PLC, The Edrington Group, the Scotch Malt Whisky Society, and *Whisky Magazine*.

The changes that have taken place in the whisky industry, even since the second edition of the book appeared in 1998, are substantial. Many companies have changed their names or changed owners; several distilleries have changed hands and been reopened; new blends have been introduced, and some established ones dropped (I have been inclined to continue to list these).

Almost every entry in this book has been adjusted. Consumption of malt whisky has doubled, and so many different bottlings have been introduced – more than five times the number available in 1993 – that I have not attempted to list them. Whisky clubs proliferate. New markets – from Russia to Taiwan, South Korea to Malaysia – continue to emerge, and negotiations with the Indian and Chinese governments to make Scotch whisky more readily available in these vast markets are progressing.

In short, at the moment the future is looking rosy for the world's greatest spirit.

Charles MacLean
June 2004
Edinburgh

www.whiskymax.co.uk

Foreword

The task I set myself in this book was to give some account of every significant brand of whisky made and bottled in Scotland. I defined "significant" as: a) every available single-malt and single-grain whisky; b) every brand of whisky blended in Scotland with a reasonable market share anywhere in the world; and c) every blended whisky with a story to tell. And the stories are abundant: generally, I have been uncritical in my inclusion of myth as well as dry fact, although I have cheerfully laid a few ghosts to rest!

My original intention was to write a comprehensive directory of Scotch whisky brands. Early in the research, it transpired that there have been in the region of 10,000 brands around at one time or another, and that merchants' lists even from ten years ago offer over two thousand brands and expressions. So I have limited myself to brands that are currently available.

There may be some interesting or "significant" brands I have missed – I apologize in advance, and hope readers and brand-owners will alert me to them. For future editions, I shall also be grateful for any additional information about the brands included in this book. The information I managed to obtain from owners and from published sources is patchy: in some cases, little or nothing is known about an individual brand; in others, marketing departments choose to be discreet, or to supply only unedifying information. The length and detail of the entries reflect to some extent the help I have had from brand-owners.

Space does not allow me to acknowledge everyone who has contributed towards the making of this book. However, I should especially like to thank the following.

First, my editorial assistant, Philip Woyka, who kept abreast of an awesome research programme (we commenced with over a thousand brands to investigate) and who made sure the book continued to progress even through periods of frustration. Second, my wife, Sheila, who detests the taste of whisky yet has endured endless whisky talk and tasting into the small hours. Third, my editors at Mitchell Beazley, past and present, whose painstaking attention to detail has ensured focus and accuracy. Fourth, and most importantly, I acknowledge a huge debt to many friends in the industry who provided me, a stranger to their ways, with encouragement, advice, and information. Space does not allow me to list them, but they know who they are.

Finally, this book would not have been possible without the support of the companies whose brands are included, to all of whom I am profoundly grateful.

How to use this book

The purpose of this book is simple: to encourage the enjoyment
and appreciation of Scotch – both single-malt (the *grands crus* of
whiskies) and blended whiskies (which account for ninety-five
per cent of Scotch consumed).

The main sections of the book are laid out alphabetically as a
directory of brands: first, Malt and Grain Whiskies (there are only
four of the latter), then Blended Whiskies (including Liqueur
Whiskies and Vatted Malts). Names given in small capitals
(*i.e. see* BELL'S) refer readers to other entries in the directory.

To understand fully some of the references in the individual
entries, I have prefaced the directory with an introduction that
comprises a brief history of Scotch and of the whisky industry, an
account of the salient features of production of the three kinds of
whisky – malt, grain, and blended – and some observations on
whisky tasting and appreciation.

The Appendices provide what I hope will be useful "support"
information: a glossary; a whisky-flavour checklist (this might be
used for practical research purposes!); a list of distilleries that
welcome visitors; details of a handful of whisky societies; a list of
whisky websites; some curious statistics about the major markets
for Scotch and the best-selling brands; something about
collecting whiskies; and a bibliography.

If this little book adds to your enjoyment of the dram in your
glass, I shall be pleased. But my hope is that you might be
sufficiently intrigued to venture forth and try whiskies with which
you are unfamiliar. Then the book will have introduced you to the
most pleasurable pursuit in the world.

A NOTE ON "PROOF SPIRIT"

Proof spirit means alcohol of tried (*i.e.* proved) strength. In early
times, 100° proof was the strength of alcohol that, when mixed
with water and gunpowder, would still allow the gunpowder to
ignite. The invention of the hydrometer allows for more precise
definition: British proof spirit is that which at 51°F (10.5°C) weighs
twelve-thirteenths of an equal volume of water at the same
temperature (*i.e.* spirit that contains 57.1 per cent alcohol by
volume).

American proof is calculated differently, and the standard is
fifty per cent alcohol at 60°F (15.5°C). So British proof spirit (i.e. at
100° proof) is equal to 114.2° proof in the US (or 14.2° over proof).
American 100° proof is the same as British 87.7° proof.

NB: *Throughout the book I have followed imperial/metric units of
measurement as appropriate.*

Introduction

A brief history of Scotch whisky

A SUBLIME REMEDY

There is a tradition that St Patrick introduced distilling to Ireland in the fifth century AD, and that the Dalriadic Scots brought the secret with them when they arrived in Kintyre around AD500. This quaint legend may hold a grain of truth, since it is certain that St Patrick brought his adoptive country into contact with Continental culture, and it is possible that the art of distilling was known in Spain and France at that time.

Taliesin, the sixth-century Welsh poet who supposedly lived in what is present-day Cumbria (where St Patrick hailed from), wrote in praise of distilled mead, but this may be a mistranslation. It is generally accepted that the secrets of distilling were perfected, if not actually discovered, by the Arabs and brought to Europe by the Moors sometime in the tenth century.

The process was originally applied to perfume, then to wine, and finally adapted to fermented mashes of cereals in countries where grapes were not abundant. The spirit was universally termed *aqua vitae* ("water of life"; in Gaelic, *uisge beatha*) and was commonly made in monasteries, for medicinal purposes. There were monastic distilleries in Ireland by the late twelfth century.

Scotland's great Renaissance king, James IV (1488–1513), was fond of "ardent spirits". The earliest written reference to distilling in Scotland dates from the Exchequer Rolls for 1494, where an entry records the sale of eight *bolls* of malt (around 1,120lb or 508kg) to one Friar John Corr, wherewith "to make *aqua vitae*", and 12 years later, when the king visited Dundee, the treasury accounts record a payment to a local barber for the supply of aqua vitae for the king's pleasure. The reference to a barber is not surprising. In 1505, the Guild of Surgeon Barbers in Edinburgh was granted a monopoly over the manufacture of aqua vitae – a fact that reflects the spirit's perceived medicinal properties as well as the medicinal talents of the barbers.

James IV also supported the alchemical researches into distilling of John Damien, an Italian whom the king made Abbot of Tongland in Kirkcudbrightshire, who unsuccessfully attempted to fly from the walls of Stirling Castle with wings of his own invention in the presence of the king. (He explained his failure by the fact that he had used hens' feathers in his flying machine, and that "hens aspire more to the midden than to the heavens"!)

During the course of the fifteenth century, the dissolution of the monasteries and better still design combined to spread the practice of distilling throughout Scotland. By the 1570s, it is safe to assume that distilling was endemic: crop failure in 1579 led to the Scottish Parliament banning distillation for a year (exempting only "lords and gentlemen, for their own use"), on the grounds that the amount of barley being used for distilling was having an adverse effect on food supplies.

The first tax on spirits was imposed by the Scottish parliament in 1644 to help finance the anti-Royalist Army of the Covenant; this was reduced by Cromwell, abandoned after the Restoration of Charles II, and reimposed in the 1690s.

Throughout the seventeenth century, distilling remained small-scale, a useful way of using up surplus grain (see HAIG'S). But whisky drinking was widespread: during the funeral wake for Sir Donald Campbell of Ardnamurchan in 1651, the largest item on the bill was for "five gallons and one quart of *uisge beatha*"; later in the century, recruits to the Earl of Argyll's regiment were allowed a gill of whisky a day (3¾ fl.oz. or 10.6cl).

The first mention of a distillery in an official document was of that at Ferintosh, established by Duncan Forbes of Culloden in the 1670s. Forbes was an ardent Whig and had supported the Protestant succession in 1688. The following year, his lands were sacked by Jacobites and his distillery burnt. As a result, the Scottish parliament granted him and his successors the privilege of distilling whisky free of duty in perpetuity, "from grain grown on their own lands". The dispensation remained in force for ninety-five years, and made a fortune for the Forbes family. By the late 1760s, they were responsible for almost two-thirds of the legal whisky being produced in Scotland.

WHISKY WARS

The Act of Union (1707) stipulated that the English duties on excisable liquors should be levied in Scotland; in 1713, this clause was applied in the form of a malt tax, despite fierce opposition. When the tax was increased in 1725 for political reasons (Walpole wanted to assert his authority in Scotland), there were riots in Glasgow. The tax led to a decline in the production of ale, which was the universal drink of the commonalty, and to an increase in the production of spirits (which tripled in a single year).

It should be understood that most whisky (this phonetic abbreviation of *uisge beatha*, usually written as *usky,* began to be widely used in the 1720s) was made on farms during the winter months, especially in the Highlands, where its production was a natural extension of the farming year and an essential part of the local economy. This was perfectly legal until 1781, provided that the spirit was not offered for sale. During the 1740s and 1750s, there was a dramatic increase in the number of small malt and (particularly in the Lowlands) grain distilleries. This growth was encouraged by the Gin Act of 1736, which imposed a heavy duty on gin manufacture, but exempted *aqua vitae*.

In 1757, distilling was prohibited throughout the United

Kingdom for three years as a result of crop failures. The ban did not extend to private stills, whose owners suddenly found they had a huge and eager English market for their product – although they could not legally sell it. Smuggling (the word embraced both the manufacture and the transporting of illicit spirits) began on a vast scale, and even after the ban on distilling was lifted in the 1760s, it was estimated that the private distillers were making ten times more whisky than the licensed distillers. Many licensed distillers were forced out of business, or had to resort to fraud to survive – producing spirit and not declaring it to the Excise. In 1777, while there were only eight licensed distilleries in Edinburgh, there were over 400 illegal stills.

During the late 1770s, the licensed distillers began to band together to defeat the smugglers, flooding the market with cheap grain whisky. They obtained the support of Parliament, which summarily banned the private production of spirits in 1781, and authorized the Excise to seize stills and equipment. In 1783, these powers were extended to include the seizure of the horses and vehicles used to transport illicit whisky.

There then began an all-out war that lasted until the 1820s. Private distilling was considered an inalienable right by the huge majority of Scots, including many landowners and magistrates who were not inclined to enforce the increasingly harsh penalties imposed by the government – especially since the money that their tenants made from smuggling guaranteed their rents. Furthermore, contraband spirits had a far better flavour than legally produced whisky because the smugglers were indifferent to the legislation that related to wash strength and still size.

The legal distillers prospered under the protection of the monopoly. Also, the application of science to agriculture – the Agricultural Revolution – vastly increased the quantity of grain available. By the 1780s, the powerful Haig and Stein families (see HAIG) were joined by a number of others who established large-scale distilleries in the Lowlands and quickly became crucial to the economy of the region. Export of spirit to England (much of it for rectification into gin) rose from 2,000 gallons (9,000 litres) in 1770 to over 450,000 gallons (over two million litres) in 1784.

Famine ravaged much of Scotland, especially the Highlands, in 1782–3. Some Lowland distilleries were mobbed, since it was thought that they were using up food supplies. In 1784, the Wash Act was introduced by William Pitt to address the problem. This important piece of legislation introduced the concept of the "Highland Line" for the first time, a diagonal boundary stretching roughly between Dumbarton in the west to Dundee in the east. Duty was cut all round and was pegged to still capacity. Highland distillers were favoured with lower tax as well as by being allowed to use smaller stills, but they were allowed to use only locally grown barley and were forbidden to export beyond the region. To get round the Act, the Lowland distillers developed a new style of still – shallow and wide-bodied – that could be worked off in a matter of minutes; within a year, Lowland production doubled to over 800,000 gallons (over 3.6 million litres). London was awash with whisky, to the annoyance of the powerful London grain distillers who first instigated a price war and then used their influence to raise duty on Scotch spirits so high that it amounted to prohibition (1786). In 1788, further legislation required Scottish distillers to give a year's notice if they intended to export to England – a state of affairs that drove many into bankruptcy. Five years later, duty was tripled to help pay for the war with France.

Highland distillers had not been included in the legislation before 1793, but the tripling of duty again encouraged widespread illegal distilling. The Highlanders had little alternative: distilling was the only feasible use for their surplus barley. Landowners encouraged it and increased rents, confident that they could be paid. Unable to afford the increased duties, tenants were forced to distil illegally. By the end of the century, a huge amount of illicit Highland whisky was pouring into the Lowlands, exacerbating the difficulties faced by Lowland distillers.

At the beginning of the next century, there was another sequence of bad harvests. Distilling was banned in 1801 and 1802, and again in 1809 and 1811; duty was once more doubled and then trebled in 1800 and 1803. Despite the fact that the Excise service in the Highlands had been strengthened, smuggling was widespread and the authorities were openly flouted: much more whisky was being produced illegally than in licensed stills.

Further enactments were made in 1814, 1816, and 1818, but these did little to check the flow of smuggled spirit from the Highlands. Clashes with the Excise sometimes amounted to pitched battles. Improved roads in the Highlands made southern markets more accessible and encouraged more landowners to become involved in (legal) distilling, but they found their profits badly eroded by the illicit trade. In 1820, their influential spokesman, the Duke of Gordon, who owned huge estates in Aberdeenshire (including Glenlivet, on Speyside), drew the attention of the House of Lords to the chaotic condition of the licensing laws and promised the landowners' support against smuggling in return for a more reasonable fiscal approach. A royal commission was set up under Lord Wallace. The resulting Excise Act of 1823 cut duty dramatically, sanctioned the weak washes that made smuggled whisky more palatable, and permitted export to England. This, together with the Illicit Distillation (Scotland) Act of the previous year, which imposed very severe penalties on anyone producing whisky illegally, encouraged distillers to take out licences (see THE GLENLIVET).

HOW THE WORLD WAS WON

Many of the distilleries listed in this book trace their histories to the mid-1820s. Landlords throughout Scotland supported the construction of new distilleries, relying mostly on the knowledge of former smugglers to run the new enterprises. The number of licensed distilleries tripled in three years from 108 to 329 (yet by 1835, this had declined to 230), and thirty-seven distilleries opened in Campbeltown alone between 1823 and 1837. Smuggling declined dramatically: 14,000 cases were awaiting trial in 1823, but by 1830, the number of prosecutions had fallen to fewer than 400.

Apart from a handful of large Lowland distilleries, production remained small-scale and continued to be a seasonal extension of the farming year, providing employment for farm workers during the winter months. Then, in 1827, the leading Lowland distiller, Robert Stein, developed a method that would allow continuous distillation (until now, whisky-making in pot stills was a batch process). By 1830, this had been perfected by a former Inspector General of Excise in Dublin, Aeneas Coffey, who patented his invention in 1831 (see GRAIN WHISKY PRODUCTION, page 22).

The vast increase in the Lowland distilleries' capacity led to over-production and increased concern about over-consumption. Temperance societies began to appear in the late 1820s, and in 1830, Parliament yielded to the pressure of these groups by abolishing the duty on beer and raising that on spirits. This measure, combined with poor harvests during the 1840s, caused many distilleries to close – especially in the Highlands.

The Lowland distilleries were better off. The coalfields of the central belt were being developed, providing a cheap source of fuel. The new railways brought supplies of grain from all over the UK and abroad. Reliable steamboat services to English ports were emerging. The repeal of the Navigation Acts in 1845 freed trade to the colonies; within a decade, grain whisky was being exported to the USA, India, Canada, Australia, and South Africa. The bland patent-still whisky suited these markets, where it was used in mixed drinks and cordials, or rectified and compounded.

In 1853, Andrew Usher, Edinburgh agent for the well-known Glenlivet Distillery (see THE GLENLIVET), produced the first proprietary "vatted" malt – a blend of malt whiskies of different ages. He named it Usher's Old Vatted Glenlivet (see USHER'S GREEN STRIPE). Blends had been made before: during the "whisky wars", legal distillers sometimes blended their own inferior products with more flavoursome illicit whiskies, and after 1823, older malts were often vatted with new spirit. Also, public houses, spirits merchants, and grocers often diluted malt whisky with grain – but in a random fashion. Usher was the first to set out to achieve a consistent product and immediately began to win markets in London and India.

The Spirits Act of 1860 turned Usher's innovation into a revolution for the Scotch whisky industry. Not only did it raise duty substantially, it permitted whiskies from different distilleries to be blended before duty was paid. Previously, only whiskies from the same distillery could be vatted in bond. In an effort to reduce the price at which he sold his whiskies, Andrew Usher applied his experience to blending malt and (cheaper) grain whiskies to a fixed and therefore repeatable recipe; the result was a drink that combined the flavour of the former with the lightness of the latter and that could be sold at a competitive price. Blended whisky has since won the enthusiastic support of the entire world.

Many firms immediately followed Usher's example, and some of their names are still familiar: Bell's, Dewar's, Haig, Lowrie's, and Johnnie Walker, among others. The early blenders were often wine and provisions merchants by profession – known as "Italian warehousemen" – but dedicated blending firms soon began to appear, selling their products in bulk to hotels and public houses, and applying themselves to winning markets in England and abroad.

The nascent industry was encouraged by the general boom that accompanied the Franco-Prussian War (1870–1). Strong-flavoured Islay and Campbeltown malts were in demand since they could "cover" as much as ninety per cent grain whisky in a blend. At the same time, the marketing of soda water, particularly in the colonies, increased demand for fiery whiskies that lent themselves to dilution. Until the 1880s, whisky was almost all sold in bulk by the cask or stone jar, and bottled by the purchaser. Whisky and soda remained the most popular way to drink whisky until at least the turn of the century.

In 1877, the Distillers Company Limited (DCL) was formed by the amalgamation of the six leading grain distillers to protect their interests, reduce expenditure and increase profits in the boom market. In the years to come, DCL became the major player in the industry, and it remains so to this day under its new name, United Distillers & Vintners.

Perhaps the most significant factor in the development of the market for Scotch whisky, however, was an insect – phylloxera – that ravaged the vineyards of France from the late 1860s until well into the 1890s. By the mid-1880s, brandy was almost unavailable, and Scotch filled the vacuum, now sold by the branded bottle and energetically promoted by a number of extremely able Scots. Men such as James Buchanan, Tommy Dewar, and Alexander Walker addressed themselves first to the London market, then to the Empire. They developed lighter, softer blends with broader appeal, and promoted them vigorously and imaginatively (*see* BELL'S, BUCHANAN'S, DEWAR'S, JOHNNIE WALKER).

During the last decade of the century, blended whisky enjoyed an unprecedented boom. Two new grain distilleries and thirty-three new malt distilleries were built – twenty-one of them on Speyside. By the 1890s, the lighter, sweeter, and more complex style of the "Glenlivet" whiskies (as Speysides were known) better suited the needs of blenders looking for smoothness. Little single-malt whisky was available beyond the districts in which it was made, although a handful of brands were bottled and more widely distributed as "selfs" (as single malts were termed), notably The Glenlivet (which had won the right to specify its uniqueness in 1880), Highland Park, Bowmore, Craigellachie, and Springbank.

The boom came to a sudden end in 1900; this was precipitated by the collapse into bankruptcy of Pattison's of Leith, one of the major and most flamboyant blending firms, whose credit network spread throughout the industry.

UNREMITTING ADVERSITY

The high level of public spending on war materials needed to wage the Boer War decreased in 1900. This and other factors brought on a recession that lasted for more or less ten years. At home, whisky consumption slumped, although exports stayed buoyant (mainly to the USA, Canada, and Australia). It became increasingly difficult to sell at a profit the large stocks of mature malt whisky that had built up during the 1890s. Many companies amalgamated and DCL began to acquire Lowland distilleries to prevent price cutting.

The smaller malt distilleries in the Highlands felt threatened by the stronger Lowland interests, and they mounted a campaign to prevent grain whisky (also, by implication, blended whisky) being referred to as "whisky", since, they claimed, the product of the pot still was "the real stuff". A decision in an English court supported their cause before DCL entered the dispute and a Royal Commission was set up in 1908. It decided that the products of both stills could be named "Scotch whisky" – a bitter blow for the Highland malt distillers. Interestingly, for a decade or so after the advent of blended whisky, pure malt whisky was often referred to in England as "Irish whiskey" (with an "e").

With the death of Queen Victoria in 1901, drinking fashions changed. On the one hand, Champagne and dry wines became fashionable in England; on the other, there was a marked growth in the anti-drinking lobby. Lloyd George, the teetotal Chancellor of the Exchequer, increased duty by one-third in his People's Budget of 1909. The effect was not as dramatic as expected, since the overall economy began to improve after 1911. The outbreak of the First World War, however, gave Lloyd George further opportunities to cut consumption. He stated that strong drink "was doing more damage in the war than all the German submarines put together", and proposed total prohibition, and, when this failed, the doubling of duty on spirits. But this measure also failed, owing to protests from the Irish Members of Parliament who held the balance of power in the House of Commons. Instead, the Central Control Board (Liquor Traffic) was introduced in 1915.

The Board took what action it could, faced as it was by an incomprehensible maze of regulations. In the face of such difficulties – compounded by wartime grain shortages – many distilleries and blending houses were sold (a number of them to DCL), and some of the larger companies (most importantly Buchanan's and Dewar's) merged.

In 1916, the Central Control Board cut production by thirty per cent, then banned pot-still production altogether; next, it set about reducing the strength at which whisky could be sold. At the time, it was being bottled at sixty per cent alcohol: the board wanted this reduced to 28.6 per cent (*i.e.* 50° under proof). A compromise was reached at 37.2 per cent (35° under proof), which has remained more or less the norm. By 1918, all whisky exports had been prohibited and duty doubled (to £1.50 a gallon; by 1920 it had been raised to £3.60, with the provision that the increased duty must not be passed on to the consumer).

Many blenders merged with or sold out to DCL; most notable among these were Haig's and Usher's in 1920, Buchanan-Dewar and John Walker in 1925, and White Horse in 1927. By 1927, DCL controlled nearly all of the major Scotch whisky brands and about one-third of the distilleries.

Domestic sales declined throughout the 1920s, but production remained high. Towards the end of the decade there was a widespread price war that significantly reduced profitability and further damaged the entire industry. Export markets looked equally gloomy. In many markets, there was a widespread anti-drink sentiment at the end of the Great War, eptomised by the voting of the Fifth Amendment in the United States in January 1920, which introduced Prohibition. It soon transpired, however, that the American thirst for Scotch was unabated – indeed, increased – and the market could be supplied by the cunning use of adjacent territories, like Canada and the Bahamas, from where the whisky could be smuggled into the States. By the time Prohibition was repealed in 1933, the foundations of what would soon become the world's leading market for Scotch had been laid.

The General Strike (1926) was followed by the collapse of the US stock market (1929) and the Great Depression; whisky output plummeted by sixty per cent. By 1933, only two malt distilleries were in production, yet still the government failed to reduce duty.

Prohibition finally ended in 1933, but for two years, the US government imposed a heavy import duty. By 1935, the economy was picking up, and the prospects for the whisky industry looked better than at any time since 1900. Most of the leading brands in the USA today were introduced and promoted either during or shortly after Prohibition (*see* J&B RARE, CUTTY SARK, BALLANTINE'S).

Alas, the boom was short-lived. When the Second World War broke out in 1939, the industry was again called upon to help pay for the coming conflict: duty immediately increased by 10/- (50p); by 1943, at £7.87 per gallon, it was over twice what it had been in 1939. During the first two years of the war, exports to the USA were maintained to earn dollars and pay for armaments, and restrictions were placed upon sales in the home market. In 1942, grain supplies to the industry were cut altogether and all distilleries were closed. Not until August 1944, with victory clearly in sight, were supplies again made available by the Ministry of Food. After VE Day, following the personal intervention of Prime Minister Winston Churchill (who was well aware of whisky's

export potential), a large allocation for the coming season*
was promised.

GOOD TIMES, BAD TIMES

It quickly became apparent that the estimated amount of available
cereals had been over-optimistic. The election of a Labour
government in 1945 committed to the slogan "Food before
Whisky" limited production to less than half the pre-war output.
Demand was rising, stocks were falling; supplies to the home
market were rationed to a quarter of the pre-war figure (later
twenty per cent) and a keen black market sprang up. The sterling
crisis of 1946–47 obliged the government to release more grain for
distilling, provided the industry would concentrate on exports.

By 1949, the situation was easing, and the government
abandoned control of home barley sales, leaving distillers free to
buy on the open market. From 1953, output recovered sharply.
Distilleries were enlarged, and the first new ones since the
nineteenth century were built (Tullibardine in 1949, Glen Keith in
1957, and Tormore in 1958). Worldwide demand for whisky soared,
especially in North America, but until stocks recovered in 1959, the
Scotch Whisky Association administered a voluntary rationing
scheme.

By 1960, four brands commanded half the world sales of
Scotch: Johnnie Walker, Dewar's, Cutty Sark, and J&B Rare. The
largest market was the USA, followed by the UK, where the most
popular brands were Haig's, Johnnie Walker, Black & White, and
White Horse (all of which were DCL brands). Towards the end of
the decade, Teacher's, Bell's, and Chivas Regal began to threaten
DCL's ascendancy. The giant reacted by cutting prices and offering
discounts, trying to use size and power to crush its competitors in
direct contravention of undertakings given to the industry in 1925.

Production was geared to cater for an export market that was
increasing by ten per cent per annum. Between 1959 and 1966,
grain whisky production doubled to ninety million gallons (over
400 million litres), and new distilleries were built at Airdrie, Girvan
and Invergordon. Malt whisky production in the same period
increased from sixteen million to fifty-one million gallons (seventy-
two million to 230 million litres). Many established distilleries were
refurbished and expanded; seventeen new ones were built, some
within existing distilleries.

The high prices fetched by mature whiskies in the late 1950s
and early 1960s encouraged investment from speculators outside
the industry. By 1968, large quantities of mature grain whisky were

---

* The fact that whisky production is still thought of as being
seasonal harks back to the time when it was part of the farming
year, a winter occupation. Nowadays, the "silent season" (when
the distillery is closed) extends for about a month; it used to last
from May to September.

available and the bottom fell out of the market. Similarly, malt sales also slumped, although not as dramatically.

The world demand for Scotch whisky seemed insatiable, however, and this small slump only temporarily halted the optimistic mood. Between 1970 and 1975, five new distilleries were built (Mannochmore, Braes of Glenlivet, Allt-a-Bhainne, Pittyvaich, and Auchroisk), and many others increased in size, most of them substantially. Mannochmore, Glendullan, Teaninich, Linkwood, Aberfeldy, Caol Ila, Tamdhu, Tormore, Aberlour, Glengarioch, Glen Grant, Glenfid-dich, Tomatin, Tomintoul, Ardmore, Tullibardine, Miltonduff . . . all were rebuilt or extended.

By the late 1970s, economic conditions were less stable and the huge US market had begun to contract. Moreover, in both the USA and the UK, there was a shift in consumer taste towards blander spirits (white rum and vodka) drunk with mixers, and white wine; younger drinkers had been especially targeted and "lifestyle" advertising was designed to appeal to them. Whisky companies responded by exploring other markets, particularly South America, Japan, Hong Kong, and Europe.

By the end of the decade, the world economy had entered a period of recession. Output of both grain and malt whisky declined sharply (in 1983, it was at its lowest level since 1959). Between 1981 and 1986, no fewer than twenty-nine distilleries were taken out of production; nineteen of these have not worked since, and several have been demolished.

Making scotch whisky

There are three kinds of Scotch: malt whisky, grain whisky, and blended whisky. The latter is a mixture of several malt and grain whiskies. A fourth category, "liqueur whisky", is also embraced by this book: to make this, sugar or honey and herbs are added to malt or blended whisky; Drambuie is the leading example.

Just under ninety-five per cent of malt and grain whisky made in Scotland is drunk as blended whisky (just under 262 million litres of pure alcohol (LPA) in 2002). Yet, although small in terms of volume consumed (16.04 million LPA in 2002), single malts have shown the best growth over the past ten years. Only a minute amount of the 220 million LPA produced by the six operational grain distilleries in Scotland is bottled as single (see CAMERONBRIDGE, BLACK BARREL, INVERGORDON).

At the time of writing, there are eighty-six operating malt whisky distilleries. In addition, there are nine distilleries that can come back into production and three that are at the planning stage – Kilchoman, Ladybank, and Shetland. This book also lists the products of a further twenty-six distilleries that are now out of production or demolished, but whose whiskies are still encountered occasionally.

It is not within the scope of a pocket book to dwell at length upon how whisky is made, but a short account of the processes and procedures involved will help the reader understand the notes that comprise the body of the book.

Distillation is the process by which the elements in a liquid are separated by vaporization and condensation. The creation of a potable spirit requires that the liquid to be distilled contains alcohol and water; the process of distillation separates the two by heating the liquid so that the alcohol vaporizes before being cooled and liquefied again.

The base liquid from which Scotch is made is not unlike strong ale – a mash of cereals and water fermented by yeast. Malt whisky is made from a mash of malted barley alone; grain whisky uses maize or wheat and a small amount of malted and unmalted barley. The differences between the processes employed to make the two kinds of whisky are considered in the following pages.

MALT WHISKY PRODUCTION

Malting

First the barley must be malted – in other words, germinated and dried to allow the starches in each grain to be converted into sugar. Distillers look for plump, ripe barley with plenty of starch and not too much nitrogen. Barley varieties are not important so long as they meet these requirements. Nor is the origin of the barley important: good Scottish barley is generally considered to be the best (on account of climatic and soil conditions), but barley is imported from England at certain times of the year.

Originally, the barley was grown locally and malted at the distillery – the familiar pagoda-shaped roofs of the malt kilns are a feature of whisky distilleries. Today, only five distilleries have their own floor maltings; Highland Park, Balvenie, Bowmore, Laphroaig, and Springbank. In several places, the old maltings have been converted into visitor centres (*see* APPENDICES), since specialist maltsters can supply distillers with malt made consistently to their own detailed specifications.

First, the barley is steeped for two or three days, then, in traditional maltings, it is spread on a stone or cement malting floor and encouraged to germinate. As each grain sprouts, heat is generated and the whole "piece" must be turned with wooden shovels and rakes to make sure the germination is even. This continues for about a week, less time in hot weather.

The barley is now termed "green malt" and is ready for drying. It is transferred to a kiln and spread out evenly on a perforated metal floor, below which is a fire. In the Highlands, until the mid-1870s, the fire was fuelled only by peat, which gave Highland malt whisky a distinctive smokiness. Lowland distilleries began to use coke and coal in the late eighteenth century, and when the railways reached the Highlands these fuels became the principal sources of heat, although a small amount of peat is still burned in many kilns.

Traditional floor maltings have several drawbacks: they are labour-intensive, limited in the amount of malt that they produce, and variable in quality. As a consequence, only five distilleries retain their floor maltings, and even these make only around twenty per cent of their requirement themselves. They have largely been supplanted by "pneumatic" malting systems that pass humidified air through the germinating grain to control its temperature and moisture. There are three kinds of pneumatic maltings: Saladin boxes; rotary drums; and "steep, germinate and kilning vessels" (SGKVs).

When the malt has been dried, the remains of the stalks and rootlets are cleaned off in a dressing machine; it is then ground, coarsely or finely depending on the distillery's mashing equipment. Many distilleries once had their own water-driven meal mills, but since the 1880s, most milling has been done by machines with steel rollers.

Mashing

The milled malt, known as grist, is mixed with hot water. The nature of the water has only a minor influence on the final product, although it used to be thought the key element in dictating the distinctive qualities of individual whiskies. Some maintain that soft, peaty water, such as that used in Islay and Campbeltown, makes for heavier whiskies, while harder water, such as that used at Glenkinchie, Highland Park, or Glenmorangie, is one of the factors that make for lighter styles. Some use springs or wells, while others favour lochs or rivers.

In the mash room, the water is heated to around 64–65°C (147–149°F), mixed with the grist in a mashing machine and pumped into a large cylindrical vessel made of cast iron or stainless steel (called a "mash tun"). In traditional mash tuns, made of cast iron, it is stirred by revolving rakes for about twenty minutes; then the sweet liquid, called "wort" or "worts", is drained off. The process is repeated three times with increasingly hot water to extract all the soluble starches from the malt; the liquid from the third mash, called "sparge", is used as the first water for the next batch. More common today are stainless-steel "lauter" tuns, in which the worts drain constantly, while the shallower bed of grist is gently stirred by fixed blades. The residue of husks and spent grains makes excellent cattle-feed, and has, therefore, always been an important part of the rural economy. Whisky production literally provided the meat and drink of Scotland!

Fermenting

The wort is cooled to between 18° and 20° C (64 and 68°F) and then pumped into fermenting vessels called "washbacks", large tubs that hold anything from 1,000 to 69,000 litres. They are made from Oregon pine or larch, or sometimes from stainless steel (which is easier to keep clean).

At this stage, the yeast is added (usually a mix of brewers' and distillers' yeast, sometimes only distillers' yeast) and fermentation takes place, causing the liquid (which is now called "wash") to bubble and froth up the washback, sometimes requiring the use of mechanical switches to keep it from foaming out of the tub. In the old days, when yeasts were less stable, fermentation could be extremely violent – the whole washback would rock and the sound has been compared to a ship in a stormy sea.

After around sixty hours, fermentation is complete. The wash is now around eight per cent alcohol, and is pumped into the wash charger to be distilled. Once discharged, the washbacks must be scrupulously cleaned to prevent bacterial infection of subsequent fillings.

Distilling

Distilling takes place in pairs of copper pot stills. One is usually larger than the other; otherwise, their shapes, capacities, and heights vary from distillery to distillery. The life of a still is between fifteen and thirty years, depending on how hard it is used. New stills will copy old ones faithfully.

The wash is pumped into the larger of the two stills, called the "wash still", where it is brought to the boil. Stills are either directly heated from below (by gas, oil, or coke) or, more commonly, from within by steam-heated coils, not unlike those found in electric kettles. The temperature has to be carefully controlled to prevent the foaming wash rising up the swan-neck and into the condenser; a little window in the neck tells the distiller how far it has risen.

The alcoholic vapours and steam pass over the neck of the still into a shell and tube condenser or, in traditional distilleries, a coiled pipe in a vat of water on the outside wall of the still-room (called a "worm tub"). Here, the vapours return to liquid at around twenty-one per cent alcohol and are termed "low wines". They pass through a sealed, brass-bound, glass-fronted box (the "spirit safe") and into the "low wines and feints charger", ready to fill the second still, which is called the "low wines still" or "spirit still".

The same process is repeated in the second distillation but this time the stillman watches the spirit carefully as it flows through the spirit safe. The early part of the run (known as "foreshots") is pungent and impure. He tests the spirit by adding water (which turns it cloudy), measuring its specific gravity, and watching the clock, and until the foreshots run clear he directs them back to the low wines and feints charger to be redistilled. This takes between fifteen and forty-five minutes, depending on the distillery.

When he is certain the run is clear, the stillman redirects the spout and begins to collect the spirit for maturing. This is "new make", and will run for between two and four hours (depending on the size of the still), commencing at between seventy-two and seventy-eight per cent alcohol and decreasing steadily down between seventy-three and sixty-five per cent; but the precise strengths, the speed at which he operates his still, and the length of time he saves spirit (known as the "cut") is part of his art and

influences the flavour and quality of the product. It varies from
distillery to distillery, but the "new make" may be as low as one-
third of the spirit distilled.

Only part of the run is collected, because about halfway
through the second distillation, various oily compounds called
"feints" begin to vaporize. They are mild and pleasant at first,
lending character and flavour to the whisky, but in time, their
intensity increases to such a degree that to continue to collect the
spirit would spoil the whole batch. The stillman will again direct
the distillate to the low wines and feints charger for redistillation.
Distilling continues until all that is left is "spent lees" (more or less
water). The distillation of 1,500 gallons (6,800 litres) of low wines
and feints normally takes about six hours.

Maturation

The "new make" (it cannot be named "whisky" until it has matured
for three years) is crystal-clear, which gives rise to it being termed
"clearic" by distillery workers, who used to receive a large dram of
the stuff before beginning work. It passes to an intermediate spirit
receiver and then to a large vat in the filling store, where its
strength is reduced (using the same water it was mashed with) to
63.5 per cent alcohol; it is then filled into oak barrels of different
sizes. This strength (111° proof) was long ago discovered to be the
best at which to mature spirit. Experiments in the mid-1960s with
maturing at higher strengths were unsuccessful.

By law, the casks used for maturing Scotch must be made of
oak. Either American white oak or European oak is used. The casks
are usually "re-made hogsheads" (250-litre capacity) or "butts"
(500-litre capacity) and sometimes "American barrels" (200-litre
capacity) or "puncheons" (500-litre capacity). They are invariably
"second hand", having previously been used for maturing
bourbon or sherry. It was long ago realized that the first

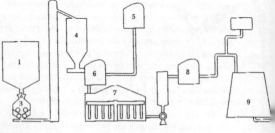

1 malt bin
2 dressing machine
3 mill
4 grist hopper
5 water tank
6 mashing machine

7 mash tun
8 cooler
9 washback
10 wash charger
11 wash still
12 condensers

incumbent seasoned the cask and benefited the whisky. New wood (previously unused), port pipes, and wine barrels are also used experimentally.

Currently, ninety-six per cent of cask imports are American oak hogsheads or barrels; only about four per cent of whisky is matured in sherry wood. The Macallan Distillery is the only one to use European oak ex-sherry casks exclusively for its single-malt fillings; some others mature their product in American oak, transferring it to sherry casks for about eighteen months to complete maturation (known as "sherry finishing"). Not surprisingly, the vast majority of whisky is matured in "refill" casks that have been used at least once for maturing whisky: such casks allow the original character of the whisky to be retained, even after many years of maturation, without masking it with wood extractives.

Much depends on the character of the individual "new make" spirit, but what is certain is that the casks in which the whisky matures are much more than storage vessels. Wood makes a vital contribution, perhaps *the* vital contribution, to the character and flavour of the final product.

The inside walls of the casks are charred (merely toasted in the case of European oak) in order to facilitate the release of vanillin (a vanilla flavour) into the spirit. In turn, the flavour of the first incumbent – bourbon or sherry (the latter more so) – lingers in the wood, and re-emerges, along with compounds in the wood itself, in the aroma and flavour of the mature whisky.

Casks are used until their qualities are deemed to be exhausted. After each maturation period they are checked and repaired, and, increasingly, de-charred, re-charred and "reconditioned". This used to be done by rinsing them with a sherry derivative called *paxarete* (named after a Spanish village, Torre de Pajarete, famous for its *vino de color*), but this is now

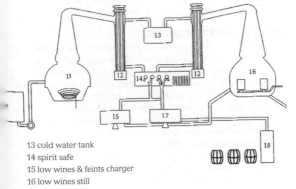

13 cold water tank
14 spirit safe
15 low wines & feints charger
16 low wines still
17 spirit receiver
18 spirit vat

deemed an additive and prohibited. After three or four fillings, the contribution made by the cask is substantially reduced, so single-malt bottlings are usually made from first- and second-fill casks. Older casks are used for "marrying" blends.

Whisky must be matured for three years, but it is by no means mature after so short a time, and most single malts are bottled after at least ten or twelve years in cask. The rate at which the whisky matures depends upon both how "active" the cask is and its size (the larger the cask, the longer maturation will take), and how often it has been filled. It is said that some whiskies peak twice, with a dull middle period. Very old whisky can become undesirably woody.

The rate of maturation also depends upon the conditions in which the spirit is matured. Traditional dunnage warehouses are low, stone-built, and earth-floored. The atmosphere is damp and cool, and the casks are stacked three high. Modern racked warehouses are like aircraft hangars, with casks stacked as many as 20 high, and the rate of maturation may vary according to where the cask is positioned in the warehouse. In traditional warehouses, evaporation is low, but the strength of the spirit drops by three to four per cent in ten years; in racked warehouses, strength remains high but evaporation is greater. Customs and Excise allows for two per cent volume loss per annum: nearly ten gallons (over forty-five litres) of spirit in ten years. This is known as the "Angels' Share".

Climate also plays its part. The rate of maturation is affected by seasonal changes in temperature, so warehouses on the coast, where there is less seasonal variation than inland, tend to mature their contents at a steadier rate.

While it slumbers, whisky does not like to be shocked by wild swings in temperature. Scotland's climate, which is temperate and oceanic, is perfectly adapted to maturing whisky, just as the end-product is so suited to cheering the heart during long northern winters and damp Scottish summers.

GRAIN WHISKY PRODUCTION

As noted in the history section, large quantities of grain whisky were made in pot stills from at least the seventeenth century until the First World War, and sold as "Irish Whiskey" in England. However, the perfection of the patent still by Aeneas Coffey in 1831 (see HAIG, CAMERON BRIG) enabled continuous production. This is how all grain whisky is made in Scotland today.

The fact that it is a continuous process is significant, since it means that vastly more spirit can be produced per annum. The six operating grain distilleries together have the capacity to produce 333 million LPA per annum. Not all the output goes into blended whisky; much of the base spirit for gin and vodka comes from the same stills. Malt whisky production is a batch process, and the equipment (mash tun, washbacks, pot stills) must be scrupulously cleaned after each round of distilling, while patent stills may be run continuously for seven days before they require cleaning. Since the bulk of the raw materials (*i.e.* any cereal that yields fermentable sugars, usually wheat and maize) is cheaper than malted barley, grain whisky is less costly to produce.

Mashing and fermenting

The mash from which grain whisky is made is unmalted wheat or maize (so distilleries are free to buy in at the best price) and a small proportion of either "green" malt (*see* page 17) or malted barley (about sixteen per cent, it varies from distillery to distillery). The unmalted cereals are milled fine, then cooked at a high temperature in a giant pressure cooker to release the starch into a slurry solution. The mixture is then added to the malted barley in the mash tun, where the mixture is mashed and the sugars extracted.

The wort, complete with any solids it contains, is then cooled and pumped to the washbacks, where yeast is added to induce fermentation. In two days, the wash will be ready to be distilled. For the most part, this is very similar to malt whisky manufacture.

Distilling

Patent stills are utterly different to pot stills. They consist of two interconnected copper-lined columns, each about fifty feet (fifteen metres) tall, known as the rectifier and the analyser. Copper lining has been found essential to achieve the flavour profile of grain whisky, although it may be dispensed with when producing plain spirit for gin or vodka.

The (cool) wash passes down the rectifier in a long, serpent-like pipe. During its passage, it is heated by hot vapour rising up the column. The (now hot) wash rises to the head of the analyser where it flows onto a series of perforated plates. On the way down, it meets ascending steam, which causes the volatile (alcoholic) elements to rise. The balance of the wash (water and grains) is drawn off at the bottom and converted into animal feed.

The alcoholic vapour now starts its return journey. From the top of the analyser, it passes to the foot of the rectifier, through which it rises, gradually being condensed by the incoming pipe of (cool) wash, which, in its turn, is heated by the hot vapour. The ascending vapour increases in alcoholic strength as it rises, until it reaches the "spirit plate" and is drawn off. Less volatile elements (the feints) condense and fall to the bottom of the rectifier as liquid, and are then pumped back to the top of the analyser to go through the process again.

Maturation

The spirit is drawn off the still at a strength not higher than 94.8 per cent alcohol. The strength is then reduced to 68.5 per cent, and the spirit is filled into oak casks; it must mature for a minimum of three years before it can be called Scotch whisky (as with malt whisky). Being lighter-bodied than malt whisky, grain whisky matures more rapidly. Some grain whisky is matured for similar long periods to malt whisky, to be used in de luxe blends or bottled as single grains. If a blend makes an age statement ("15 Years Old", "21 Years Old", and so on) its component grain whiskies must be at least of that age and so must its component malts. In most instances, however, there will be malt whiskies in the blend that are older than its age statement.

BLENDED WHISKY PRODUCTION

David Macdonald, former chairman of Macdonald Martin Distillers, has offered the following as a definition of blending: "The art of combining meticulously selected, mature, high-quality whiskies, each with its own flavour and other characteristics, with such skill that the whole is better than the sum of its parts, so that each makes its own contribution to the finished blend without any one predominating."

When the selected whiskies are all malts, the result is called a "vatted malt" rather than a "blend". Some vatted brands are described as "pure malt", or simply as "malt whisky" as opposed to "single malt", which is the product of one distillery. Blended whisky is a mix of many malt and grain whiskies from a range of first fill and refill casks, both European and American. Perhaps surprisingly, especially given the eminence of the promotion and quality of malt whisky, this style of Scotch accounts for the overwhelming majority of sales worldwide: in 2002 it was just under ninety-five per cent, in 1980, it was over ninety-nine per cent.

The first true blend (in the sense that it was produced and marketed with a view to ensuring consistency of flavour) was created in the early 1860s. Prior to this date, blends – and vattings of malt whiskies especially – had been made and offered for sale, mainly by grocers and wine shops, but with little science applied to their creation.

Selection

Typically, a blend will comprise between fifteen and forty different malt whiskies and two to three grains (although grain whisky is comparatively light in flavour, attempts to use only one grain in a blend have not been successful). The proportion of malt to grain is between twenty and sixty per cent. The cost price of the end product will reflect this and the ages of the constituent malts.

The malts that are used in a blend are categorized as follows: "base" or "heart" malts, commonly fillings from distilleries owned by the blender, around which the blend is constructed; "flavouring malts", which are sometimes called "top dressings" (there are a handful of malts that have long been famous among blenders for their flavouring properties); and "packers" or "fillers". These latter whiskies are not necessarily inferior; they simply have low aroma intensities and the contribution they make to the overall flavour of the blend is minimal.

Every malt whisky is different, and each has a different "flavour profile" – its discernible (sometimes dominant) aromatic characteristics (*see* page 25). The blender sets out to balance the characteristics of one whisky with those of another (in fact, with many others) so that the individual aromas are so well integrated that they are unidentifiable. In the perfect blend, each aroma should make its contribution to a "flavour complex" that is much more than the sum of its parts.

The goal of the blender, therefore, is to create a drink that resists analysis beyond the immediate sensation it imparts to the drinker. For this reason I have not attempted to provide tasting notes for the blended whiskies listed in this book.

Method

Although each blend is made to a formula, the formula itself is not slavishly adhered to; it cannot be, since some fillings may not be available or may be prohibitively expensive. The blender's task is to produce a product that tastes the same from batch to batch over many years. The familiar claim that a current blend is identical (in constituents and/or flavour) to that produced twenty or fifty or 100 years ago should be taken with a pinch of salt. Some distilleries cease production and others are built, and fashions and marketing strategies change (modern blends tend to be lighter in both body and colour). In 1994, for example, United Distillers took the bold step of reblending Bell's, the best-selling blend in the UK, as an eight-year-old.

With the formula to guide him, and a deep familiarity with the flavour characteristics of the blend he wants to recreate, the blender noses samples of every constituent malt and grain whisky that will go into his creation, at the ages he wishes to use them. Samples are drawn from the individual casks that will be used in that batch, since there are variations from cask to cask. He must be aware that slight changes in flavour may occur over time – the peaty dryness of some Highland or Island malts might increase, so additional sweet and fruity Speyside fillings may be required to redress the balance. On the other hand, blends which employ a large amount of Speyside malt may have to be "dried out", by adding individual malts known for their dry flavour.

Once he is satisfied that the marriage of the ingredients will create what he is searching for, the individual casks are transported from the warehouses in which they have been maturing to the blending hall. Here, the blender will check them by nosing; he will have spent years committing the individual characteristics of each whisky to memory, and is assisted by an extensive library of samples. Once he has approved their quality they are disgorged into a trough, whence they flow into a large blending vat.

Some blenders prefer to vat the malt fillings separately to the grains. In the blending vat, the mixture is roused by stirring or by blowing air through it to thoroughly mingle the ingredients. Then it is either rested for a short while and bottled, or, traditionally, run

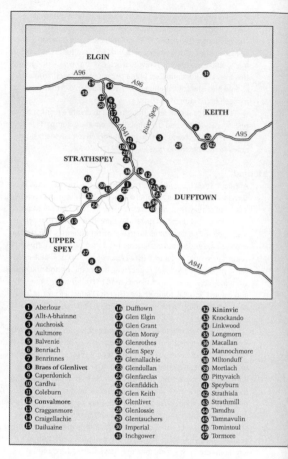

❶ Aberlour	⓰ Dufftown	㉜ Kininvie
❷ Allt-A-bhainne	⓱ Glen Elgin	㉝ Knockando
❸ Auchroisk	⓲ Glen Grant	㉞ Linkwood
❹ Aultmore	⓳ Glen Moray	㉟ Longmorn
❺ Balvenie	⓴ Glenrothes	㊱ Macallan
❻ Benriach	㉑ Glen Spey	㊲ Mannochmore
❼ Benrinnes	㉒ Glenallachie	㊳ Miltonduff
❽ Braes of Glenlivet	㉓ Glendullan	㊴ Mortlach
❾ Caperdonich	㉔ Glenfarclas	㊵ Pittyvaich
❿ Cardhu	㉕ Glenfiddich	㊶ Speyburn
⓫ Coleburn	㉖ Glen Keith	㊷ Strathisla
⓬ Convalmore	㉗ Glenlivet	㊸ Strathmill
⓭ Cragganmore	㉘ Glenlossie	㊹ Tamdhu
⓮ Craigellachie	㉙ Glentauchers	㊺ Tamnavulin
⓯ Dailuaine	㉚ Imperial	㊻ Tomintoul
	㉛ Inchgower	㊼ Tormore

off into casks to be allowed to "marry" for a period – typically
between one and six months (see EDRADOUR).

It is often remarked that while distilling is a science, blending
is an art. I hope it is clear from the foregoing summary of how
whisky is made that there is a high level of artistry – judgement,
tradition, skill, and magic – in both.

Regional differences

The first distinction was made by William Pitt's Wash Act of 1784:
a simple division of Highland and Lowland. By the middle of the
last century, four regions were acknowledged: Highland, Islay,

Distilleries

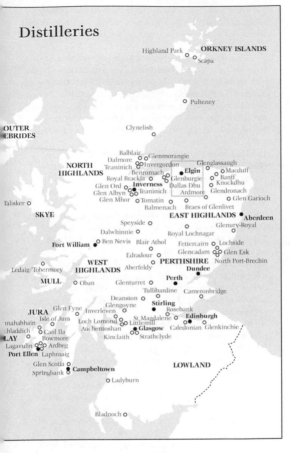

Campbeltown, and Lowland, although some writers referred quite simply to Eastern and Western malts. The whiskies of Speyside, known generically as "Glenlivets", were celebrated from at least the 1820s, and by the 1880s, this region had joined the other four.

With the growth in interest in malt whisky in recent years, the Highland region has been subdivided into North, South, West, East (once subdivided into Forfarshire and Aberdeenshire), Midlands (or Perthshire), and Islands. Authorities such as the Scotch Malt Whisky Society further subdivide Speyside (where two-thirds of Scotland's operating distilleries are located) according to the rivers that water the region: Lossie, Findhorn, Upper Spey, Lower Spey, Deveron, Fiddich, and Dullan.

In this book I have classified the malts as Highland (North, South, East, West, and Central), Lowland, Islay, Campbeltown, and Island, and divided Speyside into Glenlivet, Strathspey, Dufftown, Rothes, and Elgin.

Generalizing about the regional flavour differences in malt whisky is difficult, and nowadays it is possible to produce whiskies with similar characteristics in different regions. Every cask matures its contents differently, so bottlings can vary considerably. The notes that follow are based on proprietary bottlings where possible, on the basis that these are the flavours that owners of distilleries believe display the characters of the whiskies to best advantage.

Lowland: Light-bodied with a nose that is hay-like or grassy, often with malty or cereal notes and sometimes scents of Parma violets. The flavour tends towards dryness, or finishes dry. These whiskies are often drunk as apéritifs, and have been compared to fino sherries.

Islay: Islay produces the smokiest and strongest-tasting whiskies, although two of island's distilleries make very mild whiskies. The smoky flavour comes from the peat that is burned when the malt is dried.

Campbeltown: Although today there are only two distilleries in Campbeltown, rather than the thirty-two that were once there, the category is still recognized. Campbeltown whiskies are medium-bodied and have a slightly smoky or misty taste, with a trace of salt on the palate.

Highland: *North Highland* malts vary considerably. They tend to be medium-bodied and fresh-flavoured, with heathery, nutty, spicy, or citric notes. Peat smoke is noticeable in several, and sometimes scented smoke, such as Lapsang Souchong tea.

West Highland and *Island* malts are lighter-bodied, with some peaty or phenolic characteristics and some spice.

South and *Central Highland* malts tend to be lighter-bodied and sweeter than their cousins to the north, although they have the dry finish characteristic of Highland malts. They can be delicately fragrant.

The flavour characteristics of *East Highland* malts divide into two sections. The whiskies made north of Aberdeen tend to be malty, slightly sweet, and medium-bodied; those south of the city become richer, with some citric and toffee notes. All of them have the characteristic dry finish.

Speyside: The malts of Speyside have long been esteemed for their complexity and diversity. They tend towards sweetness and fragrance and can be divided into three styles: light-bodied malts tend to be fruity and floral-scented, with some cereal notes; medium-bodied malts are like Highlands, but more fruity/fragrant, and some are on the dry side (I include Glenlivets in this category); full-bodied malts are sometimes powerfully sherried, rich, and redolent of chocolate or fruitcake. These latter are great after-dinner whiskies.

At the time of writing, there are eighty-five malt whisky distilleries in operation in Scotland and nine that are "mothballed". All produce different flavoured whiskies and many bottle at different ages or in different styles. Maurice Walsh, an exciseman and novelist of the 1920s and 1930s, wrote in his introduction to J. Marshall Robb's *Scotch Whisky*: "I knew one small town with seven distilleries [he probably had Dufftown in mind] and I knew an expert who could distinguish the seven by bouquet alone. These seven distilleries were in one mile of a Highland river; they used the same water, peat and malt, and the methods of brewing and distillation were identical, yet each spirit had its own individual bouquet."

It is this potentially infinite variety that presents us with an inexhaustible opportunity to explore and experiment, to taste and enjoy Scotch whisky. This marvellous beverage, which is made in a tiny northern country, has won – and continues to win – the enthusiasm of drinkers of every race, in every country in the world. It is not within the scope of this book to speculate why, but if you savour the dram in your glass, dear reader, you might solve the mystery yourself!

How to appreciate Scotch whisky

Take five glasses and fill them with measures of good-quality brandy, rum, gin, vodka, and malt whisky. Dilute them with water to about thirty per cent alcohol, then sniff each one carefully. Concentrate hard and make a list of the aromas you can identify; then taste each one in turn, rolling the liquid over your tongue. Again, record your impressions, put words to the flavours you can discern. I will bet that of the five lists, the one pertaining to the malt whisky is the longest and the most varied.

Malt whisky is the most complex of all spirits. With a little application and concentration on the part of the taster, a vast range of aromas and flavours may be identified. As I have already noted, the aromas in a blend are more difficult to identify, since part of the blender's task is to integrate the flavours of the individual malt and grain whiskies so well that no individual aroma or flavour predominates. For this reason, the notes that follow relate primarily to malt whisky, although the techniques and vocabulary may be applied equally to blended whisky.

AROMA AND FLAVOUR

The latest techniques of chemical and sensory analysis identify some 300 constituents in malt whisky, and chemists estimate that there are likely to be as many more which have yet to be isolated and described.

Yet the flavour elements in an average bottle of Scotch at 40 per cent alcohol must be sought in only 0.2 per cent of the bottle's contents: the remaining 59.8 per cent is water. Apart from the essential warming effect of alcohol, both it and water are relatively neutral in smell and taste.

The word "smell" is used advisedly. The "tasting" of whisky and other spirits is done mainly with the nose, compared to which the tongue could be said to be a relatively crude organ. While there are only four primary tastes – sweet, sour, salty, and bitter (just as there are only four primary colours) – it has been estimated that there are some thirty-two "primary" aromas. These combine to provide the infinite variety detectable by the nose. Moreover, the average human nose is able to detect aromatics at concentrations as low as one part in a million!

Flavour is a combination of smell and taste. Although the former sense is often less consciously used, you have only to hold your nose to remind yourself of the vital contribution it makes to the appreciation of what you are eating or drinking.

The nose records pungency (sharpness, nose-prickle, nose-drying, even pain, which is often noted when sniffing cask-strength whisky samples) and aroma. In the case of whisky, these are the many volatile aromatics (esters, aldehydes, phenols, feints) which give rise to characteristics such as fruitiness, grassiness, smokiness, or cereal-like scents. With continued sniffing, pungency increases and intensity of aroma decreases rapidly. From a practical point of view, this means that it is pointless to nose a whisky sample for too long; if the first impression is lost, move on to another sample or simply have a rest.

The tongue and palate record "mouth-feel" (body, viscosity, drying effects, texture) as well as primary tastes. Sweetness is detected on the tip of the tongue; saltiness and sourness (also astringency and acidity) at the sides, and bitterness and dryness at the back.

Response to primary tastes deteriorates with age, but, perhaps surprisingly, it is not affected by smoking. Several of today's leading noses are heavy smokers, as are many great French wine-tasters. However, it goes without saying that smoking at the same time as tasting ruins not only the smoker's palate, but also that of everyone else in the tasting room.

TASTING

Tasting, which is more properly termed "sensory evaluation", can be either "analytical" (objective) or "hedonic" (subjective).

The first is the methodology that is employed by professional tasters, and describes a procedure in which biases are minimized and which can be verified by repetition. The goal is "to describe what is there" and to exclude personal preferences. Professional tasters are screened in order to determine their particular areas of sensitivity or insensitivity, those biases or gaps in their flavour spectrums that colour their judgements. Statistical analysis may be used to prove "significance" in the findings.

Hedonic evaluation – the word derives from the Greek for

pleasure and refers to personal preference – is the kind of tasting pursued by consumers and allows for greater latitude and subjective assessment. The tasting notes included in this book generally fall into this category.

PREPARATION

The evaluation of a whisky is bound to be affected by a variety of factors, not least the taster's mood and situation. For example, I have heard a supermarket blend (no better than second-rate) described as "excellent" by experienced tasters in a fishing hut on the Tweed, after a successful day's salmon fishing!

Other factors have a bearing on one's ability to assess accurately. Wearing perfume, aftershave, and even using strongly scented hand-soap can have a surprisingly powerful and distracting influence on the aroma of a sample. The room itself should be as free as possible from smells – such as cooking, fresh paint, and smoke. Ideally, tasters should not just have eaten a heavy meal; smokers should not smoke for half an hour before tasting.

Perhaps the most important influence on the sensory evaluation of whisky is the glass in which it is sampled. What is required is a clear, tulip-shaped glass: a large sherry copita or brandy snifter. Best is a "spirits nosing glass", which is a cross between the two. Classic, cut-crystal whisky tumblers are fine for long swigging drinks – whisky and soda, whisky and lemonade, whisky high-balls – but they are hopeless as tasting glasses since they do not collect and concentrate the aromas. The flavour of the whisky changes rapidly as it "breathes" in an open glass (sometimes improving, more often deteriorating), so for "serious" tastings, cover the sample with a watch glass or lid.

PROCEDURE
Stage 1: Appearance

As with wine-tasting, note the colour, depth, and clarity. New spirit, fresh from the still, is colourless; whisky that has been matured for twenty years in a first-fill oloroso cask will be the colour of treacle. The spectrum in between runs from pale straw, sunlight, fino sherry, and pale gold; through old gold, amber, amontillado sherry, and red gold; to bronze, oloroso, and palo cortado sherry.

The spirit's appearance should give an indication of how it has been matured and for how long. Whisky obtains its colour from the cask in which it is matured: American oak gives a xanthic (yellow) hue; European oak ambrous or umbrous tints (amber – brown). The degree of tint will depend not only upon how long it has lain in wood, but also on whether the cask is on its first, second or third filling.

To confuse matters further, it has long been the practice of the industry to add colouring (in the form of caramel) prior to bottling in order to make for colour uniformity in a batch or brand, and for historic marketing purposes (North America prefers pale whisky; the Far East likes rich amber). It is maintained that this additive is tasteless, but this depends how robust and flavourful the individual whisky is. In my view, it is a useful practice in relation to blends, but unforgivable for malts. It certainly means that one cannot judge age and origin by appearance alone.

Stage 2: Aroma (Straight)

Swirl the neat whisky in the glass, and nose it gingerly. A deep sniff of cask-strength spirit may anaesthetize your sense of smell for a time (known as "palate fade"). You may note "nose-prickle" or "nose-drying" – even "nose-burn" – which indicates the strength of the whisky. How "forward" or "shy" is it? How intense and complex? You should also note the key aromas; they may be somewhat subdued, and, at high strengths, spirity and vaporous. You may well want to sip the whisky before you add water, especially if you are tasting an old digestif malt.

Stage 3: Aroma (Dilute)

For tasting purposes, whisky should be diluted to about thirty per cent alcohol. The strength at which it is presented will be marked on the bottle; this is usually forty to forty-three per cent in the UK and forty-six per cent in the US, but there are variations: cask-strength – unreduced spirit – is normally about sixty per cent.

Here, an aside. How you enjoy whisky – straight, on the rocks, with water, soda, ginger, Coca-Cola – is a personal preference. It will vary, both according to the nature of the whisky (a venerable sherry-finished malt is best savoured neat, like brandy, and sipped in small quantities – your saliva acts as the dilutant), and according to the occasion (serious drinkers on the West Coast of Scotland favour dilution with lemonade).

For "sensory evaluation", however, whisky is diluted to between thirty per cent and twenty per cent alcohol (blenders tend to work at twenty per cent). It is not a bad idea to reduce to thirty per cent, nose and taste, then add a little more water. This agitates and "awakens" the spirit; you will be able to judge its viscimetric potential by observing the oils eddying, unlocking aromatics.

Swirl the glass again and sniff, first over the top of it (the bouquet), then deep within it (the aroma). Note your immediate impressions; try to put words to the scents that first strike you. Then, perhaps after a couple of deep sniffs of fresh air, repeat the performance. Now more subtle nuances may become apparent: elusive fragrances and "notes". It may be useful to run through a checklist of characteristics (see APPENDICES).

Stage 4: Mouth-feel

Take a large enough sip to fill your mouth and roll it over your tongue. What is your first impression of the intensity of flavour?

Then, consider the "texture" of the whisky, the feeling as it slides across your palate. Malt whiskies can usually be divided into three textures: "mouth-coating" (viscous), "mouth-warming" (spirity), and "mouth-furring" (slightly astringent and dry).

Stage 5: Primary taste

What are the initial flavours you pick up? Is it sweet on the tip of your tongue? Is there any saltiness, sourness, or acidity? Does the flavour change (it does with most whiskies) as it reaches the back of your tongue, becoming drier or more bitter?

Stage 6: Overall taste

As you swallow, is the back-palate flavour consistent with that promised by the bouquet and first taste? Or is it changing, beginning to play a different tune? It has been said that taste is like a golf ball: it rarely travels in a straight line, but bends, loops, and curves. As you go through the tasting process it can take several different directions, and you will also notice that even over a brief time, the flavour of the whisky will change slightly.

Stage 7: Finish

What can you taste, if anything, about a minute after swallowing? Did the taste fade rapidly, or did it linger like a northern sunset? Are there any echoes of earlier flavours or aromas which return for good or bad?

One might add a final stage, when you lay down your pencil and pad, suspend your super-critical judgement, and abandon yourself to inarticulate enjoyment. Pure hedonism!

The industry today

Until the 1980s, single-malt whiskies remained rare outside Scotland. Of course, there were exceptions (*see* GLEN GRANT and THE GLENLIVET, in particular), but the larger whisky companies, those whose fortunes had been made by blended whisky, were historically opposed to devoting money and effort to promoting single malts.

By the mid-1970s, however, stocks of whisky in bond were the highest they had ever been, and rising fast: from 168 million proof gallons in 1955 to over a billion gallons in 1975. In 1963, the directors of William Grant & Sons, owner of the Glenfiddich Distillery, resolved to set aside stock with a view to promoting its whisky as a single malt. A number of other independent distillers were to follow suit, notably Macallan and Glenmorangie in the mid-1970s, and by the early 1980s DCL had quietly launched its "Malt Whisky Cellar", which was a selection of singles from Lagavulin, Linkwood, Rosebank, Royal Lochnagar, and Talisker Distilleries.

Between 1970 and 1979, overall whisky consumption was in line with general consumption. The industry continued to expand and build new distilleries until 1976, when there was a sharp slump produced by the oil crisis and the end of the Vietnam War (which had stimulated the US economy). By 1979, the world economy was moving into recession, and the early 1980s saw a spate of distillery closures. In 1983 and 1985, DCL closed twenty-one of its forty-five distilleries; only seven of these have re-opened. Other owners followed suit, and during the same period, fifteen other distilleries were mothballed or dismantled; only six of these are currently operational.

Following a 1977 EC ruling concerning "parallel exports" (*see* JOHN BARR), DCL was obliged to withdraw a number of its leading brands from the UK market, including Johnnie Walker Red Label (which commanded about ten per cent of the market) and Haig Dimple, in order to protect its export trade. The company increased domestic prices on other major brands, introduced a number of new brands with mixed success (*see* JOHN BARR, BUCHANAN BLEND, THE CLAYMORE) and sold the UK rights of others to Whyte & Mackay (*see* WHYTE & MACKAY, HAIG). DCL's market share slumped from thirty-seven per cent to just under eighteen per cent in 1985, and although the company won a relaxation of the EC edict in 1983, which permitted the return of Red Label to the UK market, the brand never recovered, and DCL's morale was badly affected.

So badly, in fact, that the mighty Distillers became vulnerable to takeover. In December 1985, the Argyll Group, a UK food-retailing chain, made a bid to buy the company. This was rejected outright, but the management was shaken by the equivocation of shareholders and government and recommended the acceptance of an offer by Guinness, the brewing giant that had acquired Arthur Bell & Sons the year before (*see* BELL'S). There followed the most acrimonious takeover battle of modern times, and the greatest change in the whisky industry this century.

Guinness was ultimately successful, in May 1986, and became the largest drinks group in the world. The Scotch whisky industry was initially nervous, but United Distillers (UD), the subsidiary established by Guinness to run its spirits interests, won back its confidence with a statesmanlike approach and effective leadership. Led by UD, the industry resolved to reverse the cut-price and low-quality policy of the 1960s and 1970s, and set about restoring Scotch whisky's reputation as a product of infinite variety with a high-quality image.

In 1988, UD launched "The Classic Malts", a selection of six malt whiskies that displayed regional differences to their advantage, with a massive repackaging and promotional campaign. Other companies followed suit, bottling and promoting their malt whiskies, repositioning their blended brands, redesigning labels and packaging, and introducing new up-market expressions. So successful was this move, that the market for malt and de luxe blended whisky grew dramatically. This trend has continued.

At the same time, the 1980s was a decade of increased concentration of distillery and brand ownership in the hands of a few large international companies, many of which had interests beyond that of Scotch. At the opening of the decade, ownership generally belonged to companies whose main interests were in whisky (Seagram was the exception, while DCL had major interests in gin and Cognac).

By the end of the decade, major diversified conglomerates – including Guinness, Allied Lyons (with Allied Distillers as its whisky subsidiary), and Grand Metropolitan/International Distillers and Vintners (the main whisky subsidiary is Justerini & Brooks) – had bought distilleries and brands and joined the industry's principal players. This continued in the 1990s with the merger of Guinness and Grand Met in 1997 to form the world's largest drinks company, Diageo plc. In order to allow the merger to go through, Guinness was obliged to sell some of its leading brands, principally Dewar's (along with five distilleries), which went to Bacardi in 1998.

Three years later, the giant Canadian company, Seagram, disposed of its drinks business, with Diageo acquiring the non-Scotch whisky interests and Pernod Ricard the Scotch whisky business, including Chivas Brothers (under which name the company now trades) and nine distilleries (including The Glenlivet and Glen Grant). In parallel with these agglomerations, there were significant "un-bundling" moves within the industry. Inver House Distillers bought Pulteney Distillery in 1995 and Balmenach the next year. Highland Distillers bought The Macallan, in partnership with Suntory, and then, in 1999, Highland itself was taken over by its long-term partner, The Edrington Group, and removed from public ownership. Glenmorangie bought Ardbeg from Allied (1997). The long-established firm of indepenedent bottlers, Gordon & Macphail of Elgin, reopened Benromach Distillery, which they had bought in 1993). Other independent bottlers were to follow their example: Murray MacDavid bought Bruichladdich in 2000, Signatory bought Edradour, and Peter J. Russell & Co bought Glengoyne, both in 2003. The same year, Tullibardine Distillery was sold to a private consortium. It is currently being refurbished, with an impressive retail development adjacent, and will be back in operation in 2004, after nine years of silence.

In April 2004, J. & A. Mitchell & Co, owners of Springbank Distillery, built a new distillery called Glengyle nearby, on the site of a distillery of the same name which closed in the 1920s. At the time of writing, three further distilleries are proposed: at Kilchoman on Islay, Ladybank in Fife, and Blackford in Shetland. All are private ventures.

Many distilleries followed the example set during the 1970s by Glenfarclas, Glenfiddich, Glenlivet, and Glenturret, and opened or revamped visitor centres. Distillery visits are now an established feature of holidays in Scotland and the facilities are generally excellent (*see* APPENDICES).

Export sales of Scotch began to recover in 1985 and sales have increased every year by an average of 3.8 per cent, topping 200 million LPA for the first time in 1993. Growth has been most dramatic in the new markets of the Far East, although major increases have also occurred in Europe, particularly among traditional wine-drinking countries such as France, Spain, Greece, and Portugal.

In Scotch whisky's most important mature market, the US, sales declined every year since 1974 (from 97 million LPA to 30.30 million LPA in 2002), although there are signs of a revival of interest, particularly in single malts and de luxe blends.

In the UK, the pattern has been similar (a decline in consumption from 41.34 million LPA to 32.08 million LPA), but here the main reason for the decline is fiscal. Between 1974 and 1994 duty on spirits tripled, and although it has remained unchanged in every budget since 1998, this is still more than twice the rate, per unit of alcohol, on wine or beer.

Furthermore, with a level of spirits tax which is two and a half times the European average, it is impossible for the government to argue in favour of reducing duties within the European Community.

The collapse of Asian economies in 1998 hit the Scotch whisky industry hard, particularly those companies supplying the super-de luxe blends so popular in the Far East. In 1996, South Korea was the fifth-largest global market for Scotch and Thailand the eighth (the latter having been in fourteenth place in 1992). In December 1998, South Korea sank to fifteenth place, and Thailand to sixteenth. But there are strong indications that sales in the region are picking up, with South Korea now back in fifth place,

Japan in sixth place, Thailand in ninth and Taiwan emerging in eighteenth place.

The establishment of the World Trade Organisation has provided the Scotch whisky industry with a new opportunity to fight fiscal discrimination around the world; by 1999, it was the only industry to have successfully fought three such cases, against Japan, South Korea, and Chile. In spite of the fact that exports, which account for ninety per cent of the sales of Scotch, are still burdened by the strength of the pound, more whisky was exported in 1997 and at a higher value than ever before in history, and this has continued year on year ever since (to time of writing, 2003).

Conclusion

The year 1994 marked the 500th anniversary of the first written record of whisky-making in Scotland. The past five centuries have seen a cottage craft grow into a world industry, without altering the essentials of the way in which whisky is produced. They have witnessed the fortunes of a trade characterized by periods of great growth, followed by dramatic downswings. They have seen the product itself win worldwide acceptance. And at the end of this era, it is pleasant to report that the appreciation of Scotch whisky reaches broader and deeper than ever before in the spirit's history.

When he visited Edinburgh in 1822, King George IV was able to savour some Glenlivet which was "long in wood, mild as milk, and with the real contraband *goût* in it" (*see* THE GLENLIVET). A hundred years later, Aeneas Macdonald (in *Whisky*) bemoaned the decline of whisky as a civilized pleasure, properly understood by only "a handful of Scottish lairds, farmers, gamekeepers and bailies, relics of a vanished age of gold when the vintages of the north had their students and lovers", and promoted by its makers as "a mere brute stimulant . . . to the swillers, the drinkers-to-get-drunk who have not organs of taste and smell in them but only gauges of alcoholic content . . . [for whom] there are no whiskies but only one whisky – and, of course, soda".

Today, there are more single malts available to the general market than ever before. Bottlings of single malts from individual casks, at full strength and without chill-filtration, have proliferated. A genus of "super-de luxe" whiskies has emerged: blends that make use of very old fillings and demonstrate the contention that a blend is greater than the sum of its parts. Nearly twice as many books about Scotch whisky have been published since 1990 than were published between 1650 and 1970.

Only punitive taxation prevents widespread celebration.

Directory

Malt & grain whiskies

KEY

Abbreviations: Names of major companies are abbreviated as follows: the Distillers Company Limited – DCL; Jim Beam Brands – JBB; United Distillers & Vintners – UDV. All these are now historical. The Scotch Malt Whisky Society is also abbreviated as SMWS.

Category: Scotland is divided into Lowland, Campbeltown, Island (Islay, Mull, Jura, Orkney), Highland (North, South, East, West, Central), and Speyside. Sub-regions or districts are also provided. See also page 26: REGIONAL DIFFERENCES.

Distiller: In many cases the owning company will have licensed the distillery to a subsidiary.

Owner: About one-third of the distilleries in Scotland are owned by Diageo, the largest spirits company in the world (twenty-seven malt distilleries; 2.5 grain distilleries; this company arose out of the DCL to become UD, then UDV. The name Diageo was adopted in 2000). Other major owners are: Chivas Brothers Ltd (a subsidiary of Pernod Ricard; eleven malt distilleries), Allied Distillers (a subsidiary of Allied Domecq plc; nine malt distilleries, one grain distillery), John Dewar & Sons (a subsidiary of Bacardi Ltd; five malt distilleries), The Edrington Group Ltd (formerly Highland Distillers; five malt distilleries, 0.5 grain distillery), Inver House Distillers Ltd (a subsidiary of Pacific Spirits Ltd; five malt distilleries).

Tasting notes: Professional tasters, or "noses", attempt to be as objective as possible in their definition of a whisky's characteristics and flavour profile. I have allowed myself a little more latitude. Sensory evaluation is bound to have a subjective content – one's mood, health, appetite (or lack of it), circumstances, even the time of day, all have a bearing on what one will perceive in the whisky. I approach the task as a consumer, eager to get the most out of the dram before me. These notes, therefore, should be read as "one (or more) person's impression at a particular moment in time". Unless otherwise stated, the comments made apply to the proprietory bottling.

Where possible, the notes have been augmented by notes from the Scotch Malt Whisky Society's nosing panel, which I chair.

Aberfeldy

Category: Central Highland Distiller: John Dewar & Sons, Glasgow Owner: John Dewar & Sons.

Aberfeldy Distillery was built between 1897 and 1898 on a small area of land bought by Dewar's from the Marquis of Breadalbane. It lies on the outskirts of the spa town of the same name, and close to Taymouth Castle, the Marquis' seat. It was an ideal site for a distillery, having the main railway line at its door, which provided a direct link to Dewar's blending and bottling operations in Perth. It was close to the Pitlie Burn, which had supplied a previous distillery on the site with abundant water.

The distillery opened in 1898. Apart from the war years, it has remained in production ever since. In 1925, when Dewar's, Buchanan's, and Walker's joined DCL, Aberfeldy was taken over by Scottish Malt Distillers, which was the subsidiary responsible for the business of DCL's malt distilleries. Following the merger of Guinness and Grand Metropolitan, UDV was obliged to sell Dewar's, and Aberfeldy distillery, to Bacardi Ltd. It is the heart malt for Dewar's famous White Label blend, the number-one Scotch in the USA, and is bottled by its proprietor in limited amounts only. An excellent visitor centre opened in Spring 2000, "Dewar's World of Whisky", which admirably displays material from the archive in an interactive way.

Tasting notes: Aberfeldy offers a perfumed aroma of pear-drops, violets, vanilla, some peppermint, and a trace of biscuits. The flavour is pleasant but plain, somewhat syrupy, well-rounded, and sweetish, with a hint of oranges. It ends in a bitter-sweet finish.

Aberlour

Category: Speyside (Strathspey) Distiller: Aberlour-Glenlivet Distillery Co, Aberlour Owner: Chivas Bros, Paisley

Aberlour lies at the heart of Speyside, and its distillery was first noted in 1826, although whisky was almost certainly made on the site before this time, drawing water from St Drostan's Well.

St Drostan (or Dunstan) was made Archbishop of Canterbury in ad960. Previously, as Abbot of Glastonbury, he led a mission into the Highlands and established a cell at Aberlour. The well was used for baptisms, and later, more prosaically, to power a meal-mill and a sawmill.

The distillery was rebuilt after a fire in 1898. Much of the existing building dates from this time, with extensions in 1945 and more recent modernization by Campbell Distillers, which acquired it in 1974. Aberlour's distillery manager, Ian Mitchell, who died in 1992, was one of the longest-serving and best-regarded members of the industry. He was born within the distillery grounds, and both his father and his grandfather worked there before him.

Aberlour uses only Scottish barley and has very broad-based stills; the product is matured partly in sherry casks, partly in bourbon. Cork bungs are used instead of wooden ones; these, it is believed, allow the harsher vapours to evaporate more easily. Aberlour is available in all the major malt whisky markets, has worldwide popularity, and is particularly strong in France. In 2001 it was the seventh-best-selling malt worldwide (having risen from twenty-second place).

It is the heart malt for the Clan Campbell blends and is the only malt whisky to have won both the Pot Still Trophy and the gold medal at the International Wine and Spirit Competition twice (in 1986 and 1990). Strangely, the week the first award was announced, St Drostan's Well, which had dried up, gushed forth once more!

Tasting notes: Aberlour possesses a rich nose, with a strong caramel aroma when nosed straight (it is delicious drunk neat), with traces of pine (fresh sawdust) and smoke, and a hint of peat as in a mountain burn. It has a voluptuous body and a typical Speyside flavour: sweet, estery, bubblegum and pear-drops. Well-balanced, with a clean, sweetish finish.

Allt-a-Bhainne

Category: Speyside (Glenlivet) Distiller: The Chivas & Glenlivet Group Owner: Chivas Bros, Paisley

Allt-a-Bhainne (correctly pronounced "Alta-vanya", although the owners refer to it as "Alta-Bane") means "the burn (*i.e.* stream) of milk". The distillery was built in 1975 on the eastern slopes of Ben Rinnes, overlooking Glen Rinnes, between Dufftown and Glen Livet. The buildings are stylishly modern, with satisfyingly varied roof lines and "traditional" features. It has two stills and is capable of producing a million gallons of whisky a year (4.5 million litres). The use of computers makes it possible for the plant to be run by only two operators.

It was built by Seagram to provide fillings for Chivas Regal, and has never been bottled as a single by its owner. The distillery is currently mothballed.

Tasting notes: Designed as a "filling", not as a single malt, the rare casks that have been bottled are variable, some richer than others. It has a typical Speyside profile, fragrant and toffeed, with hints of coffee. Light-weight, generally, with a sweet flavour and spicy undertones.

An Cnoc (aka Knockdhu)

Category: East Highland Distiller: The Knockdhu Distillery Co, Knock, Banffshire Owner: Inver House Distillers, Airdrie, Lanarkshire

Knockdhu Distillery (pronounced "nock-doo") was originally opened in 1894. A showpiece of its day, it was the first distillery to be built by DCL, and its two original stills are still in production today.

The site is on the River Isla, beneath Knock Hill (from which the distillery draws its water), close to the fertile Laich o'Moray which provided abundant barley. For nearly a hundred years, Knockdhu's product went mainly into Haig's blends; then, in 1983, it was closed. Five years later, it was acquired by Inver House, with a view to making Knockdhu available as a single malt. The name of the proprietory bottling was changed in 1993 to prevent it being confused with Knockando.

Tasting notes: (*12 Years Old*) The nose is malty and sweet, with some fruit and a whiff of wood smoke; the mouth-feel is soft and smooth; taste is sweet with orange notes and a surprisingly dry, smoky, lingering finish.

Ardbeg

*Category: Island (Islay) **Distiller:** Ardbeg Distillery, Port Ellen*
***Owner:** Glenmorangie plc, Broxburn, Midlothian*

It is said that the location of Ardbeg Distillery, on the south coast of Islay, was once the hideout of a gang of smugglers who dispersed after their cache was discovered by the Excise. What is certain is that there was a family of MacDougalls here from 1798, one of whom started a legal distillery in 1815 which was producing around 500 gallons (2,270 litres) per annum by 1835. The family retained its interest in the distillery until 1977, when it was sold to Hiram Walker. Allied Distillers bought it in 1989, and sold it to the present owner, Glenmorangie, in 1997.

Until the early 1980s, Ardbeg Distillery had its own floor maltings. Unusually, there were no fans in the pagoda-roofed malting houses; the trapped peat smoke thoroughly permeated the malt, producing an extremely pungent whisky.

The strong character of Ardbeg tended to be too dominant for the blenders, and the distillery's history has been punctuated by closures. Between 1989 and 1998 it worked at only a third of its capacity. It no longer uses its own maltings, although the bought-in malt is among the most heavily peated in Scotland, at 50 parts per million phenols. Only about 200 cases were bottled as single malt every year by Allied Distillers. There are independent bottlings and these are very highly regarded by connoisseurs of Islay whisky.

Tasting notes: Peat smoke, iodine, seaweed, and sawdust on the nose. Smoky, salty flavour, with a medicinal bite in the finish. The older expressions gain in depth; the younger have a somewhat shallow flavour range, with all the powerful aromas associated with Islay malts.

Ardmore

*Category: East Highland **Distiller:** Ardmore Distillery,*
*Kennethmont, Aberdeenshire **Owner:** Allied Distillers, Dumbarton*

The Ardmore Distillery was established by William Teacher's successors in 1898 (*see* Teacher's). Until this time, the company had been concerned exclusively with blending, but during the 1890s, whisky boom, it quickly realized the importance of securing its own fillings.

The distillery stands deep in rural Aberdeenshire, near the ancient villages of Spynie and Kennethmont, close to the river Bogie. Despite some extensive modernization in the 1950s and 1970s the buildings still retain several of their original features and the stills were direct fired until 2002.

Ardmore is rarely bottled as a single malt by its owners, but is available from independent bottlers.

Tasting notes: A dryish nose, with malty, cereal notes; slightly oily; "meaty". The flavour shows traces of silage, salt, and vegetable mash. Overall, a balance between sweet and dry.

Auchentoshan

Category: Lowland Distiller: Morrison Bowmore (Distillers), Glasgow Owner: Morison Bowmore

It is likely that Lowland malts were the first whiskies to be drunk in any quantity in England – their lightness had more appeal than the heavily flavoured Highland malts. However, following the arrival of consistent and well-made blended whiskies after about 1870, the entire output of the Lowland distilleries went for blending.

The growing appreciation of malt whisky led to several Lowland malts being made available as singles, but alas, most Lowland distilleries are now closed (*see* ST MAGDALENE, ROSEBANK). Auchentoshan is one of the survivors and its malt is unique in being created by "triple distillation", formerly a common Lowland practice, which makes for a lighter distillate and helps the spirit mature more quickly.

Auchentoshan Distillery is on the northern edge of Glasgow, where the city gives way to the Kilpatrick Hills from which it draws its water. It was founded as early as 1800, largely rebuilt after the Second World War and re-equipped in 1974. A decade later, it was bought by Stanley P. Morrison & Co to complement its Highland and Islay distilleries (*see* BOWMORE, GLEN GARIOCH).

Tasting notes: Nosed straight, the aroma is of sweet hay or straw, fresh and meadow-like. With water, this persists with cereal notes (dry barns); slightly oily. Hay notes are also apparent in the flavour, now with a slightly lemony tinge. The overall impression is well-balanced, clean, and dry, and the finish is dry.

Auchroisk

Category: Speyside (Keith) Distiller: Auchroisk Distillery, Mulben, Banffshire Owner: Diageo plc

Auchroisk Distillery was opened in 1974 and is something of a showpiece. Its total production is bottled as a single malt, launched in 1986. Pronunciation of the name Auchroisk ("athrusk") was considered too hard for non-Scots, so when its make was first marketed, it was named "The Singleton of Auchroisk".

As well as indicating that it is a single malt, the word "Singleton" is an expression that was used by the industry earlier this century to describe single casks of malt whisky at auction. The fact that they came as single items, rather than in "parcels", often implied exceptional quality or age.

The water used at Auchroisk comes from Dorie's Well, a local spring which rises from granite through sandstone, and produces the soft water which is traditionally sought by distillers; the distiller at Auchroisk claims it accounts for the whisky's character. This is enhanced and enriched by part of each bottling being matured for two years in ex-sherry butts, and part in ex-bourbon barrels.

The resulting whisky has done well in tastings, winning gold medals at the International Wine & Spirit Competition and at the

Monde Sélection in 1992. The brand is well-established in North America, Japan, Spain, and Portugal, as well as the UK.

Tasting notes: Gives little away on the nose: traces of cereal, spirity, with straw or hay notes. The taste is inoffensive and somewhat bland; there are some beeswax notes, some nuts, very slight wood smoke; a clean flavour, with a sudden fade.

Aultmore

Category: Speyside (Keith) Distiller: John Dewar & Sons, Glasgow
Owner: John Dewar & Sons

Built in 1896 by Alexander Edward, the owner of Benrinnes Distillery, Aultmore is Gaelic for "the big burn", and derives its name from a neighbouring stream. The distillery is situated two and a half miles north of Keith, in the hills between that town and the Moray Firth. The district was popular with smugglers in the old days on account of its relative remoteness and the peat-rich springs of the Foggie Moss, from which the distillery draws its water.

In 1898, Alexander Edward bought Oban Distillery, and the following year, the new company was nearly brought down by the collapse of a principal customer, Pattison's of Leith. Production was cut, and times remained difficult until 1923, when the two distilleries were offered for sale. Aultmore was bought by John Dewar & Sons for £20,000, and thus, two years later, became part of DCL, which licensed it to John & Robert Harvey & Co.

In 1952, DCL embarked on a programme of modernization at the distillery, including a pioneering scheme for treating and making use of distillery residue: the protein-rich draff and pot ale left after distillation has taken place. The experiments here and at Imperial Distillery were successful, and now "dark grains", an animal feed, is made by all distilleries. In 1970–1, Aultmore was rebuilt and expanded, and another pair of stills was added.

Aultmore has long been well-respected by blenders, and is ranked "top class". The distillery was sold to Bacardi by UDV in 1998.

Tasting notes: Sweet and estery, with apple notes, and traces of walnuts. Surprisingly dry, with maltiness and a floral finish.

Balblair

Category: North Highland Distiller: Balblair Distillery Ltd
Owner: Inver House Distillers, Airdrie

On the southern shore of the Dornoch Firth, close to the village of Edderton, sits Balblair. Said to have been founded in 1790, it claims to be the second-oldest distillery in Scotland. The location of the original distillery is uncertain, but some of the present buildings may date from the eighteenth century; the rest have not changed for a hundred years. It is among the most attractive distilleries in Scotland, and, unusually, has three stills.

As with many areas where water and peat are in generous supply, this was a favourite site for smuggling activities. Edderton is known as the "parish of peat", and the peat here is curiously dry and crumbly – presumably because of the plants from which it is composed, or perhaps because it is relatively young, which some distilleries deem to be an advantage (see HIGHLAND PARK). The water used by the distillery trickles through this peat, which is said to account for the whisky's distinctive spicy character.

Balblair was bought by Hiram Walker in 1970. Its successor, Allied Distillers, sold the distillery to Inver House in 1996. Inver House resumed production and commenced bottling in May 1997. **Tasting notes:** The nose has a distinctly salty tang, with some spice and an elusive freshness (pine sap?). The taste is also fresh, clean, sweet-sour, with pinewood traces and perhaps a dash of lemon.

Balmenach

Category: Speyside (Strathspey) Distiller: Inver House Distillers, Airdrie Owner: Inver House Distillers

Early in the nineteenth century, three Macgregor brothers left Tomintoul for Cromdale, a small village about five miles away across the hills. James Macgregor settled in Balmenach and established a farm there, on which he kept an illicit still. Sir Robert Bruce Lockhart, one of Macgregor's direct descendants, and the author of *Scotch,* describes how, in 1823, his great-grandfather received a visit from the local exciseman, whose suspicions had been aroused by seeing a building with a mill-wheel and lade. Asked what it was, the farmer told him that it was a peat shed. Later, after receiving generous hospitality, and as he was about to leave, the exciseman gently advised Macgregor to take out a licence for his peat shed.

James Macgregor died in 1878, and was succeeded by his brother, who was summoned home from New Zealand, where he had made his fortune, to take control of what was by then a well-established distillery. Alas, the following year, during the great storm which blew down the railway bridge across the River Tay (immortalized by William McGonagall), the distillery chimney collapsed and a catastrophic fire was only averted by a stillman opening the discharge cocks and preventing the fire from spreading. In 1897, a limited company was formed as the Balmenach-Glenlivet Distillery Co, and in the same year a private railway line with sidings was laid down, linking the distillery to the station at Cromdale.

The distillery was closed during the First World War. Having been acquired by Scottish Malt Distillers in 1930, it closed again and was used as a billet for the Royal Corps of Signals during the Second World War.

The distillery was extended from four to six stills in 1960 – an indication of the demand for this "First Class" malt from blenders – but it was mothballed in 1993. Four years later it was sold to Inver House Distillers, who plan to make it more widely available. **Tasting notes:** Has a sweet, slightly sherried, very slightly smoky, rich, and perfumed nose. The perfume comes through in the taste, with some maltiness, and the flavour embraces every area of the tongue: sweet to start, then an appetizing tinge at either side (like acid drops), even a slight dry note as it slides over the back of the tongue. Beautifully balanced, complex, satisfying whisky.

Balvenie

Category: Speyside (Dufftown) **Distiller:** *William Grant & Sons*
Owner: *William Grant & Sons, Dufftown*

In 1892, five years after building Glenfiddich Distillery, William Grant bought the ground adjacent to it and built a second distillery. Its nucleus was "new" Balvenie Castle, which had been designed in the neoclassical style by James Gibb and built in 1724 for the first Earl of Fife.

The ruins of "old" Balvenie Castle stand on the hill behind. This was founded at the turn of the thirteenth century by the third Earl of Buchan, who entertained King Edward I of England there and forfeited it to the Earls of Douglas in 1326. The "Black" Douglases themselves forfeited the castle to the Crown in 1355, but James II returned it to Lady Douglas, on condition that she marry his supporter, Sir John Stewart, and pay an annual rent of a single red rose. Stewart was created first Earl of Atholl and Lord Balvenie, and his descendants lived there until 1610. The rose is a feature of the coat of arms that decorates Balvenie's label. In 1673, the castle was bought by Alexander Duff of Braco, who gave his name to nearby Dufftown and whose descendants became Earls of Fife.

Balvenie is unusual in having its own maltings and growing (some of) its own barley. It also has its own coppersmith's shop and cooperage (which it shares with Glenfiddich), and eight stills, which have much longer necks than those at its sister distillery. It matures its product in situ – partly in new wood, partly in fino sherry casks, and partly in oloroso casks (the latter are used for the final year's maturation only).

Tasting notes: (*10 Years Old*) Deep amber colour; medium body; sherried, honeyed, orangey nose. The flavour is rich and chocolatey, with a balance of sweet and dry, finishing on the dry side. A first-rate after-dinner malt.

Banff

Category: East Highland **Distiller:** *distillery closed 1983*

The distillery was founded in 1824 by James McKilligan & Co at the Mill of Banff, close to the ancient town of the same name. Some years later, it was taken over by James Simpson & Co, but closed in 1863.

Simpson's son then built a new distillery at Inverboyndie, a mile west of Banff and strategically placed to take advantage of the recently established railway line. In 1877, a fire destroyed the new distillery, apart from its maltings and warehouses; when it was rebuilt, a fire engine was installed to prevent further disasters.

During the Second World War, the distillery was closed and the buildings used to billet soldiers from the King's Own Scottish Borderers. On the afternoon of Saturday, August 16, 1941, a single enemy aircraft bombed the site; no one was injured, but the warehouse was burned to the ground. Exploding whisky casks were seen to fly into the air, and those remaining were smashed to prevent the fire spreading. *The Banffshire Journal* reported that "thousands of gallons of whisky were lost, either by burning or running to waste over the land . . . and so overpowering were the results that even farm animals grazing in the neighbourhood became visibly intoxicated". It is said that ducks and geese dabbling in the Boyndie burn were recovered at the seashore, some dead, some drunk, and that cows could not stand to be milked.

At one time, Banff (it was more commonly known as Inverboyndie) was purveyed to the House of Commons, but for many years before its final closure in 1983, the entire production of the distillery was sold for blending.

Tasting notes: Malty, sweet but slightly astringent nose with a whiff of smoke. The flavour is bland and light, with a quick, slightly soapy finish. Pleasantly unassertive.

Ben Nevis

Category: West Highland – also Standard Blend Distiller: Ben Nevis Distillery, Fort William Owner: Nikka Whisky Distilling Co, Japan

The distillery was built in 1825 by "Long John" Macdonald (*see* Long John), who produced the famous blend Dew of Ben Nevis, which, like the distillery itself, is named after the highest mountain in Scotland. Macdonald stood six feet four inches tall (1.93 metres) and was a renowned figure in the whisky industry. His distillery was the first licensed operation in the area.

In 1955, it was bought by Joseph Hobbs, a colourful character who had made and lost a fortune in Canada during the 1920s in shipping, building, and wines and spirits importing. One of his ventures was to use a converted naval vessel, the *HMCS Stadacona*, to run spirits into the USA during Prohibition. He arrived in the UK about 1938, and having bought a manufacturing company in Leicester, began to buy distilleries in Scotland. At one time he owned (through his trading company Associated Scottish Distillers, itself funded by National Distillers of America) Benromach, Bruichladdich, Glenury Royal, Glenlochy, Glenesk and Fettercairn Distilleries.

Hobbs later started an American-style cattle ranch along the Great Glen, allowing his beasts to roam semi-wild on the mountain slopes (this is still in existence). Some of his ranch hands took the idea a stage further and dressed as cowboys, complete with stetsons, chaps, and spurs!

After he sold his interest in Associated Scottish Distillers, Hobbs bought Inverlochy Castle (now a luxurious hotel), Ben Nevis and Lochside distilleries, and introduced patent stills into their operations in order to produce both malt and grain whiskies under the same roof; however, the move was not a great success. The brand name had been sold to Seager Evans in the 1920s, before Hobbs bought the distillery.

In 1981, the name and the distillery were reunited when the latter was bought by Long John International, a subsidiary of Whitbread & Co, the major brewer. Ben Nevis Distillery had been silent for many years after Hobbs' death and its new owner took it out of production in 1983. The distillery was sold to Nikka, the Japanese distiller, in 1991, and production has resumed.

Tasting notes: *(21 Years Old)* The nose is very rich – rum toffee, coconut, fruitcake, caramel, and sherry – but with intriguing herbal and floral notes: sherbet and violets. The taste is full-flavoured – sweet, smooth, and rich, reminiscent of chocolate and coconuts – and the finish is smoky and slightly dry. An impressive whisky.

Benriach

Category: Speyside (Elgin) Distiller: The Chivas & Glenlivet Group
Owner: Chivas Bros, Paisley

This distillery was built in 1897–8 by John Duff & Co, the founder and owner of Longmorn Distillery, which is less than a quarter of a mile away. The distillery was closed between 1900 and 1965. In 1985, two new stills were added to the complex to boost its annual output to over 780,000 proof gallons (3.5 million litres) of pure alcohol. It is one of the few distilleries to retain its own floor maltings, which also supply malt to Longmorn. Until recently it was rare as a single, but in 1995 its owner began to promote it as part of its Heritage Selection.

Tasting notes: A big, toffeed nose when nosed neat. A noticeable sherry aroma, some floral fruitiness, with a hint of liquorice. Taste is positive, malty with a trace of toffee. Sweetish with a dry finish. Sound but uninspired.

Benrinnes

Category: Speyside (Strathspey) Distiller: A&A Crawford, Leith
Owner: Diageo plc

Benrinnes Distillery was built 700 feet (213 metres) above sea level on the northern slopes of the mountain of the same name which dominates eastern Speyside. Its make is ranked "top class" by blenders.

The earliest reference to a distillery in this location was in 1826 at Whitehouse Farm, some distance away from the present site, but this was washed away by a great flood three years later. The farmstead at Lower Lyne of Ruthrie was adapted in 1835 to form the present distillery, although little now remains of these buildings. The first licensee was Peter McKenzie.

In 1864, it was bought by David Edward and his son Alexander, who owned and promoted many distilleries on Speyside, including Aultmore and Craigellachie. Alfred Barnard described the Scurran and Rowantree burns, from which the distillery draws its water, as rising "from springs on the summit of the mountain and [it] can be seen on a clear day, some miles distant, sparkling over the prominent rocks on its downwards course, passing over mossy banks and gravel, which perfectly filters it".

The Benrinnes-Glenlivet Distillery Company was formed in 1897, but suffered badly when Edward's brokers collapsed two years later. However, production continued and it attracted the attention of John Dewar & Sons, which acquired control in 1922, taking Benrinnes into DCL with it in 1925. Ownership was transferred to Scottish Malt Distillers, the DCL subsidiary, in 1930.

In 1955, major reconstruction was undertaken in the interests of more efficient production; unfortunately, the new buildings do nothing for their picturesque setting. Today the licensed distiller is A&A Crawford, which used to use much of Benrinnes' output for its 3 and 5 Star blends (*see* CRAWFORD'S).

Tasting notes: (15 Years Old) Pleasant, fruity aroma – rich, with some sherry, traces of beeswax, and a hint of liquorice. Medium body. Smooth and rich-tasting, with traces of fresh brambles and some smoke (cigar boxes). Clean and surprisingly dry finish.

Benromach

Category: North Highland Distiller: Gordon & MacPhail
Owner: Gordon & MacPhail, Elgin

Benromach Distillery was founded in 1898 by Duncan MacCallum of Glen Nevis Distillery (Campbeltown) and FW Brickmann, a broker from Leith. They were encouraged by Alexander Edward, the well-known promoter of Scotch whisky on Speyside, who granted them the land on which to build the distillery.

Unfortunately in 1900, before the distillery had commenced production, Pattison's of Leith collapsed, and Brickmann, who was closely associated with the company, had to withdraw from the partnership. MacCallum only maintained production for a short time, then had to fight a lengthy battle with the Inland Revenue.

The distillery remained silent from 1909 until 1939, when it was acquired by Joseph Hobbs (*see* BEN NEVIS) and Hattim Attari, a London financier. Having bought up several distilleries, they then sold them to National Distillers of America, which in turn returned them to the Scottish ownership of DCL in 1953. Its subsidiary, Scottish Malt Distillers, managed the Benromach Distillery, which was licensed until its closure in 1983 to J&W Hardie of South Queensferry. In 1992, the distillery was sold to Gordon & MacPhail, the independent bottler based in Elgin. Gordon & MacPhail has refurbished Benromach and resumed production in 1998, exactly a century after the distillery's foundation.

Tasting notes: A pleasant, estery nose, with walnuts predominating and some light solvent and toffee notes in the background. Joined by sweet, fresh, pine-and-geranium scents when water is added; even some turpentine. Smooth mouth-feel; sweet start, malty middle, and a sweet-dry finish. Lean, fresh, and complex.

Ben Wyvis

Category: North Highland Distiller: distillery closed

The Ben Wyvis Distillery was established in 1965 as part of The Invergordon grain distillery complex on the northern shore of the Cromarty Firth. Its product was used entirely for blending although it is thought that one cask was bottled as an 8-year-old in 1974 and sold in the USA. The only recent bottling is a 1967, bottled Spring 2000 by Signatory. The distillery was closed and dismantled in 1977.

It should be noted that there was an earlier distillery called Ben Wyvis, built in 1879 at Ferintosh, near Dingwall and renamed "Ferintosh" in 1893 when it was bought by a Belfast firm. It was closed in 1926, but the warehouses continued to be used until the early 1980s. They have now been converted into flats and there are no known examples of this distillery's make.

Tasting notes: "Round and smooth and heavy in style. Subtle rather than robust" (Norman Mathison, Master Blender).

Black Barrel

Category: Single Grain **Distiller:** *William Grant & Sons, Girvan* **Owner:** *William Grant & Sons*

Black Barrel (or BlackBarrel, as its owners prefer) is one of only four grain whiskies bottled as singles. The brand was launched in 1995 in Spain, France, and Portugal, and is now also available in South America, South Africa, Scandinavia, Germany, the Czech Republic, and Canada.

Girvan Distillery was built by William Grant & Sons in 1963 to provide fillings for its blended whiskies (at that time named Standfast, now William Grant's – *see* entry). It has one Coffey still, a column still for neutral spirit production. It also once had a pair of pot stills to produce the single malt Ladyburn (*see* entry).

BlackBarrel is matured in "freshly charred casks, used once only for this whisky" and its owner claims that this makes for smoothness and mellowness.

Bladnoch

Category: Lowland **Distiller:** *Bladnoch Distillery Co* **Owner:** *Raymond Armstrong T/A Co-ordinated Development Services*

Bladnoch Distillery lies deep in the pastoral southwest corner of Scotland, on the Machars Peninsula in Wigtownshire, by the River Bladnoch from whence it draws its water. *Machars* signifies flat or low country in Gaelic, and well describes the landscape in which Scotland's most southerly distillery is located. It is a landscape rich in early Celtic remains, and inspired Sir Walter Scott's *Bride of Lammermoor*.

The distillery itself has been producing whisky since 1814, when it was established by two brothers, John and Thomas McClelland. It flourished as a typical winter-operating distillery until the 1930s, when it was closed for eighteen years and its equipment sold to Sweden. Since reopening, it has been expanded twice and been sold twice, the second time to Bell's in 1983, which brought Bladnoch with it when it joined United Distillers.

The distillery was again closed in 1993 and taken over by the local authority, which sold it to its present owner, Raymond Armstrong. He established a visitor centre and resumed production in 2001.

Tasting notes: Bladnoch is an example of the Lowland style: the colour of pale straw and smelling of damp hay and cereal mash. The keynote on the nose is Parma violets and there is a hint of grappa. This whisky begins sweetish and finishes dry.

Blair Athol

Category: Central Highland **Distiller:** *Arthur Bell & Sons, Perth* **Owner:** *Diageo plc*

Blair Athol Distillery was founded in th late 1790s by John Stewart and Robert Robertson – not at Blair Atholl (double "l") village itself, but eleven miles south at Pitlochrie. The whole district around Pitlochrie was once involved in the production of whisky: there were over thirty distilleries in the area, although only three have survived.

Alfred Barnard wrote in 1887 that the water of the Allt Dour Burn ("the burn of the otter"), which flowed from Ben Vrackie, rising above the snow-line close to Blair Athol Distillery, was "of the purest description, sparkling as clear as crystal".

It was revived in the mid-1820s and bought by P. Mackenzie & Co in the 1880s, which considerably enlarged the buildings and added two new granaries and malting floors. By the turn of the century, there was a capacity for 100,000 gallons (over 454,000 litres). However, the distillery was closed in 1932 and was out of production until 1949.

In 1933, P. Mackenzie & Co was bought by Arthur Bell & Sons, an event one writer describes as Bell's "coming of age". In 1949, Bell's substantially rebuilt the distillery, happily without spoiling its attractive character. It was described as "almost a model distillery" by Professor McDowall, who considers its product "one of the best malts". The distillery went with Bells to United Distillers (and thence to Diageo) in 1985.

Tasting notes: It has a dry, sharp nose, becoming sweeter and creamier as the alcohol settles – and finishing deep and orangey with some cereal notes (fresh baking), vanilla, and heathery overtones. Its flavour is very smooth and sweet, with a gingery finish and mossy overtones.

Bowmore

Category: Island (Islay) **Distiller:** *Morrison Bowmore*

Midway along the southern shore of Loch Indaal is the village of Bowmore, considered to be the "capital" of Islay. It is a fine example of a late-eighteenth century planned village, with its quirky round church sitting at the head of the main street, which runs down to the shore through a huddle of houses. The distillery buildings are on the quayside.

Bowmore Distillery was established in 1779 by John Simpson, a local merchant. It was one of the earliest legal distilleries on the island and it was also owner-operated, which at that time was unusual, since most proprietors on Islay leased out their distilleries. Bowmore was later taken over by James Mutter and his family. Mutter, in addition to being a farmer and distiller, had the unlikely role of Ottoman, Portuguese, and Brazilian vice-consul in Glasgow.

Mutter considerably expanded the distillery, using his own steamship to bring barley and coal to Bowmore and deliver the whisky to Glasgow; thus, the Bowmore name began to travel and demand grew. The family kept the distillery until the 1890s, when it was sold and became the Bowmore Distillery Co. During the Second World War, the buildings were used as a coastal command base by the Air Ministry. After a brief spell of ownership by William Grigor & Son of Inverness in the 1950s, the distillery was acquired by Stanley P. Morrison in 1963.

Morrison rebuilt and renovated many of the buildings, retaining the malting floors that are still used today and supply about twenty per cent of its malt requirement, the rest coming from Port Ellen Maltings and from a maltings on the mainland.

Black Bowmore, a limited edition from 1964 that was bottled at fifty per cent, is something of a legend and extremely rare.
Tasting notes: A much more complex nose than the southern Islays, and fuller than their northern cousins. The nose is peaty, but not medicinal; there is a powerful scent of air freshener, artificial lavender, and butterscotch. The flavour is big, sweet, and resonant: there are traces of linseed oil and pure turpentine, reminiscent of a painter's studio; a salty tang and billows of smoke.

Braeval (formerly Braes of Glenlivet)
Category: Speyside (Glenlivet) Distiller: The Chivas & Glenlivet Group Owner: Chivas Bros, Paisley

This distillery, not far from Dufftown, was built by Seagrams, the Canadian distilling giant, in 1973 during that company's expansion in Scotland and was originally named "Braes of Glenlivet", which is where it is located. The entire output is used for blending. The architecture of the complex follows traditional distillery designs while employing the most advanced modern production technology. It can be operated by one man and a computer.

The distillery was renamed in 1995 to avoid any possible confusion with its sister distillery, The Glenlivet. It is very rare as a single, since it is not bottled by its owner. Ownership passed to Pernod Ricard (Chivas Brothers' holding company) in 2000. The distillery is currently mothballed.
Tasting notes: The colour is deep gold, with copper lights. The unreduced nose is of treacle toffee, with some tobacco; flattens out with water, becomes more estery; fresh pears are a keynote and some ozone. Flavour starts sweet but is predominantly sour. Bitter aftertaste.

Brora
Category: North Highland Distiller: distillery closed 1983

Brora, the original part of Clynelish Distillery, stands close to the village of the same name on the east coast of Sutherland (*see* CLYNELISH). In 1967–8, a new distillery was built at Clynelish.

The old distillery was closed for seven years before being refurbished and renamed "Brora" in order to distinguish it from the new Clynelish Distillery. Brora was closed in May 1983, and true Brora malt is becoming increasingly hard to find (*see* CLYNELISH for G&M 1972).

Tasting notes: (*20 Years Old+Rare Malt*) Sweet, vanilla nose. No sign of peat smoke appears until water is added, and, even then, very little (which is of a light medicinal character). There are some natural turpentine traces. Smooth, sweetish mouth-feel with a dryish finish.

Bruichladdich

Category: Island (Islay) Distiller: The Bruichladdich Distillery Co Ltd, Islay Owner: The Bruichladdich Distillery Co Ltd (incorporating Murray McDavid)

Bruichladdich (pronounced "brewickladdie"), which means "the brae on the shore", is the most westerly of Scotland's distilleries, situated in that western peninsula of Islay known as the Rhinns.

The distillery was built in 1881 by William, Robert, and John Harvey, with money from a trust established by their father, a well-known distiller in Glasgow (*see* HARVEY'S). The building used a newly patented material in its construction (concrete) and has changed little in appearance since its construction, with smart, whitewashed buildings overlooking the pebbled shore of Loch Indaal. Much of its equipment, including cast-iron brewing tanks and mash-tun, and one of its stills (which is riveted rather than being welded) date from the distillery's foundation. The warehouses have traditional earthen floors. (Visitors are welcome, but should make an appointment.) In 1929, the Harveys were obliged to close the doors on this, their last remaining distillery. It was bought by the redoubtable Joseph Hobbs (*see* BEN NEVIS) for Associated Scottish Distillers.

Bruichladdich became part of the Invergordon Group in 1968. It passed into the ownership of Whyte & Mackay in 1994, which mothballed it the following year and then sold it to a consortium of (mainly local) investors led by the independent bottling company Murray McDavid, in 2000. The new owner has done a splendid job of restoring the distillery and its archaic equipment, has opened a visitor centre and now bottles a range of years and expressions issued by an independent bottler in 1997, labelled Lochindaal.

Tasting notes: A delicate nose, biscuity, slightly oily, with a hint of seaweed; there is no trace of peat until water is added, and then it is only slight – little to betray its Islay origin. Flavour is fresh at first, with almonds, moss (rather than peat), and sea breeze, developing into a sweetish finish (marzipan). A complex and subtle malt.

Bunnahabhain

Category: Island (Islay) Distiller: Bunnahabhain Distillery, Port Askaig, Isle of Islay Owner: Burn Stewart Distillers plc, East Kilbride

The inspiration for building a distillery on the Sound of Islay came from W.A. Robertson (of Robertson & Baxter, blenders in Glasgow) and his partner J.C.R. Marshall. In 1878, they approached the Greenless brothers of Campbeltown for technical advice and purchased a site at the mouth of the river Margadale: "Bunnahabhain" (pronounced "Boonahaven") means "mouth of the river". Building commenced in 1881. Their company, the Islay Distillery Co, amalgamated with Glenrothes-Glenlivet Distillery in 1888 to become The Highland Distilleries Company.

The attraction of the site was the abundant supply of fresh, peaty water that tumbled down a burn from Loch Staoinsha, combined with ready access to the Sound of Islay for shipment. Otherwise, it was remote and desolate, without a tree in sight, let alone a human habitation. A mile-long road had to be constructed up a steep slope behind the distillery to join the track from Port Askaig; a strong pier had to be built and stone quarried for the distillery buildings, warehouses, and accommodation. In due course, an entire village grew up in the shadow of the distillery, complete with a school and a village hall.

Bunnahabhain's make was used almost exclusively for blending until the late 1970s, when the 12 Year Old was launched, labelled with an illustration inspired by the old song "Westering Home". The UK, the USA, France, and Holland are its main markets. In 1984, a bottling was made of casks filled in 1963 (this was the last year that the distillery's floor maltings were used) to celebrate Bunnahabhain's centenary. These are now very rare.

Bunnahabhain is the lightest of the Islay malts, and the distillery ensures this by using unpeated malt, by drawing spring water from underground (before it has run through peat), and by taking a very narrow cut from the second distillation. Maturation is done on site, in a mix of sherry and bourbon casks. The style may change, however, since the distillery was sold by Edrington to Burn Stewart in 2003, who plan to introduce a peated expression. **Tasting notes:** Light in colour, Bunnahabhain has a very fresh, salty nose and a light to medium body. Its flavour is smooth and subtly phenolic – a faint whiff of smoke, with a malty sweetness. Flavour develops well, and the finish is refreshing.

Cameronbridge

Category: Single Grain Distiller: John Haig & Co, Markinch, Fife
Owner: Diageo plc

The Haigs have a good claim to be the oldest Scotch whisky distillers in Scotland. Their first recorded association with distilling was in 1655, when Robert Haig was summoned before the Kirk Session, charged with working his still on the Sabbath! The distilling interests of the family continued over many years; it was 21-year-old John Haig who built the Cameronbridge Distillery in 1824, near the house in which he was born and brought up.

The distillery's original product was a Lowland malt, but Haig was a keen experimenter. In 1827, the year that his cousin, Robert Stein, invented the continuous still, Haig installed one at Cameronbridge. After the repeal of the Corn Laws in the 1840s (which made grain cheaper), he installed a pair of Coffey stills and concentrated on the production of grain whisky. By the 1870s, the distillery was producing 1.25 million gallons (over 5.6 million litres) of spirit a year – a remarkable amount for that era.

In 1877, only a year before he died, John Haig was instrumental in the merger of Cameronbridge with five other grain whisky producers to become the Distillers Company. He and his son Hugh became directors of the new company; another son, Henry, was appointed company secretary. In 1878, John Haig died, leaving Hugh to manage the distillery and the whisky blending company John Haig & Co, which had been excluded from the merger (see HAIG'S). Two other brothers set up Haig & Haig to concentrate on exporting to the expanding American market. Another brother, who was a young soldier at the time, was later to become Field Marshall Earl Haig, commander-in-chief of the British forces in France during the First World War.

In 1919, John Haig & Co was taken over by DCL and a great many technological improvements were made to Cameronbridge distillery, which operated without interruption until 1941, when wartime grain shortages halted production for six years. Further modernization took place during the 1960s, and again between 1989 and 1992 (when £20 million was invested and output trebled), making Cameronbridge one of the most efficient distilleries in Europe.

Although most of the product goes for blending, a small amount is bottled as single-grain whisky and sold as Old Cameron Brig, the main markets being local and in Edinburgh. Grain whiskies are lighter than malts owing to the extended rectification process used in distillation. As no peat is used in the production of grain whisky, it also lacks the smoky, phenolic flavour that is common to malt whisky.

Tasting notes: Grain whiskies do not posses the range of aromas and flavours offered by malts (they are somewhat monochrome) but they have a robust, industrial attractiveness of their own, and tasting them provides a fascinating insight into blending. Cameron Brig is richly coloured (caramel?). The nose is oily (reminiscent of machinery) with hay-like tones and, to me, a trace of haggis! The taste is sweet and viscous, with an indefinable spiciness. The finish is disappointingly short.

Caol Ila

Category: Island (Islay) Distiller: Bulloch, Lade & Co, Glasgow Owner: Diageo plc

Coal Ila (pronounced "cull-eela") is Gaelic for "the Sound of Islay" (the strait separating that island from the Isle of Jura). The distillery was built in a cove overlooking the sound in 1846 by Hector Henderson, who had been in partnership at Littlemill Distillery. The site was chosen for its abundant supply of good water from Loch Nam Bam – of which Alfred Barnard wrote, "over which ever and anon the fragrant breeze from the heather and myrtle is wafted" and which, more prosaically, was used to power the distillery's generator as well as to make its whisky.

Henderson soon went out of business. The distillery was

bought in 1857 by Bulloch Lade & Co, which, among other things, built a mission hall at Caol Ila, where each Sunday a seminary student from Edinburgh or Glasgow preached to the distillery workers and their families.

In 1927, its management passed to DCL. The distillery remained in production until 1972, when it was decided to demolish the entire structure (apart from the warehouses) and build a larger distillery in the same architectural style as the original, but with new and better equipment and another pair of stills. Production resumed in 1974. Today, Caol Ila obtains its malt from Port Ellen, and the whisky once dispatched by DCL's own vessel from the distillery's private pier now travels by road and ferry from Port Askaig and Port Ellen.

For many years, Caol Ila was only available in independent bottlings, but it has been bottled by its owners since 1988–9.
Tasting notes: Very pale in colour, with a greenish tinge. Malty, biscuity, heather-smoke nose, with a hint of rhododendrons and wet spring mornings – especially once water is added – and a whiff of smoke. The flavour is well-balanced, sweet, and dry, with good body and a bitter charcoal finish.

Caperdonich
Category: Speyside (Rothes) Distiller: The Chivas & Glenlivet Group Owner: Chivas Bros, Paisley
Caperdonich was built as Glen Grant No 2 Distillery (see GLEN GRANT) in 1897, across the road from its parent. Although it used the same source of water, the same malt, and the same distilling practice, its make turned out to be quite different. Owing to the market slump at the turn of the century, it was only in production for three years.

The distillery was rebuilt in 1965 by Glenlivet Distillers, and doubled in size (to four stills) two years later. It passed to Seagrams in 1977, and thence to Chivas Bros in 2000. The distillery was mothballed by its new owner in 2002.
Tasting notes: (G&M 1980) The colour is that of pale straw; it has a thin, spirity nose, sweet with malt and vinous notes. There is a hint of cloves and green apples and a whiff of smoke. Sweetish taste and short finish.

Cardhu
Category: Speyside (Strathspey) Distiller: John Walker & Sons, Kilmarnock Owner: Diageo plc
Cardhu – the name derives from the Gaelic for "black rock" – looks down upon Strathspey from Upper Knockando, on the slopes of the Mannoch Hill. For over 150 years, the Cumming family farmed and made whisky here; John Cumming leased the property in 1811, and like so many in the district, he had been involved in illicit distilling for many years. His wife, Helen, was famous for her skill in avoiding the excisemen: when the officials were on their rounds of the area, they would lodge for the night at the farm, and when she had them safely seated at table she would steal into the farmyard and raise a flag above the barn, which was

a sign for the neighbourhood smugglers to hide their gear. Despite the efforts of his wife, John Cumming was convicted of unlicensed distilling three times before 1824, when he acquired a licence and went on to build up a thriving business.

In 1846, he died and left the farm to his son Lewis, who in turn died in 1872, leaving the running of both the farm and distillery (not to mention three young children) to his wife, Elizabeth.

Elizabeth Cumming was a remarkable woman, overseeing the distillery and business at Cardhu (pronounced "car-doo") for nearly twenty years and becoming known as "the queen of the whisky trade".

During this period the "Glenlivets", as Speyside malts were termed, were in great demand for blending. Realizing that if the firm were to take advantage of this, the distillery had to be expanded and updated, Elizabeth acquired a lease of four acres (1.6 hectares) of land adjacent to the farm and, in 1886, built a new distillery capable of producing 60,000 gallons (over 270,000 litres) annually. With her son John, Elizabeth Cumming determined the business of the distillery, dealing directly with agents and brokers herself. By 1888, Cardhu was in demand by blenders, and was being sold in London as a single malt called "Cardow").

Such success attracted interest from larger companies. Over the years, Elizabeth turned down several takeover bids on the grounds that the distillery should be retained by the family. However, in 1893, she negotiated a deal with John Walker & Sons of Kilmarnock (see JOHNNIE WALKER), Cardhu's major customer, whereby her son would become a salaried director of the larger company while remaining at Cardhu to manage the distillery. John Walker & Sons then bottled Cardhu (as Old Vatted Cardhu, then, post-1908, as Cardow).

John Cumming retired from the board in 1923, when John Walker & Sons was floated as a public company, and spent the rest of his days farming. He was succeeded on the board by his son Ronald – later Sir Ronald – who eventually became chairman of Walker & Sons and then of its parent company, DCL. During the war and the postwar period of barley shortage, all the distillery's production went into the Johnnie Walker brands, but in the 1960s, Ronald Cumming reintroduced Cardhu as a single malt. It is now among the world's top-ten best sellers and is especially popular in Spain – so much so that there is not enough to meet the demand, leading Diageo to rebrand Cardhu as a vatted malt in 2003, a move which aroused the ire of some other whisky companies. Although the move was perfectly legal, it was undoubtedly confusing for consumers, and after discussion, Diageo withdrew the planned "Pure Malt".

Tasting notes: Cardhu has been described as a ladies' whisky. Lightly scented with violets and sweet almonds; notes of peach-stones and honeycomb, a whiff of smoke. The flavour is fresh, sweet, and smooth, with traces of pencil shavings (cedarwood) and aromatic spices (cinnamon?). The spiciness is reminiscent of a Highland, but the sweetness is pure Speyside.

Clynelish

*Category: North Highland **Distiller:** Ainslie & Heilbron (Distillers), Glasgow **Owner:** Diageo plc*

Clynelish Distillery was established in 1819 at the fishing port of Brora, on the northeast coast, by the Duke of Sutherland to provide a use for the barley grown by the tenants on his farms. He was the son of the Marquis of Stafford, and acquired the vast Sutherland estates by marriage to the Countess of Sutherland. He is remembered in history for ordering the removal by force of some 15,000 men, women, and children from his estates in order to make room for the more economical Cheviot sheep.

Many of the crofters were forced to emigrate; others moved to the coast at Brora where the land was better for growing barley, and where there was a coal field, which it was hoped would power the distillery's machinery. The duke sank a pit, but the coal turned out to be of inferior quality and ran out quickly.

James Ainslie & Co bought the distillery in 1896 (*see* AINSLIE'S). Soon after the years of the whisky boom at the turn of the century, there followed a collapse of the market for fillings. Ainslie's barely survived bankruptcy until 1912, when the distillery and company were bought jointly by one John Risk and DCL. In 1925, Risk was bought out and the Clynelish Distillery became part of DCL. In 1967, a new distillery was built, also named "Clynelish". The original, renamed "Brora", was closed in 1983, although the buildings still stand.

Clynelish is very highly regarded. The great Victorian connoisseur, Professor George Saintsbury, declared it a favourite (he believed a blend of it with The Glenlivet to be a sublime dram). **Tasting notes:** (*12 Years Old*) Fresh, fragrant, waxy, complex nose, with a dash of seaweed and a whiff of scented smoke. Medium-bodied. Sweet-tasting, with a slightly smoky, dry finish. Unmistakably Highland.

Coleburn

*Category: Speyside (Elgin) **Distiller:** distillery closed 1985*

John Robertson & Son, which was established in Dundee in 1827, built the Coleburn Distillery in 1896–7, six miles south of Elgin. Coleburn was situated near the Glen Burn, which provided the water for production, and the Great Northern Railway, which provided a goods station for the distillery traffic. The distillery was designed by Charles Doig, the leading distillery designer of the day. The owners described the appearance of the complex as "faced on one side by a . . . plantation of Scotch firs and birches, and swept by the cool mountain breezes of Brown Muir . . . in a snug corner shut off from the surrounding country . . . complete itself, compact and clean with a cleanliness that can only be attained in Highland air".

In the early years of the twentieth century, Coleburn was the site of a number of successful experiments at purifying effluents.

The process perfected there was used in other distilleries in the area. In 1916, Coleburn was bought by the Clynelish Distillery Co (*see* CLYNELISH), and went into DCL with that company in 1930.

Although the buildings retain their original appearance, some conversion was done in the late 1950s and 1960s: the mash house was rebuilt, condensers replaced the worm tubs, and the stills were provided with internal steam coils. The licensed distiller at Coleburn was J&G Stewart, the well-known Edinburgh blender (*see* USHER'S GREEN STRIPE). Coleburn closed in 1985, has been dismantled and is currently for sale as a property development.

Tasting notes: Coleburn has an unusual aroma reminiscent of dried seaweed, with some salt and a trace of rubber, and a faint floral mustiness. Smooth and sweet-tasting, with an interesting "fishiness" and a smooth, short finish.

Convalmore

Category: Speyside (Dufftown) Distiller: distillery closed 1985

The distillery takes its name from the Conval Hills, north of Dufftown, from whence it draws its water; it was built in 1894 by the Convalmore-Glenlivet Distillery Co. The *Elgin Courant* announced that "Its situation (close to the railway and within a mile of the town of Dufftown) is most convenient and central and will save considerable time and money in cartage . . . the natural contour of the ground has been largely taken advantage of."

The company was bought by W.P. Lowrie & Co, of Glasgow, in 1905, following a recession in the whisky trade. Lowrie was a very successful stockholder, blender, and bottler for wholesale whisky merchants who had no premises of their own (*see* LOWRIE'S). James Buchanan was one of his customers, and in 1906, he acquired most of the company from Lowrie, whose business was suffering from the lack of demand for mature whiskies.

In 1909, a fire broke out at Convalmore and much of the distillery was destroyed. The rebuilding that immediately followed included some innovations, one of which was a continuous still with the capacity to distil 500 gallons (2,270 litres) of wash every hour, using a similar process to that used in grain distilleries. This experiment was not a success, however, since the spirit would not mature evenly. It was abandoned in 1915.

The distillery passed to DCL in 1925. In 1964–5, it was extended to four stills. It closed in 1985, and the site was sold to William Grant & Sons in 1990 for warehousing purposes.

Tasting notes: A full-bodied aroma including scents of beeswax, some sherry, malt, and a curious, sweet, caramel note that can best be described as fresh meringues. The taste is sweetish, slightly salty, and vaguely musty.

Cragganmore

Category: Speyside (Strathspey) Distiller: D&J McCallum, Edinburgh Owner: Diageo plc

John Smith, the founder of Cragganmore Distillery, is said to have been the most experienced distiller of his day. He had been manager of Macallan, Glenlivet, and Wishaw distilleries, among others, and was lessee of Glenfarclas distillery when, in 1869, he persuaded his landlord, Sir George Macpherson-Grant, to lease him the land to build a new distillery at Ballindalloch beside the Strathspey railway line.

Cragganmore (which is the name of the hill behind the distillery, whose springs supply the water for production) was the first distillery to be deliberately sited to take advantage of railway transport, and a private siding was built on the Speyside railway to accommodate distillery traffic. John Smith himself was a great railway enthusiast, but since he weighed 308 pounds (140 kilograms) and was too wide to enter a railway carriage, he was obliged to travel in the guard's van. He died in 1886, leaving the business to his son Gordon, who largely rebuilt the distillery in 1901.

In 1923, Gordon's widow sold the distillery to the Cragganmore Distillery Co, a subsidiary of White Horse Distillers (*see* WHITE HORSE). When White Horse merged with DCL in 1965, Cragganmore became a wholly owned subsidiary.

The licensed distiller is D&J McCallum, of Edinburgh (*see* MCCALLUM'S PERFECTION), which for many years exported Cragganmore mainly to Australia and New Zealand. Cragganmore has always been well thought of by blenders (it is the heart malt of McCallum's Perfection and the Old Parr blends), but was uncommon as a single. However, in 1988–9, the brand was deservedly chosen by United Distillers to represent Speyside in its Classic Malts series. It was magnificently relabelled and widely promoted, and as a result it has become much better known.

Tasting notes: Nosed straight, Cragganmore has a polished leather aroma, with a hint of sherry; when water is added, other sweet scents emerge: pine essence, spices, cider apples, leather. The overall impression is complex, clean, and fresh. The taste begins dry and finishes sweet; there is plenty of sherry, but it doesn't mask a variety of other herbal notes. There is some restrained peat smoke. Overall, it fills the mouth with flavours and has a long finish.

Craigellachie

Category: Speyside (Strathspey) Distiller: John Dewar & Sons, Glasgow Owner: John Dewar & Sons, Glasgow (a subsidiary of Bacardi Ltd)

The Craigellachie Distillery Co, founded in 1898 during the whisky boom, overlooks Thomas Telford's famous single-span bridge across the Spey. It was established by Peter Mackie, who, after inheriting Lagavulin Distillery on Islay, formed a partnership with Alexander Edward (*see* AULTMORE DISTILLERY), whose father, David, was a leading Speyside distiller (*see* BENRINNES).

Mackie eventually took over complete ownership of Craigellachie, and thus it came under the mantle of White Horse Distillers. Mackie, or "Restless Peter" as he was known by his employees for his unrelenting energy, held his annual general meetings at Craigellachie, during which he was wont to air his views on the industry and the Empire in forceful terms. He was made a baronet in 1922 for his services to the whisky industry (*see* WHITE HORSE).

The distillery became part of Scottish Malt Distillers (DCL) in 1930 and was rebuilt in the mid-1960s, when two stills were added. Relatively well known as a single before the First World War, Craigellachie is now uncommon, although it has been bottled by its owners. The distillery was sold to Bacardi with the Dewar's brand in 1998.

Tasting notes: (*14 Years Old*) Pale gold in colour, Craigellachie has a light, sweetish nose, with distinct traces of cereal and smoke. Light- to medium-bodied, syrupy mouthfeel, with oranges and walnuts. Somewhat bitter finish.

Craiglodge

Category: South Highland Distiller: Loch Lomond Distillery Co, Alexandria, Dumbartonshire Owner: Loch Lomond Distillery Co

Craiglodge is made in Lomond-style stills at Loch Lomond Distillery (*see* LOCH LOMOND). It is the third-smokiest of the stable, being made from a mash which is half made up of malt peated to forty parts per million phenols and half the standard unpeated malt. One spirit-still run is mixed with one wash-still run.

Croftengea

Category: South Highland Distiller: Loch Lomond Distillery Co, Alexandria, Dumbartonshire Owner: Loch Lomomnd Distillery Co

Croftengea is a further variation from Loch Lomond Distillery (*see* LOCH LOMOND), and like its sister products (*see* CRAIGLODGE, INCHMURRIN, OLD ROSDHU, GLEN DOUGLAS) it is named after a local landmark on Loch Lomondside.

This variant is the smokiest of the stable, employing malt peated to 40 parts per million phenols and blending one spirit-still run with two wash-still runs to produce a much heavier spirit than if it was simply a spirit-still run. Like the others in the Loch Lomond stable, it is a blending whisky, although a single cask was bottled by SMWS in 2004.

Dailuaine

Category: Speyside (Strathspey) Distiller: Dailuaine-Talisker Distilleries, Owner: Diageo plc

Dailuaine (pronounced "daal-yewann") is Gaelic for "the green vale", and must refer to the site of the distillery, built in 1854 by William Mackenzie on the lush ground between Ben Rinnes and the River Spey, near Ballindalloch. Twelve years later, the Strathspey railway reached the opposite bank of the river, and when a new road bridge was constructed close to the distillery, Dailuaine could reach its distant markets directly.

In 1890, Mackenzie & Co became a limited company and in 1898, it merged with the successful Talisker Distillery of Skye to form Dailuaine-Talisker Distilleries. By this time, the business was in the hands of Mackenzie's son, who had built the Imperial Distillery at Carron and owned another in Aberdeen. During the pre-war recession, however, the company came under increasing

pressure, and in 1916, it was bought jointly by Dewar's, the
Distillers Company Limited, W.P. Lowrie, and John Walker & Son,
thus becoming part of DCL.

Dailuaine has traditionally been a filling malt, and until
recently the distillery's entire production went for blending, apart
from the occasional cask that was bottled independently. Since
1988–9, a small quantity has been bottled by the proprietor at 16
years old.

Tasting notes: (*16 Years Old*) Nosed straight, Dailuaine has a
rich, rum-toffee aroma. With the addition of water, this becomes
gentler and more sherried. The nose is quite hot and peppery,
which adds to an already dry impression; however, there is plenty
of rich malt present. The flavour is an interesting balance of sweet
and dry, with more than a little sherry, some fruity and woody
notes, and a bitter finish.

Dallas Dhu

*Category: Speyside **Distiller:** distillery closed 1983; now a
museum **Owner:** Historic Scotland*

Alexander Edward, the eminent Speyside distiller, laid the plans
for Dallas Dhu Distillery in 1899 and sold the rights to build it (on
his own land) to Wright & Greig, the Glasgow blender. The name
of the distillery (pronounced "dallas doo") is taken from the Gaelic
Dalais Dubh, which means "black-water valley".

In 1919, ownership passed to J.P. O'Brien & Co, then, in 1921,
to an English consortium which had set up a company called
Benmore Distilleries, based in Glasgow, "with a view to creating
an organization of brewers, merchants and others interested in
the whisky trade, for the purpose of assuring supplies of Scotch
malt whisky, and also for securing the manufacturers profits".
This company was, in turn, bought by DCL in 1929, and
ownership of Dallas Dhu was subsequently transferred to
Scottish Malt Distillers.

A fire in 1939 caused considerable damage, gutting the
stillhouse and damaging most of the production equipment.
Fortunately, the warehouses, which contained hundreds of
thousands of pounds worth of maturing stock, were saved. Apart
from the war years, production continued during most of the last
century, until the distillery was closed in 1983. Today, it is
preserved as an industrial museum by Historic Scotland.

Tasting notes: Dallas Dhu has a rich nose, which is perfumed
with a distinct barber-shop aroma. It is a medium-bodied whisky.
The flavour is smooth, complex and well-balanced, being neither
sweet nor dry; with some maltiness, traces of wood and some
pleasant mustiness.

Dalmore

*Category: North Highland **Distiller:** Dalmore Distillery, Alness,
Ross-shire **Owner:** Whyte & Mackay Ltd, Glasgow*

The Dalmore Highland Malt Distillery was founded in 1839 and
acquired by the Mackenzie brothers, a local farming family, in
1878. It has a fine position overlooking the Cromarty Firth and the

Black Isle, and its appearance has been compared to that of an old-fashioned country railway station, its offices partly panelled with carved oak from a shooting lodge. The harbour here was once an important embarkation point for timber that was being shipped to Newcastle and South Shields. It has exclusive rights to the water of the River Alness, and one of its stills dates from 1874.

A diary dating from this time is still in the possession of the Mackenzie family. It holds detailed entries of tastings and day-to-day transactions, showing the importance of whisky as a part of the agriculture and commerce of the area. During the First World War, when the distillery was closed, it was used for assembling mines.

The Mackenzie brothers were friendly with James Whyte and Charles Mackay, and Dalmore had always been a key component in their leading brand, Whyte & Mackay. In 1960, the two companies merged, although the Mackenzie connection was not lost: until recently there was still a representative of the family on the board of the larger company. Much of the distillery's output now goes to Whyte & Mackay blends, although Dalmore has an established market as a single malt.

Tasting notes: The nose is dense and oily, with a heavy, smoky note, like burnt rubber. With water, these scents become lighter, more complex, and sweeter. The mouth-feel is smooth and well-rounded, and the flavour at once malty and dry, with some dried fruit, a trace of oil, and a dry finish.

Dalvey

Category: Speyside (Strathspey) Distiller: Glenfarclas Owner: Grants of Dalvey, Alness, Ross-shire

This unusual bottling of Glenfarclas was done for Grants of Dalvey, the well-known manufacturer of high-quality gifts and "gentlemen's accessories" in Alness. It was selected by the company's founder and chairman, the eponymous Sir Patrick Grant of Dalvey, fourteenth Baronet, and the label depicts his ancestor dressed to meet King George IV in 1822.

Dalwhinnie

Category: North Highland Distiller: James Buchanan & Co, Glasgow and London Owner: Diageo plc

Dalwhinnie, the highest distillery in Scotland, stands in the Drumochter Pass at the head of Strathspey. The area is steeped in history. The place name itself means "meeting place", where cattle drovers and smugglers met on their way to markets in the south. Prince Charles Edward Stuart passed down Drumochter after raising his standard at Glenfinnan in the Jacobite rebellion of 1745. Part of General Wade's road, built after the "Fifteen" to help control the Highlands, remains in the distillery's grounds.

The distillery was originally named Strathspey when it was established during the whisky boom of the late 1890s by three men from Kingussie. They chose the site for its access to a supply of clear spring water from Lochan-Doire-Uaine, above the snow-line, and abundant peat from the surrounding moors.

It was sold in 1898, renamed Dalwhinnie, and, five years later, acquired by the largest distilling company in America, Cook & Bernheimer. This gave rise to great concern within the whisky industry in Scotland, which feared that the Americans might attempt to take over the market. Worries were dispelled by the introduction of Prohibition in 1920, and in 1926, the distillery passed into the ownership of DCL, which licensed it to James Buchanan & Co (*see* BLACK & WHITE).

Until 1988–9, the brand was only available locally, but it was chosen by United Distillers for its Classic Malts series, and is much better known today as a result.

Tasting notes: The advertising slogan for Dalwhinnie is "The Gentle Spirit", but this does not mean it lacks character. Pale gold in colour, its nose is very aromatic, with traces of heather flowers and peat smoke, and malty and fruity undertones. The taste is very sweet, slightly oily, and smooth – honey and flowers, with a malty and heathery finish. "Heather-honey" is promised on the label.

Deanston

Category: Central Highland **Distiller:** *Burn Stewart Distillers plc East Kilbride* **Owner:** *Burn Stewart Distillers*

Deanston Distillery is situated at Doune in Perthshire, just north of the Highland Line. It is about a mile upstream of the picturesque ruins of Doune Castle, seat of the "Bonnie Earl o'Moray", who was brutally murdered in February 1592 near North Queensferry.

The distillery is housed in a cotton mill built in 1785, and was designed by Richard Arkwright, the inventor of the "spinning jenny", and one of the fathers of the Industrial Revolution.

The mill was closed in the early 1960s, and converted to a distillery in 1965–6. It was perfectly suited to such a purpose on account of its good supply of clean water from the River Teith (the mill had been powered by this source), and its airy weaving halls, designed to maintain a constant temperature and humidity in the days before air conditioning. It was thus ideally suited to the maturing of whisky. The conversion was inspired by Mr Brodie Hepburn, a well-known figure in the industry. The internal reconstruction involved removing three very solid floors in order to accommodate four stills.

Deanston prospered during the 1970s, then ceased production temporarily during the difficult mid-1980s. It was acquired by The Invergordon Distillers in 1972, which sold it to Burn Stewart Distillers in 1991.

Tasting notes: It is pale in colour and light-bodied. The nose is sweet and cereal-like. This breakfast-cereal note continues when water is added, becoming drier. In flavour, it is well-balanced, with malty notes and some fruitiness. Sweet with a dry finish.

Deerstalker

Category: Speyside (Strathspey) **Distiller:** *Balmenach Distillery* **Owner:** *Aberfoyle & Knight, Glasgow*

The brand was first registered in 1880 by J.G. Thomson and Co, the well-known wine merchant and whisky blender in Leith.

Andrew Usher, "The Father of Blending", sat on the board
at that time. In 1991, Deerstalker was relaunched as a single
malt exclusively in export markets by Hedges & Butler, having
been attractively repackaged (the packaging won design
awards), with colourful remarks on the label penned by the
current writer.

In 1994, the brand was sold to Aberfoyle & Knight, a small,
independent spirits company in Glasgow, whose managing
director formerly worked for Bass Export (the parent of Hedges &
Butler). He has obtained permission from United Distillers to
reveal that the malt is the rare and excellent Balmenach. Its new
owner is now selling it in the home market, focusing on Scottish
hotels, restaurants, and golf clubs.

Tasting notes: Light in colour and body. Grassy aroma with
some estery notes and perhaps a trace of smoke, becoming more
like damp hay. The flavour is thin and dryish, with some
sweetness, which is out of balance. The finish is dry, becoming
bitter.

Drumguish

*Category: Speyside (Upper Spey) Distiller: Speyside Distillers Co
Ltd, Glasgow Owner: Speyside Distillers Co*

Drumguish is the brand name of a five-year-old malt made at
Speyside Distillery (*see* SPEYSIDE).

Dufftown

*Category: Speyside (Dufftown) Distiller: Arthur Bell & Sons, Perth
Owner: Diageo plc*

In 1895, two Liverpudlian entrepreneurs, Peter Mackenzie and
Richard Stackpole, visited Speyside with the aim of purchasing a
property on which to build a distillery. Having toured the Kirkton
of Mortlach, they settled on a meal mill near Dufftown on land
owned by John Symon, one of whose farms, Pittyvaich, stood at
the top of the hill overlooking the mill (*see* PITTYVAICH). A deal was
struck, and the Dufftown-Glenlivet Distillery Company was
founded (soon incorporated as P. Mackenzie & Co).

Within a year, the mill was converted and barley from
Pittyvaich farm was being mashed for distillation. The first batch
filled nine hogsheads. Water came from "Jock's Well", famous in
the district for its quality and quantity, and just a few miles from
the distillery. On more than one occasion, men from the nearby
Mortlach distillery attempted to divert the water.

As business prospered, the company acquired Blair Athol
Distillery and expanded its outlets for the firm's whisky, even
including the USA shortly before Prohibition. In 1933, P.
Mackenzie & Co was bought by Arthur Bell & Sons (*see* BELL'S).

Apart from the war years, when grain shortages forced most
distilleries to shut down, Dufftown has been in continuous
production, its product well-regarded by blenders.

In 1968, a major expansion programme doubled the capacity
of the distillery; in 1979, further expansion led to the introduction
of a stainless-steel Lauter mash tun and two more stills, allowing

Dufftown to produce over six million gallons (over twenty-seven million litres) of whisky per annum.

In 1985, Arthur Bells & Sons was acquired by Guinness; two years later Guinness went on to take over the Distillers Company Limited, so Dufftown, along with the other former Bell's distilleries, is now part of Diageo.

Tasting notes: Dufftown has a light body and traces of biscuits and diesel oil on its nose. It is sweet and estery, but this is balanced by a dryish smokiness. In flavour, the smoke and oiliness persist, and to my mind, it has a somewhat cloying finish.

Edradour

Category: Highland (Perthshire) Distiller: Glenforres-Glenlivet Distillery Co, Pitlochry Owner: Signatory Vintage Scotch Whisky Co Ltd, Edinburgh

Edradour is Scotland's smallest distillery and, many would say, her prettiest. It is a classic example of a farm-distillery, and was established as such in 1825 by a group of Perthshire farmers. The fact that it has been preserved is thanks largely to William Whiteley, known as the "Dean of Distillers", one of the characters of the industry in the 1920s, who bought Edradour in 1922 with a view to keeping it as it was.

Apart from the conversion of the malt barn into a visitors centre, and the reluctant installation of electricity in 1947, little has changed at Edradour. There is no automation; much of the equipment is still made of wood, the stills are the smallest permitted by the Excise, and the brewing and distilling methods are entirely traditional.

William Whiteley's principal reason for purchasing Edradour was his belief that its product was perfect for blending; indeed, with it he produced King's Ransome, the blend that in the 1920s was considered "the world's most excellent and expensive whisky". Until the late 1980s, Edradour was not available as a single malt, except in rare bottlings by, for example, Gordon & MacPhail. The distillery was acquired by Pernod Ricard in 1992, and sold to the independent bottler Signatory in 2002.

Tasting notes: Edradour shows an extraordinarily floral nose (with scents of dog roses and almond blossom) and a light but substantial body. At ten years old, this is a beautifully developed whisky, with layers upon layers of flavour that unravel across one's tongue. It is sweetish to start with and spicy to finish, with just a trace of sherry, but more of mint and a buttery aftertaste. Clean and fresh, this is a dram for any time of the day or night.

Fettercairn

Category: East Highland Distiller: Invergordon Distillers, Leith Owner: Whyte & Mackay Ltd, Glasgow

Fettercairn is situated at Laurencekirk, in the heart of the Mearns, one of Scotland's most fertile areas. It began trading in 1824. The Fettercairn Distillery Co was formed in 1887; Sir John Gladstone, father of the great Victorian prime minister, was chairman.

In 1939, Fettercairn was acquired by Associated Scottish

Distillers, through its Glasgow subsidiary, Train & MacIntyre, which controlled it until 1970, when it came under the private ownership of an Aberdeen businessman. The distillery was later bought by Whyte & Mackay, which markets the brand in the UK, Europe, and the Far East. It is currently mothballed.

Tasting notes: A light nose – sweet and estery, with traces of fudge. The light toffee note persists in the flavour, and there is a very slight rubbery taste on the back of the tongue. Despite these sweet-associated notes, the overall impression (and the finish) is dry. An unusual and well-balanced flavour.

Finlaggan

Category: Island (Islay) Distiller: not stated (Bruichladdich)
Owner: The Vintage Malt Whisky Co, Glasgow

It was on a tiny island in Loch Finlaggan, Islay, that the Lords of the Isles (formerly styled "Kings of the Isles") held court. At the high point of the lordship, the patronage of the chiefs was legendary. Poets, musicians, silversmiths, and sculptors all prospered under the benign and cultured support of the mighty chiefs of Clan Donald. Alas, they over-reached themselves – they were forfeited by the Scottish Crown in 1492, and their lands were confiscated. The poets mourned: "It is no joy without Clan Donald . . . the best race in the round world." The island depicted on the label of this whisky supports a romantic tower quite unlike the heap of stones that is today the great Council Chamber of the Lordship. But no matter.

Brian Cook, the founder of the Vintage Malt Whisky Company, joined Auchentoshan Distillery in the 1970s and established his own venture in 1992, principally to supply smaller outlets in Europe with good-quality single-malt whisky. Finlaggan's main market is in France. A small amount is available through Harrods and Fortnum & Mason in London.

Glen Albyn

Category: North Highland Distiller: distillery closed 1983 and demolished

Glen Albyn was founded in 1846 by the then provost of Inverness, James Sutherland, using the site of an abandoned brewery. It is thought that its owner was attracted to the prospect of sales to the great urban markets in the south which could be reached via the Caledonian canal, on whose bank stood Glen Albyn. However, the main buildings were destroyed by fire three years later, and although rebuilding commenced immediately, Sutherland went bankrupt in 1855.

The complex was briefly used as a flour mill; then for twenty years, Glen Albyn lay silent. A.M. Gregory, a grain merchant, acquired the site in 1884 and built an entirely new distillery with the same name and its own railway siding connecting it to the main line.

During the First World War, Glen Albyn became a US naval base for the manufacture of mines. Then, in 1920, Mackinlays & Birnie, which had built a neighbouring distillery called "Glen

Mhor" (see entry), bought Glen Albyn and worked the two as a single operation.

In 1972, DCL took over both distilleries; they remained in production until the early 1980s, when they were closed and demolished. Glen Albyn was considered typically Highland and is now rare.

Tasting notes: (G&M 1972) Estery, with some maltiness and fruit, and a trace of nail varnish remover (Cadenhead's notes make mention of lavender). The flavour is well-rounded, sweet, but with a dryish finish, and some light smokiness.

Glenallachie

Category: Speyside (Strathspey) Distiller: Glenallachie Distillery Co, Leith Owner: John Dewar & Sons, Glasgow

Glenallachie Distillery was built in 1967, near Aberlour in the heart of Speyside, by Mackinlay & McPherson, a company which at that time was owned by Scottish Newcastle Breweries. It was managed by Charles Mackinlay & Co and was a constituent of the Mackinlay brands (see MACKINLAY), and became part of the Invergordon Group in 1985.

The distillery was designed by W. Delmé Evans, as were Tullibardine and Isle of Jura distilleries (both part of The Invergordon Group). After being closed for a time during the late 1980s, the distillery was sold to Campbell Distillers (the Scotch whisky subsidiary of Pernod Ricard) in 1989. Campbell Distillers was merged into Chivas Bros when Pernod bought Seagrams Scotch whisky interests in 2000. Uncommon as a single malt.

Tasting notes: (12 Years Old) A rather closed and nondescript nose – some heather notes; some malt. The flavour is smooth and medium-bodied; sweet and syrupy with hints of digestive biscuits.

Glen Andrew

Category: Speyside Distiller: not stated Owner: The Vintage Malt Whisky Co, Glasgow

(see FINLAGGAN) This bottling of a "well-known Elgin malt" is only available in the USA. Presumably, the brand is named for Scotland's patron saint, or perhaps HRH the Duke of York, since there is no actual Glen Andrew in Scotland.

Glen Avon

Category: Speyside (district unknown) Distiller: undisclosed Owner: Avonside Whisky Co, Elgin (a subsidiary of Gordon & Macphail)

(see MACPHAIL'S, AVONSIDE) Avonside Whisky is a subsidiary of Gordon & MacPhail of Elgin, which, for longer than any other company, has been buying new spirit at the distillery and holding it in its own warehouses for an exceptionally long time. It is not disclosed which distillery Glen Avon comes from; however, it is on Speyside and still in operation.

Glen Bannock

Category: Speyside (Glenfarclas) Distiller: undisclosed Owner: J&G Grant, Glenfarclas

Glen Bannock is an export brand, bottled in various years by the owners of Glenfarclas Distillery.

Glenburgie

*Category: Speyside (Forres) **Distiller:** James & George Stodart, Edinburgh **Owner:** Allied Distillers, Dumbarton*

Glenburgie Distillery was established as early as 1810 by William Paul, and was originally known as "Kilnflat". In 1884, it was acquired by Alexander Fraser & Co of Elgin. As the demand for Speyside malt increased, so did the distillery's output: by 1890, the wash still capacity had grown to 1,500 gallons (6,800 litres) from its original ninety gallons (400 litres).

In 1925, Fraser & Co went into liquidation, and control passed into the hands of an Elgin lawyer, Donald Mustard. Hiram Walker Ltd bought Glenburgie in 1936 (a year later it acquired Ballantine's – see entry); since then, there has been a steady programme of rebuilding and upgrading, with great pains being taken to preserve the original character of the buildings. Floor malting ceased at Glenburgie during the 1950s.

From 1958 to 1981, Glenburgie was producing two different whiskies. This came about because, during that time, the distillery housed a pair of Lomond stills (*see* INCHMURRIN) as well as its conventional stills. The spirit produced was quite different and was known as Glencraig (*see* entry), after the director of Ballantine's Highland Malt Distilleries. Some of this whisky remains in bond but it is unlikely to be distilled again as the two Lomond stills have been replaced by traditional Highland malt stills. Glenburgie is not presently bottled as a single malt by its owner.

Tasting notes: The aroma is slightly astringent and oily, with traces of rum toffee, sherry, and some maltiness. The flavour is strangely nondescript, sweetish with a touch of saltiness in the finish.

Glencadam

*Category: East Highland **Distiller:** The Glencadam Distillery Co **Owner:** Allied Distillers, Dumbarton*

Glencadam is situated about half a mile outside the ancient Royal Burgh of Brechin (*see* NORTH PORT). The distillery was built in 1825, and from 1827 until 1837 it was owned by David Scott. A succession of owners followed before it was acquired by Gilmour, Thomson & Co in 1891. The latter, an established firm of blenders, retained ownership until 1954, when it sold Glencadam to Hiram Walker. The distillery later became the responsibility of Stewart & Son of Dundee, which uses it in the popular Cream of the Barley blend. It is currently mothballed.

Tasting notes: Glencadam has a relatively closed nose; the aroma is of damp wool, with some sherry and distinct tangerine notes. The flavour is light, smooth, and sweetish, with some traces of tangerine.

Glencraig

*Category: Speyside (Elgin) **Distiller:** James & George Stoddart **Owner:** Allied Distillers, Dumbarton*

Glencraig was a brand of malt whisky produced on Lomond stills between 1958 and 1981 at Glenburgie Distillery, Forres, when the distillery was owned by Hiram Walker & Sons, which later became Allied Distillers. The Lomond stills were dismantled in 1981 (*see* INVERLEVEN for a description of Lomond stills).

Glen Deveron

Category: East Highland Distiller: William Lawson Distillers Owner: John Dewar & Sons, Glasgow

Macduff Distillery was built in 1963 by a consortium, Glen Deveron Distilleries, and sold to William Lawson Distillers (a subsidiary of Bacardi-Martini) ten years later. Its owner uses it for its William Lawson's Finest blend, marketing its product as Glen Deveron, after the distillery's source of water, the River Deveron. Independent bottlings name it after the distillery (*i.e.* Macduff), and it is rare. Both the distillery and the brand passed into the ownership of John Dewar & Sons in 1998, when Bacardi acquired this company from UDV.

Tasting notes: Pale-straw in colour with gold lights; the nose is reminiscent of boiled sweets and rum toffees, with a trace of diesel oil and a whiff of smoke. Salt and pepper show on the palate, which is sweet overall.

Glen Dochart

Category: region unknown Distiller: undisclosed Owner: Winerite, Leeds

This is Winerite's own-label single malt, launched in 1991 and available from the company's retail outlets throughout the UK. Glen Dochart's origin is kept secret, and it may be that the company will change the malt marketed under this label from time to time (*see* ROYAL GAME), so no tasting notes are provided.

Glen Douglas

Category: South Highland Distiller: Loch Lomond Distillery Co, Alexandria, Dumbartonshire Owner: as above

Glen Douglas is made in Lomond-style stills at Loch Lomond Distillery (*see* LOCH LOMOND). It is made in the traditional way (unlike some of its stable-mates – *see* CRAIGLODGE, CROFTENGEA, INCHMOAN) from lightly peated malt, collected from the spirit still at the very low strength of fifty-five per cent, to produce a "standard well-rounded malt". It is only used for blending.

Glendronach

Category: Eastern Highland Distiller: The Glendronach Distillery Co Owner: Allied Distillers, Dumbarton

The distillery straddles the Dronac burn in Glen Forgue, near Huntly (West Aberdeenshire). Built in 1826 by James Allardes, the son of a local landowner, its product was favoured by the fifth Duke of Gordon – the peer responsible for the 1823 Act that provided for the licensing of distilleries and reduction of taxation. The duke was so impressed by this whisky that he introduced Allardes into London society, which resulted in him neglecting the management of his distillery to such an extent that it burned down in 1837 and was sold to one Walter Scott (no relation).

> *Redcurrant jelly is good for the belly.*
> *Ginger and nuts are good for the guts.*
> *But the wine of Glendronach is good for the stomach!*

In 1960, the distillery was bought by William Teacher & Sons, which has doubled its production capacity while preserving the traditional production methods. These include old-fashioned floor maltings (much of the barley used is grown locally, to order), Oregon pine washbacks, a peat-fired drying kiln, and four coal-fired stills. The whisky is matured at the distillery and all the malt bottled as a single by the owner comes from sherry casks. The distillery was closed between 1996 and 2002 to allow for stock adjustments, but is now in operation again.

Tasting notes: (*12 Years Old*) Deep amber colour, with red tinge; intense, sherry nose with some vanilla; luscious body; a good balance of sherry and malt, some caramel notes and peat smokiness; surprisingly dry.

Glendullan

Category: Speyside (Dufftown) Distiller: Macdonald Greenlees, Edinburgh Owner: Diageo plc

Founded in 1897 by William Williams & Sons of Aberdeen, this was the last of the seven distilleries to be built in Dufftown during the nineteenth century, which prompted the saying "Rome was built on seven hills and Dufftown stands on seven stills". The location was chosen for its proximity to the River Fiddich, which not only provided water for production, but drove a water-wheel for power.

At the outset, Williams & Sons used most of the output for its own blends (Strathdon and Three Stars), although a small amount of the single malt was known to have been supplied to Edward VII in 1902.

Following the hardships of the First World War, the company merged with Macdonald Greenlees to become Macdonald Greenlees and Williams (Distillers) in 1919 (*see* OLD PARR). It was acquired by DCL in 1925, rebuilt in 1962 and substantially expanded (to eight stills) in 1972. The original distillery was closed in 1985.

Tasting notes: Pale-coloured; spirity/biscuity nose, turning to damp grass. Markedly dry aroma. Very sweet, smooth, and clean as it slides over the tongue; fresh-tasting but with few noticeable characteristics. Short finish. Warming.

Glen Elgin

Category: Speyside (Elgin) Distiller: White Horse Distillers, Edinburgh Owner: Diageo plc

The distillery was established in 1898 (during the years of the whisky boom) by a former manager of Glenfarclas, William Simpson. During construction, however, Pattison's, the Leith blender and one of the country's principal buyers of malt fillings, went into liquidation, taking with it the market for malt whisky.

Thus Glen Elgin ended up much smaller than originally planned, and it was the last distillery to be built on Speyside until Tormore in 1958. Within six months of commencing production, the distillery was taken over by a consortium of local businessmen who registered themselves as the Glen Elgin-Glenlivet Distillery Co. In turn, they sold on to J.J. Blanche, a Glasgow distiller and blender.

In 1936, the company was sold to DCL, which placed it under the management of its subsidiary, Scottish Malt Distillers, and licensed it to White Horse Distillers (Glen Elgin had long been a key ingredient of White Horse). Glen Elgin is ranked "top class" by blenders, and its rarity as a single is because there is such a demand for it from blenders.

Tasting notes: A positive, aromatic nose, offering a combination of heather flowers, herbs, sherry, a trace of mint, and a whiff of smoke. Medium-bodied and oily in appearance. Honey-sweet, with an attractive fruity finish. It remains sweet and clean throughout.

Glenesk

*Category: East Highlands **Distiller:** distillery closed 1985*

Originally a flax mill at the mouth of the River South Esk at Montrose, Highland Esk Distillery (as it was known at first) was converted in 1898 by James Isles, a wine merchant from Dundee.

The site enjoyed both a ready supply of water and access to the Mearns, one of Scotland's great barley-growing regions. Before the First World War, the distillery was bought by a J.F. Caille Heddle, who changed the name to North Esk Distillery. During the war, operations ceased and the buildings were used to billet soldiers. Part of the distillery was burnt down at this time and remained in disrepair; for some years, only the distillery's maltings were in use.

In 1938, it was acquired by Associated Scottish Distilleries (ASD), Joseph Hobbs' company (*see* BEN NEVIS). The distillery's name was changed again (to Montrose) and it was also converted to grain whisky production. Following the Second World War, ASD ran into difficulties and Montrose was bought by DCL, which used only the warehouses and maltings until 1964, when it was reconverted to malt whisky production with the name "Hillside". A large mechanical drum malting was also installed, which enabled the distillery to supply a number of Scottish Malt Distillers' other operations.

The complex was renamed Glenesk Distillery and Maltings in 1980, but finally closed in 1985. The distillery had its distilling licence cancelled in 1992.

Tasting notes: (*Prop. at 25 Years Old (58.3%) Rare Malt*) Mid-gold colour and a sweet, toffeed nose, with a green, sappy note. This flattens out into a combination of sweet malt, malt barns, and hay. The flavour is well-balanced, the finish short, with a pleasant hint of apples in the aftertaste.

Glenfarclas

Category: Speyside (Strathspey) Distiller: J&G Grant International, Ballindalloch, Banffshire Owner: J&G Grant

Glenfarclas is one of only two malt whiskies of world status that remain in the ownership of the families responsible for creating them. The company's directors, George and John Grant, are the great-grandson and great-great grandson of the founder.

The first licence was granted to Rechlerich Farm in 1836, but distilling was low-key. The property was bought by a neighbouring farmer, John Grant, in 1865, but distilling remained a "hobby" until 1896. For some time, the distillery in the corner of the field was let to John Smith (*see* CRAGGANMORE). In 1896, it was entirely rebuilt, and within ten years the founder's son, George, was shooting with the king at Balmoral – such was the fame of his whisky.

Glenfarclas means "the valley of the green grass", and the Grants still breed pedigree Aberdeen Angus cattle, as did their forebears. The distillery stands in meadows at the foot of Benrinnes and draws its water from a spring fed by snow-melt high in the mountain: soft water filtered through heather and over granite. The still-house itself is modern, and its stills are the largest on Speyside. The distillery was one of the first to build a visitor centre (in 1973), and includes an exhibition, a film theatre, and a tasting room constructed from a stateroom in the *RMS Empress* of Australia (which was built in 1913).

Glenfarclas is mainly matured in European oak, ex-sherry casks – some first-fill, some refill. This lends a sherried quality to the end product: an assertive, vigorous character, typical of the robust school of Speysides, yet with all the finesse one associates with these superb whiskies. It is popular in Scotland and has a well-developed market throughout Europe and North America; it is also found in Australasia, the Far East, and South Africa.

Tasting notes: Glenfarclas is a whisky of classic status; usually it is numbered among the top handful of Speysides by professional tasters. The fact that it is available at so many ages (and at cask strength) makes for fascinating comparative tastings. The older expressions become more sherried, as one would expect, and fill out the subtle wood notes and sweetness of the more youthful members of the tribe.

Glenfiddich

Category: Speyside (Dufftown) Distiller: William Grant & Sons, Dufftown, Owner: William Grant & Sons

Glenfiddich is not only the world's best-selling malt whisky, it is also the whisky that introduced the world to the pleasures of single malt. The statistics relating to the brand's sales performance are impressive: twenty-five per cent share of the total world export market for malt whisky, with a high market-share in South America (65%), Australasia (31%), Germany (26%), Scandanavia

(40%), Spain (15%), France (18%), the USA (15%), and Canada (25%). The brand is the UK category leader, outselling its nearest competitor by two to one.

William Grant (1839–1923) was the son of a tailor in Dufftown. He served an apprenticeship as a cobbler, then learned the art of distilling at Mortlach Distillery, where he worked for twenty years. Although he earned only £200 a year, he patiently saved part of his wage until he had enough to establish his own business. He chose a site close to Dufftown, in the field of Glenfiddich ("the valley of the deer"), drawing his water from the Robbie Dubh spring and buying his stills and plant second-hand from Cardhu Distillery for £120. The first whisky ran from the stills of Glenfiddich on Christmas Day, 1887.

William Grant brought his eight children into the business, and the company is still directed and managed by his descendants (see GRANT'S). This sense of family tradition and continuity runs through all the company's operations: Glenfiddich still has its own cooperage and coppersmiths, retains open mash tuns and traditional Douglas fir washbacks, and fires its 29 stills directly with coal furnaces. The distillery also bottles on site, reducing the spirit with the same water from the Robbie Dubh as is used in its making.

Throughout its history, all but a minute amount of Glenfiddich went for blending. Then, in the early 1960s, the directors of William Grant & Sons decided on a bold plan: to sell it in southern Scotland and England as a single malt, marketing it in the same way as blended whisky. Single-malt whisky had never been widely promoted, as the popular palate found it too strong in flavour and body. However, Glenfiddich is a delicately flavoured, light-bodied whisky, and within a few years it had won markets in England and abroad. In 1964, 4,000 cases were sold in export markets; ten years on, the figure was 119,500 cases; in 1999, 745,000 cases were sold. In 1974, William Grant & Sons became the first whisky company to be honoured with the Queen's Award for Export Achievement.

William Grant & Sons has always been adept at packaging its products. In 1957, the firm introduced a triangular bottle – wildly eccentric at the time – and was the first to put its products in tubes and gift tins. It was also the first to realize the significance of the duty-free trade and take advantage of these worldwide outlets. Many foreign distributors have been handling the firm's products for decades, and it supports them with advertising and promotions tailored to their individual markets. Above all, Glenfiddich's success is attributable to the fact that it is a most "accessible" malt, easy to drink at any time of the day. The result is that, today, one in every three bottles of malt whisky sold in the world is Glenfiddich.
Tasting notes: Very pale in the standard version (which makes no age statement, but is usually bottled at eight years), becoming deeper in older expressions; light, fresh, sweet, slightly oily nose; dry finish, with a hint of smokiness and some malt and citric notes. Often described as the "perfect beginner's malt".

Glen Flagler

*Category: Lowland **Distiller**: dismantled 1985*

Built in 1965 within the Moffat grain distillery complex on the
eastern outskirts of Airdrie, by Inver House Distillers (then a
subsidiary of Publicker Industries of Philadelphia). The complex
comprised five continuous stills for neutral spirit and grain whisky
production, and two pot stills for malt whisky. All were housed
within a converted paper mill (the complex was originally known
as Garnheath). It closed in 1985, and is now extremely rare.

Tasting notes: (*S 23 Years Old – 51.1%*) Amber, with a delicate,
malty/nutty nose and a good body. Surprisingly fresh, with a hint
of apples and spice. Sweetish to start and dry in the finish.

Glen Garioch

*Category: East Highland **Distiller**: Morrison Bowmore (Distillers),
Glasgow **Owner**: Morrison Bowmore*

The distillery (pronounced "glen geerie" and written as one
word: *Glengarioch*) is located in a small glen near the village of
Oldmeldrum in Aberdeenshire. It was founded in 1798, but had
a patchy history, owing to the unreliability of its water source. In
1884, William Sanderson bought Glen Garioch (*see* VAT 69), and
in 1937, it passed into the DCL empire.

After sporadic periods of closure, the distillery was bought
by Stanley P. Morrison in 1970, as part of his plan to build a
portfolio of distilleries that represented all the geographical
areas of whisky production. After digging a deep well in a
nearby field, a reliable source of water was secured. An innovative,
ecologically sound development meant that the waste heat from
the distillery was piped into hothouses nearby for the purpose of
growing tomatoes and other greenhouse fruits. The distillery was
mothballed 1995–7.

Tasting notes: The initial aromas are of lavender and sawdust,
with sandalwood traces. This quickly develops into a remarkable
ginger aroma – the nose is complex, with spices. Ginger persists
in the flavour and the finish is hot and spicy, almost oriental,
with traces of cinnamon and spiced rum. Glen Garioch is,
however, more variable than any other malt I have come across.
I have tasted supermarket bottlings that were mere shadows
of the proprietory bottlings, and I once tasted a single-cask
bottling from a "rogue" cask that was heavenly – like a divine
ginger cordial.

Glenglassaugh

*Category: East Highland **Distiller**: Highland Distillers, Glasgow
Owner: The Edrington Group*

Glenglassaugh Distillery was built between 1873 and 1875 on
land known as "Craig's Mills", after the three mills situated
there. Two were watermills, and powered the distillery until
well into this century; the third was one of the few windmills in
Scotland and formed the entrance to the distillery, even though
it is some way off, since the road passed through it.

Highland Distilleries (sic) bought Glenglassaugh (pronounced

"glenglassoh") in 1892 and completely refurbished it in 1959.
It has always been in demand by blenders, but its owners have
never felt that it stands up as a single malt. From time to time
great efforts have been made to "improve" it – its owners going
so far as to transport water in from their distillery at Glenrothes.
This was not a success and the distillery has been mothballed
since 1986.

Tasting notes: *(G&M 1983)* Grainy, with some floral notes
(gorse?), unusual but unintegrated. Sweetish and floral to taste,
again with a trace of gorse (very slight coconut); a fresh, almost
minty finish. A pleasant dram.

Glen Gordon

Category: Speyside (district unknown) Distiller: undisclosed
Owner: The Glen Gordon Whisky Co, Elgin

Glen Gordon Whisky Co is a subsidiary of Gordon & MacPhail
of Elgin (*see* MACPHAIL'S, JAMES GORDON'S, GLEN AVON).

Glengoyne

Category: South Highland Distiller: Lang Brothers, Glasgow
Owner: Peter J. Russell & Co, Broxburn, Midlothian

The distillery lies in a wooded glen on the western edge of the
Campsie Fells, not far from Loch Lomond. It is one of the most
attractively sited in Scotland, with a pretty waterfall plunging
into the natural hollow which forms the distillery's dam,
where ducks swim and preen. The distillery retains many of
its nineteenth-century features, and its layout is well-adapted
to viewing the distilling process in a compact space.

Glengoyne was established in 1833 (when it was known as
Glenguin, later as Burnfoot of Dumgoyne). It was bought by Lang
Brothers in 1876, and its product is used in the Lang blends. The
Highland Line, which nationally divided Highland from Lowland
Scotland, runs through the distillery grounds, and until the late
1970s, Glengoyne was numbered among the Lowland malts. Its
flavour actually combines characteristics from both Highlands
and Lowlands.

What distinguishes Glengoyne, however, is that it is the
only malt distillery to make a virtue of using unpeated malt. It
is suggested that by avoiding peat smoke in the drying process,
the more subtle flavours in the barley (Golden Promise is the
leading variety used) are allowed to emerge. About one-third
of the output (and all of the whisky bottled as single) is matured
in refill sherry casks.

Lang Bros, and Glengoyne Distillery, were bought by
Robertson & Baxter in 1965, which rebuilt and expanded the
distillery the following year and sold both to the established firm
of blenders and brokers Peter J. Russell & Co in 2003.

Tasting notes: *(10 Years Old)* Pale straw with gold highlights,
the nose is lightly sherried, fresh, and fruity (the word that comes
to mind is "gentle"). The mouth-feel is smooth and creamy, with
nutty notes. The primary tastes are well-balanced and the overall
impression is of a nicely rounded whisky.

Glen Grant

Category: Speyside (Rothes) Distiller: The Chivas & Glenlivet Group Owner: Chivas Bros, Paisley

In 1840, an Elgin lawyer, James Grant, went into partnership with his older brother, John, to establish Glen Grant Distillery in the village of Rothes on the River Spey. Their father farmed six miles away (John had worked on the farm and had established a grain merchant's business) and both brothers had been engaged in illicit distilling before going into partnership with the owners of Aberlour Distillery in about 1833.

In 1839, the brothers leased some land from the Earl of Seafield and proceeded to build the first Glen Grant distillery. James Grant was a railway enthusiast and was instrumental in the completion of the Morayshire Railway (indeed, he is best remembered in Elgin, where he became lord provost, for his work on the railway enterprise), and this was vital for the efficient transport of the brothers' new product, which was one of the first malt whiskies to be sold outside its locale.

The distillery used water from the Back Burn close by, and coal-fired stills were installed. The technical innovation of electric light was introduced to the buildings and workers' houses, making Glen Grant one of the first industrial premises in Scotland to be so equipped.

When the brothers died in 1864 and 1872, the distillery passed to James Grant's son, also named James and known universally as "The Major". The Major extended the distillery (although it was already one of the largest), built a mansion for himself nearby, and created a romantic woodland garden in the glen behind. The latter was restored in 1995; the house has been demolished.

Rated "top class" by blenders, Glen Grant was one of the first single malts to be made widely available throughout Scotland (about 1900). Major Grant built another distillery across the road to meet the demand: Glen Grant No 2. It lasted only four years – Pattison's, the large Edinburgh firm of brokers and blenders, was a major client, and when it collapsed in 1898, Glen Grant No 2 ceased operation. (It reopened in 1965 as Caperdonich Distillery.)

When James Grant died in 1931, he left the business to his grandson, Major Douglas Mackessack, who set about increasing production and expanding the market for Glen Grant. During the Second World War, the distillery had to close (Major Mackessack was captured at St-Valèry and spent four years as a POW).

In 1953, Glen Grant merged with George and J.G. Smith, to form The Glenlivet and Glen Grant Distilleries. In 1972, there was another merger: with Hill, Thomson & Co and Longmorn Distilleries. Then, six years later, the company was acquired by The Seagram Company, Canada (*see* CHIVAS REGAL). In 2000, Pernod Ricard acquired Seagrams Scotch whisky interests, including Glen Grant Distillery.

Glen Grant is a world brand, one of only two malt whiskies that feature in the top twenty export best-sellers. It has long done especially well in Italy, owing to the efforts of Armando Giovinetti, a Milanese hotelier, who travelled to Scotland in the late 1950s to investigate malt whisky and returned with fifty cases of Glen Grant, with which he literally introduced his country to malt whisky. By 1970, 60,000 cases were being sold in Italy each year; today, the number is in excess of half a million.

Tasting notes: There is a marvellous range of Glen Grant expressions, and it is fascinating to compare one with another to see the mellowing effects of ageing. The younger versions are spirity and dry; then an attractive nuttiness develops and the whisky becomes sweeter, gaining delectable honeycomb notes. Sherry notes also develop with age, but these depend on the wood in which the spirit has been matured. In terms of flavour, Glen Grant's hallmark is probably its nuttiness: hazel in the younger expressions, almonds in the older (even marzipan). A well-made whisky, Glen Grant strikes a delicate balance between sweet and dry.

Glen Keith

Category: Speyside (Keith) Distiller: The Chivas & Glenlivet Group Owner: Chivas Bros, Paisley

In 1957, Seagram acquired the site of an old meal mill on the opposite bank of the River Isla from its beautiful distillery of Strathisla, and built this complex. It was the first distillery to employ gas-fired stills, and pioneered the use of computers in the monitoring and control of production. Vast bonded warehouses were also built at Keith, which are now used to house the products from most of the Chivas & Glenlivet Group's distilleries. Formerly uncommon, since 1995, Glen Keith has been more widely promoted as part of its owner's Heritage Selection. The distillery is the "Home of" Passport blended whisky.

Tasting notes: Slightly oily texture and nose; rum toffees, rich and sherried aromas. Flavour is sweet and slightly salty; very smooth, viscous. Fairly rapid finish. A pleasant, full-bodied dram.

Glenkinchie

Category: Lowland Distiller: John Haig & Co, Markinch, Fife Owner: Diageo plc

Glenkinchie is a Lallans corruption of "de Quincy", the name of a family that owned tracts of East Lothian (known as the "garden of Scotland") in the fourteenth century.

The distillery was founded in 1837 by the Rate brothers near the village of Pencaitland. They were originally farmers, and grew and malted their own barley on the premises to produce a high- quality Lowland whisky that has only recently become available as a single malt (1988–9) as part of United Distillers' Classic Malts range.

In 1853, the Rate brothers went bankrupt, and the distillery was used primarily as a cowshed, with part converted into a sawmill. In the 1880s, Glenkinchie was bought by a consortium of whisky merchants and blenders from Leith and Edinburgh which re-established production after rebuilding the distillery and maltings.

In 1914, Glenkinchie was a founder member of Scottish Malt Distillers, which was established to consolidate the resources and interest of malt distillers in the Lowlands. In 1925, the members of Scottish Malt Distillers all joined DCL, and Glenkinchie was licensed to join John Haig & Co.

Tasting notes: The colour of Sauternes. A fragrant nose, sweet, slightly estery with hay or grassy notes. The flavour is very clean and fresh – sweet to start, then bone dry. Light, but by no means insipid; a good, positive flavour. An interesting gingery note in the finish.

The Glenlivet

Category: Speyside (Glenlivet) Distiller: George & J.G. Smith Owner: Chivas Bros, Paisley

In 1823, an act was passed that gave encouragement to licensed whisky distilling by cutting duty dramatically and permitting weaker washes (which made for more palatable distillates). The Act had been steered through Parliament by the Duke of Gordon, whose estates in northeast Scotland included Glenlivet. He encouraged one of his tenants, George Smith, to build a legal distillery on his farm.

The fame of Glenlivet was already well-established. In 1815, there were reputed to be 200 illicit stills in the area. Elizabeth Grant of Rothiemurcus recorded in her Diary of a Highland Lady that, on her father's instructions, she sent some Glenlivet whisky – "long in wood, mild as milk, and with the real contraband goût in it" – to George IV, when he visited Edinburgh in 1822. While the king was in Scotland, he would drink nothing else.

Like his neighbours, George Smith had been involved in illicit production and smuggling; unlike them, he saw the opportunity presented by legal distilling and seized it, the first distiller on Speyside to take out a licence. He did this with some trepidation, however, since his neighbours were still committed smugglers and considered him a turncoat. He wrote in his journal: "The outlook was an ugly one. I was warned that they meant to burn the distillery to the ground, and me in the heart of it. The laird of Aberlour presented me with a pair of hair-trigger pistols worth ten guineas, and they were never out of my belt for years . . . " Captain William Grant, the officer in command of guarding the distillery, courted and married George Smith's daughter.

George Smith took his son, James Gordon Smith, into partnership in about 1850. In 1858, they built a larger distillery close by at Minmore to meet the growing demand for their product – notably from Andrew Usher & Co (*see* USHER'S GREEN STRIPE). This location benefited mightily from the construction of the Speyside railway line in 1863, and the following year, the first bottle of The Glenlivet was sold south of the border.

J.G. Smith succeeded his father, who died in 1871. By this time, the name Glenlivet had become the benchmark for fine malt whisky, and had been adopted by some eighteen other distilleries, none of them situated in the glen itself. In 1880, J.G. Smith took legal action and the court ruled that there was only one Glenlivet (hence the definite article: *The* Glenlivet). The others could only use the appellation as a suffix to their brand-names.

The distillery passed to J.G.'s nephew, Colonel George Smith Grant of Auchorachan. In 1921, his son, Captain Bill Smith Grant MC, assumed control. Even before the end of Prohibition, Captain Grant had visited the United States and laid the foundations of what was to become the brand's principal market. In 1953, he guided the company into a merger with Glen Grant Distillery and subsequently (1970) the company merged with Hill, Thomson & Co to form The Glenlivet Distilleries. This company was acquired by Seagram in 1978, whose marketing power helped establish The Glenlivet as the largest-selling single malt in the American market. In 2000, Pernod Ricard acquired Seagram's Scotch whisky interests, including Chivas Brothers, which is the current owner of The Glenlivet Distillery.

The expression at 18 Years Old won Best Single Malt over fifteen years and Most Outstanding Single Malt in the 1995 International Wine and Spirit Competition, and a gold medal in 1996.

Tasting notes: (*18 Years Old*) Rich and fruity with some spice, malt, and floral notes. With water, it becomes sweeter, with some vanilla and baking tones. The taste is smooth, clean, and marvellously balanced: the first impression is sweet and lightly sherried with some honey and light fruit, becoming drier and spicier.

Glenlochy

Category: West Highland Distiller: distillery closed 1983

Glenlochy Distillery was established in 1898 by David McAndie of Nairn. It was built a mile outside Fort William, on the bank of the River Nevis and in the shadow of Ben Nevis, which afforded a good supply of water – described as "coming off the mountain at great speed" – with which to power the distillery. The West Highland Railway was close by. However, the distillery's owners could not have chosen a worse time to commence business. The whisky boom of the 1890s turned to recession the year Glenlochy opened, and it ran at only a fraction of its capacity, even going out of production for several seasons.

In 1920, the shareholders sold out to a group of English breweries, but production remained patchy. In 1937, Joseph Hobbs, a colourful character who had made and lost his fortune in Canada, bought the distillery in association with the Glasgow firm of blenders Train & McIntyre, and funded by the National Distillers of America. Production resumed the following year, and the distillery was transferred to a subsidiary, Associated Scottish Distillers (ASD). Production resumed in 1938 (*see* BEN NEVIS).

In 1940, Hobbs sold his interest in ASD and retired to Inverlochy Castle (now a luxurious hotel) to develop plans for his

Great Glen Cattle Ranch, where beef cattle roamed semi-wild and largely fended for themselves as they did on the North American prairies. ASD was sold to DCL in 1953, and its distilleries were managed by Scottish Malt Distillers (SMD), which re-equipped Glenlochy in the 1960s and undertook renovations in the 1970s.

Due to world recession, Glenlochy was closed in 1983. Its closure was one of the measures taken by SMD to reduce output in order to bring the level of maturing stock into line with the anticipated level of future sales.

Tasting notes: Rich nose, sherried, and perfumed, with some spicy notes and a trace of orange. Its flavour is sweet, some sherry; a good balance, but somewhat nondescript. Fades rapidly.

Glenlossie

Category: Speyside (Elgin) Distiller: John Haig & Co, Markinch, Fife
Owner: Diageo plc

Glenlossie Distillery was built in 1876 by John Duff, a publican who had been the manager of Glendronach for several years. He had two partners in the business, Alexander Grigor Allan, procurator fiscal for Morayshire, and H. Mackay, a land agent and burgh surveyor of Elgin. By 1887, John Hopkins & Co was entirely responsible for the sale of the fillings. John Duff & Co was liquidated in 1897, and the Glenlossie-Glenlivet Co was formed. A private railway siding constructed on the line that ran between Elgin and Perth cut the costs of transporting incoming supplies and consignments of whisky to the markets in the south.

Many improvements and extensive additions to the buildings were made over the years (including the installation of a horse-drawn fire engine, which the distillery preserves to this day), and in 1930, Glenlossie became fully owned by Scottish Malt Distillers, a subsidiary of DCL. During the 1950s and 1960s, new warehouses were built and the distillery was fully powered by electricity. In 1971, Mannochmore distillery was built within the same complex and John Haig & Co became the licensed distillers. Glenlossie is rated "top class" by blenders.

Tasting notes: Slightly green tint. Full, fresh nose, with some sherry. Heather-honey predominates. Taste is sweet and sherried, with more honey, but the finish is smooth and dry.

Glen Mhor

Category: Highland (Inverness) Distiller: distillery closed 1983

Glen Mhor Distillery faced Glen Albyn across the Great North Road on the western outskirts of Inverness. The manager of Glen Albyn, John Birnie, tried in vain to gain a significant shareholding in his distillery, and so formed a partnership with Charles Mackinlay & Co of Leith (*see* MACKINLAY). He bought a site opposite Glen Albyn and built a new distillery, designed by architect Charles Doig of Elgin. Named Glen Mhor, the distillery was completed and in production by 1894. The partnership became a private company in 1906, with the participation of John Walker & Sons, which held forty per cent of the shareholding.

In 1920, Mackinlay & Birnie bought Glen Albyn and set about

an extensive modernization plan for both distilleries. DCL made a successful offer for Mackinlay & Birnie's shares in the distilleries in 1972, and in 1983, both distilleries were closed.

Tasting notes: The aroma is malty, with cereal, grassy, and nutty notes. The taste is sweet, fresh, and smooth, but unremarkable.

Glenmorangie

Category: North Highland Distiller: The Glenmorangie Distillery, Tain, Ross-shire Owner: Glenmorangie plc, Broxburn, Midlothian

For many years, Glenmorangie has been the best-selling malt in the UK and the third-ranking malt whisky worldwide in volume terms. So it comes as a surprise to discover that the distillery itself is relatively small.

It is situated on the southern shore of the Dornoch Firth, near the Royal Burgh of Tain in Ross-shire – one of the oldest towns in Scotland, with a bishopric dating from the ninth century – on the site of a brewery which was established in 1738. The site is attractive because of the nearby Tarlogie Spring, which provides a copious supply of extremely hard and mineral-rich water – unusual, this, since traditional wisdom maintains that soft water is best for whisky-making. Illicit distilling took place on Morangie Farm from at least the 1660s.

The foundation of the distillery dates from 1843, when the farm was bought by William Matheson, a partner in Balblair Distillery. Matheson lacked capital, so was unable to realize his plans to develop the distillery. His first pair of stills were second-hand and of an unusual pattern (they are immensely tall, the highest in Scotland, and were originally gin stills), but were so successful that they have been copied ever since. When Alfred Barnard visited in the mid-1880s, he described Glenmorangie Distillery as "certainly the most ancient and most primitive we have seen, and now almost in ruins". He was amazed that, in spite of its condition, it produced 20,000 gallons (over 90,000 litres) of whisky a year.

Indeed, by this time Glenmorangie was selling throughout Britain, and even abroad, wherever Ross-shire expatriates travelled. The *Inverness Advertiser* reported that a consignment had been seen en route to San Francisco, and another to Rome.

The distillery was incorporated in 1887, and the directors immediately undertook its complete renovation. The new stills, modelled on the old, were heated by internal steam coils rather than by direct firing – a pioneering move, and one which was to be followed by the industry generally. By the outbreak of the First World War, Glenmorangie was being exported all over the world, although principally trade remained in the home market, including such prestigious outlets as the Savoy Hotel in London.

During the war, barley rationing and a shortage of manpower (seventy-five per cent of the local men aged between fifteen and thirty-five signed up) caused the distillery to close for two years. In 1918, the need for capital persuaded the directors to sell the distillery to their largest single customer, the Leith-based distiller and blender Macdonald & Muir (*see* HIGHLAND QUEEN).

By 1920, production exceeded pre-war levels, but that year Prohibition was introduced. This, combined with high taxation and the General Strike of 1926, kept profits down. In 1929, the collapse of the American Stock Market heralded the first great world recession. This proved nearly fatal for Glenmorangie, and the distillery was closed from 1931 to 1936.

By the outbreak of the Second World War, production had again reached unprecedented levels, but barley was rationed once more, and whisky production ceased between 1941 and 1944. Not until 1948 were pre-war levels reached, but these were soon exceeded: during the 1960s and 1970s, stock rationing had to be introduced. In 1980, the number of stills was doubled (to four), but even this was not enough; ten years later a further four were added.

By maintaining traditions and adhering to the strictest production standards, Macdonald & Muir did much to promote the enjoyment of malt whisky throughout the world. The company pioneered the study of the effects of wood upon maturation, and it exercises the most stringent "wood regime", buying its oak as standing timber in the Ozark Mountains of Missouri, air-drying the staves, and filling the casks with Kentucky bourbon. The company eschews the use of sherry wood but has pioneered the procedure known as "sherry finishing", where whisky is transferred into sherry (or wine) casks for the final years of maturation. Macdonald & Muir took the name of its most famous distillery in 1996, becoming Glenmorangie plc. The entire production of the distillery is bottled as single malt. None goes for blending.

Tasting notes: (*10 Years Old*) Clean fragrance, with floral and citric notes (mandarin, vanilla) and a trace of smoke. (A leading Parisian perfumier has identified no fewer than twenty-six individual aromas, including apricot, bergamot, cinnamon and quince.) Medium-bodied, smooth-tasting, well-balanced. Almonds, some spice, and wood smoke. The overall effect is fresh and aromatic; the finish is clean and dryish. Glenmorangie is the quintessence of a "well-mannered" Highland malt. The older expressions fill out and enrich the flavours above: caramel and butterscotch appear, marzipan and increased nuttiness, but the finish is still fresh and dry, even minty.

Glen Moray

Category: Speyside (Elgin) Distiller: Glen Moray-Glenlivet Distillery Co, Elgin Owner: Glenmorangie plc, Broxburn, Midlothian

Glen Moray Distillery was established in 1897, on a site which was famous for the quality of its water (which drains off the Dallas Moor into the River Lossie) and which had been occupied by a brewery since the eighteenth century. The buildings on two sides of the distillery's central courtyard date from this time.

The distillery's site was also on the main road west out of Elgin, and until 1680, the town's gallows stood here – a grim warning to visitors. Excavations in 1962 at Gallowcrook Hill, within the distillery's grounds (to make room for a new warehouse), revealed seven skulls, one with a musket ball embedded in its jaw.

The Royal Burgh of Elgin is the gateway to Speyside, and the "capital" of the whisky industry. It was once the centre for the extensive whisky trade with the Baltic states. The surrounding area, known as the Laich o'Moray, is famous for its barley crop: according to an old saying (repeated on Glen Moray's label), "The Laich o'Moray has forty days more summer than any other part of Scotland."

The distillery was acquired by Macdonald & Muir in 1920 (see HIGHLAND QUEEN, GLENMORANGIE) after a lengthy period of closure, and was considerably expanded in 1958. Its product has a good name among blenders and the huge majority of its 1.6 million litre (over 350,000 gallons) annual output is used for this purpose. Since 1976, some has been bottled as a single malt, but it was made more generally available after 1981 and it is now found in global markets and many different expressions.

Tasting notes: (12 Years Old) A typical estery, Speyside nose: cereals, hay, fresh-mown grass, a trace of smoke and violets (the malt is hardly peated at all; the peat flavour comes from the water). Light but smooth-bodied; fresh-tasting, clean, with barley coming through. Well-balanced with a clean, dry finish.

Glen Ord

Category: North Highland Distiller: John Dewar & Sons, Perth Owner: Diageo plc

Built on the site of an illicit still at Muir of Ord in Ross-shire, the distillery was licensed in 1838 by a Mr Maclennan. Its product has been known variously as Ord, Glenordie, and Glen Ord.

In 1924, Muir of Ord Distillery was acquired by Dewar's, and accordingly passed to DCL the following year. Ord has long been a contributor to Dewar's blends. The distillery has its own drum maltings, and an unusual feature of production is that heather is thrown into the kilns during malting – this is believed to impart a dry, rooty flavour.

The distillery was rebuilt in 1966. Glen Ord was only available locally until 1993, and since then has won gold medals at the Monde-Sèlection (Brussels) and the International Wine and Spirit Competition (trophy and gold medal 1994, gold medal 1995).

Tasting notes: Medium-bodied, very smooth. Heather flowers, green sticks and a whiff of peat smoke emerge. A clean, malty taste, slightly sweet; well-balanced, very smooth. The finish is dry and spicy; slightly smoky, with a trace of ginger.

Glenrothes

Category: Speyside (Rothes) Distiller: Glenrothes-Glenlivet, Rothes, Morayshire Owner: The Edrington Group, Glasgow

Glenrothes Distillery was started in 1878, the year in which the City of Glasgow Bank collapsed. This had dire consequences for the firm building the distillery: it had borrowed heavily to finance the venture, and two of the directors were employed by another bank, which might well have gone the same way.

As it happened, all went well. Work continued on the distillery and the owning company, William Grant & Co, amalgamated with the Islay Distillery Co to become the Highland Distilleries Co. The distillery was completed in 1878 and the partners appointed James Booth Henderson as brewer. Henderson, a renowned judge of livestock, used to stable his stock of horses and cattle in the distillery, to the displeasure of his employers.

Glenrothes is ranked among the top six malt whiskies by blenders, who pay a premium for it and take all they can get. It is also a key constituent of the popular Famous Grouse brand. Thus it is difficult to find as a single malt, and apart from the occasional cask bottled by independents, only Berry Brothers & Rudd, the established London wine merchant, has the exclusive licence to issue the proprietory bottling.

The still-house was extended in 1980, and for a short time after this it was haunted. Only the intervention of the well-known psychic investigator, the late Professor Cedric Wilson, laid the spirit to rest.

Tasting notes: A deep, fruity nose, slightly sherried, with a medium to full body and a well-rounded, raisiny palate. There is a trace of malt, and the sweetness this implies, but this is balanced by a smooth dryness in the finish.

Glen Scotia

Category: Campbeltown **Distiller:** *Glen Scotia Distillery Co, Campbeltown, Argyll* **Owner:** *Loch Lomond Distillery Co, Alexandria,*

Glen Scotia is one of only two distilleries in Campbeltown (the other being Springbank), where once there were over thirty distilleries. First registered in 1835, it was overhauled in the early 1980s to increase efficiency and capacity. In spite of this, the distillery was closed in 1984 and only reopened after it had been sold to Gibson International in 1989. The company went into receivership in 1994, and Glen Scotia was sold to Glen Catrine Bonded Warehouse, the sister company of its present owner. The distillery was put on sale in 1996, and is currently working part time.

Glen Scotia is small, has the appearance of a good townhouse, and is reputed to be haunted by a previous owner who drowned himself in Campbeltown Loch after being swindled. The brand is especially popular in North America and Germany.

Tasting notes: Campbeltown malts are famous for their briny, "sea-mist" character. Glen Scotia has this in full measure. The nose is aromatic, fresh, and slightly peaty; it is medium-bodied and very smooth, full, rounded, and salty, with some peat. Finishes long.

Glen Spey

Category: Speyside (Rothes) Distiller: Glen Spey Distillery, Rothes, Morayside Owner: Diageo plc

The distillery was built in 1884 by James Stuart, and was named Mill of Rothes. In 1887, it was sold to Gilbey Vintners, which was expanding its interests into whisky distilling (*see* THE SINGLETON OF AUCHROISK, KNOCKANDO, STRATHMILL). The distillery was substantially reconstructed in 1970.

Glen Spey is a key ingredient of the J&B whiskies and is rare as a single malt, although it was sold as a house malt by Unwins, the off-licence chain for a period. It is now bottled in small quantities by its owner.

Tasting notes: (*SMWS 10 Years Old – 60.8%*) A slightly oily nose, with aromas of hazelnuts and old leather car seats. With water the scent resembles Lapsang Souchong tea – scented smoke, tar, and saddles. The flavour is like sweet tea to start, with some tannic astringency and a trace of linseed oil.

Glentauchers

Category: Speyside (Keith) Distiller: Allied Distillers, Dumbarton Owner: Allied Distillers, Dumbarton

The Glentauchers-Glenlivet Distillery was built by James Buchanan (*see* BUCHANAN'S) in 1898, when he realized that in order to complete the range of his operations he should secure a supply of malt whisky. By this time, Buchanan's was one of the "Big Three" whisky houses, along with Dewar's and Walker's, and in 1925, they merged their interests with DCL. The ownership of Glentauchers (pronounced "glen-tockers") eventually passed to Scottish Malt Distillers, the DCL subsidiary. Between 1923 and 1925, extensive alterations and improvements had been made and a large new spirit store was built to the design of the distillery architect, Charles Doig of Elgin. Glentauchers was closed in 1985, then sold to Allied Distillers, which reopened it in 1989. It is available in independent bottlings only, mainly from Gordon & MacPhail.

Tasting notes: A sweet and estery nose, with a trace of solvent and an interesting "waxy" development (scented candles). The taste is smooth and sweet, with rich biscuity traces; the waxy flavour is still discernible. The finish is surprisingly dry, and quite lengthy.

Glen Torran

Category: Region unknown, probably Speyside Licensee: Roderick & Henderson, Edinburgh and London Owner: London & Scottish Spirits, Guildford, Surrey

I know of no glen Torran, although there is a skerry of fierce rocks off the south coast of the Isle of Mull called the "Torran Rocks". This malt is available in export markets only (principally Scandinavia, the Far East, and the USA), and its colourful blurb states that "Glen Torran Malt Whisky is about barley and water, time and stillness".

Glenturret

Category: Central Highland **Distiller:** *Glenturret Distillery Co, Crieff, Perthshire* **Owner:** *Highland Distillers, Glasgow*

Glenturret makes a claim to being the oldest distillery in Scotland, having apparently being established by 1775 (some of the original buildings still exist), on a site that had been used by illicit distillers since 1717. Whisky-makers, then and now, use the water of the fast-flowing River Turret, said to be "as fine as any in the kingdom for distilling purposes". The site also appealed to smugglers on account of the vantage points provided by the surrounding hills.

The distillery itself was dismantled in the 1920s, then revived in 1957 by noted whisky enthusiast James Fairlie, with a view to preserving the craft traditions of malt distilling and developing its appreciation. To the latter end, he was well ahead of his time in organizing visitor facilities and making arrangements for tours and tastings. In 1964, he showed the British Prime Minister, Sir Alec Douglas-Home, round the distillery. Fairlie retired in 1990, and Glenturret joined Highland Distilleries in 1993. A 1996 bottling won Best Single Malt in the 1991 International Wine and Spirit Competition.

Today, the distillery is a major tourist attraction (some 250,000 visitors per annum) and is provided with a heritage centre, exhibition museum (complete with life-size figures), an audio-visual display, a shop (selling souvenirs and the complete range of Glenturret products, including a limited-edition ten-year-old, which is available nowhere else), and a substantial restaurant.

Tasting notes: (*12 Years Old*) Pale, with a slightly green tinge. Dryish, malty nose, some flowery aromas (elderflower?), and a hint of wood; fairly closed and unyielding. Malty flavour, hint of nuts and vanilla. Dryish finish. Older expressions differ wildly, becoming more sherried, richer, creamier, and more scented.

Glenugie

Category: East Highland **Distiller:** *distillery closed 1983*

First recorded in the early 1830s, Glenugie was converted into a brewery in 1837, and then rebuilt as a distillery in 1873; six years later, the owning company was wound up. Having passed through the hands of several owners, it was silent from 1925 until 1937, when it was taken over by Seager Evans. Seager Evans became Long John International in 1956 (*see* LONG JOHN) and was taken over by Whitbread & Co in 1975. The new owner sold Glenugie to a consortium of oil men who were unable to make a success of it. The distillery was closed in 1983 and later demolished.

Tasting notes: (*1965*) There is an intriguing trace of incense on the nose – spicy and lightly sherried. The flavour is disappointingly flat: sweet turning to bitter.

Glenury-Royal

Category: East Highland **Distiller:** *distillery closed 1985*

Glenury Royal Distillery used to stand close to the coastal town of Stonehaven, south of Aberdeen. Founded in 1825, it was built in 1836 by Captain Robert Barclay of Ury, MP for Kincardine, a prominent farmer and landowner, and a renowned long-distance athlete. In 1799, he walked from London to Birmingham in two days, and, in 1808, he became the first man to walk 1,000 miles in 1,000 successive hours. He also had a friend at court (whom he referred to as "Mrs Windsor"), through whose influence he was permitted to suffix "Royal" to his product.

Barclay died in 1847, and the distillery was put up for auction. In 1857, it was bought by William Ritchie of Glasgow, and it remained in his family until 1938, when it was sold by its landlord, Lord Stonehaven, to Associated Scottish Distilleries (see BEN NEVIS). In 1953, it became part of DCL and was licensed to the small Glasgow blender, John Gillon & Co (see GILLON'S).

Glenury was closed in 1985 and the site sold for residential development in 1992. Uncommon though it is as a single malt, it was bottled as a Rare Malt by United Distillers, and won Most Outstanding Single Malt and Best Single Malt Over 12 Years in the 1996 International Wine and Spirit Competition.

Tasting notes: (*Proprietor 23 Years Old – 57.4%*) Full, gold colour, with bronze lights; the nose is aromatic, with a trace of sherry and some peat smoke. A sweetish nose, although the taste is on the dry side – rich and complex, with malt, indeterminate floral flavours, and spice. The finish is long.

Highland Park

Category: Island (Orkney) Distiller: James Grant & Co, (Highland Park), Kirkwall, Orkney Owner: The Edrington Group, Glasgow

The world's most northerly whisky distillery was founded in 1798 by Magnus Eunson of Gallowhill, near the Parks of Rosebank, Kirkwall. Until it was licensed in 1825, its production was illicit, and Eunson was assisted in evading the excisemen by a kinsman, who was a kirk elder and hid the contraband under the pulpit.

By the 1880s, Highland Park had an established reputation. In 1883, Sir Donald Currie, the founder of the Union Castle shipping line, took a party of distinguished guests to Kirkwall on the maiden voyage of the *Pembroke Castle*. They were entertained by one Baillie Peace,

> "who produced his well-known big bottle of Old Highland Park whisky. No sooner had this famous brand been tasted than they one and all agreed that they had never met with any whisky like it before; that what was called Scotch in England was as different from this as chalk from cheese . . . A supply of Old Highland Park was at once sent on board . . . At Copenhagen, where the vessel called after leaving Kirkwall, the King of Denmark, the Emperor of Russia and a very distinguished party were entertained on board. The Highland Park was procured and pronounced by all to be the finest they had ever tasted".

In 1888, James Grant, whose father was manager of The Glenlivet Distillery, became managing partner and later owner of Highland Park. The Grants relinquished control to Highland Distilleries in 1937. The distillery has its own floor maltings and peat beds (the peat is cut shallow to impart a light, "rooty" character) and two traditional peat-fired kilns. During kilning, a little heather is burned.

Highland Park has been promoted as a single malt since the early 1970s, and is one of the largest-selling malts worldwide. Sales are currently growing at ten per cent per annum.

Tasting notes: Michael Jackson describes Highland Park as "the greatest all-rounder in the world of malt whiskies". Its aroma is heathery, slightly sweet, with clean, smoky echoes. Its flavour is succulent and smoky, with leafy, spicy, and heather-honey notes. A subtle balance of sweet and dry, and a clean, dryish finish.

Imperial

Category: Speyside (Strathspey) Distiller: Allied Distillers, Dumbarton Owner: Allied Distillers, Dumbarton

The Imperial Distillery was built in 1897, the year of Queen Victoria's Diamond Jubilee, by Thomas Mackenzie, who already had substantial interests in the Dailuaine and Talisker distilleries. The buildings were designed by the renowned distillery architect from Elgin, Charles Doig, and were constructed entirely from red Aberdeen bricks within a frame of iron beams. This specification was made in order to restrict the possibility of damage by fire, a common problem in so volatile an environment.

The progress of the distillery was reported by a local journalist, who noted that the malt kilns were being surmounted with a large imperial coronet that "once gilded, would flash and glitter in the sunlight like the crescent on a Turkish minaret . . . among the dark pine woods of Carron and the brown hills which encircle it".

During the 1890s, the demand for whisky outstripped supply, so Mackenzie merged his interests to form Dailuaine-Talisker Distilleries, to which Imperial was transferred. Following the crash in 1898 of Pattison's, the blender in Leith, demand for malt fillings slumped and Imperial closed in 1899. It remained closed for twenty years. In 1925, production resumed for one season only, then the distillery was beset with problems of effluent disposal. During the next thirty years, Imperial operated purely as a maltings. In the 1950s, it transpired that effluents could be recovered by drying, and used as a high-protein animal foodstuff, so the earlier disposal problems were overcome. Production recommenced in 1955.

The business of Dailuaine-Talisker Distilleries was wound up in 1982, and Imperial was subsequently taken over by Scottish Malt Distillers, the DCL subsidiary responsible for malt whisky production. It was closed in 1985, then sold to Allied Distillers, which reopened it in 1989, but mothballed it again in 1998.

Tasting notes: The nose is spirity, slightly sherried with some smoky notes; generally lightweight. The flavour is also lightweight and sweet, with smoky traces and cereal undertones, and lacks integration. The finish is sweet.

Inchgower

*Category: Speyside (Keith) **Distiller:** Arthur Bell & Sons, Perth*
Owner: Diageo plc

The distillery was built in 1871 in an area renowned for illicit distilling. Although it is described as a Speyside, it is a long way from the region on the Moray Firth, near the fishing port of Buckie.

Bell's acquired Inchgower in 1938 and undertook an extensive modernization programme, converting the power from coal to steam, and renovating the warehouses, which were so vast that they provided bonding space for other distilleries in the region.

Tasting notes: Dense floral notes, with some caramel and an aroma of mint toffee. The flavour is rich and very smooth, with toffee notes persisting, a trace of salt, an overall dryness, and a curious impression of steam engines. A pleasant, rich whisky.

Inchmoan

*Category: South Highland **Distiller:** Loch Lomond Distillery Co,*
*Alexandria, Dumbartonshire **Owner:** Loch Lomond Distillery Co*

This curiously named malt takes its name from a small island in Loch Lomond (see INCHMURRIN), and is made in Lomond-style stills at Loch Lomond Distillery (see LOCH LOMOND). It is basically the same spirit as Inchmurrin, except that the malt has been peated to 40 parts per million phenols, so it is much smokier. It is made in the traditional way, allowing one wash still to charge one spirit still (unlike some of its stable-mates – see CRAIGLODGE, CROFTENGEA). It is not bottled by its owner at present.

Inchmurrin

*Category: South Highland **Distiller:** Loch Lomond Distillery Co,*
*Alexandria, Dumbartonshire **Owner:** Loch Lomond Distillery Co*

This malt is named after an islet in nearby Loch Lomond upon which stand the ruins of an ancient castle built by the Dukes of Lennox. More recently, the island was used as a naturists' resort (see LOCH LOMOND).

Inchmurrin was first sold as a vatted malt, but now that it has had time to mature it is marketed as a single malt. It is made in Lomond stills (see INVERLEVEN) which have rectifying columns within the still head, and can produce different styles of whisky at different strengths. Old Rosdhu is made in the same stills.

Tasting notes: Nosed straight, the impression is of a weighty whisky with rum toffee notes. This becomes lighter when water is added; there is still a slight toffee aroma but malty, grainy notes appear, becoming grassy and hay-like. The flavour is smooth and well-integrated; some initial sweetness but the overall impression is dry. The finish is fairly quick.

The Invergordon

*Category: Single Grain **Distiller:** The Invergordon Distillers,*
*Invergordon **Owner:** Whyte & Mackay Ltd., Glasgow*

The Invergordon Distillery occupies an eighty-acre site on the northern shore of the Cromarty Firth in the northeast Highlands, surrounded by some of the best arable land in Scotland.

The place takes its name from an eighteenth-century laird, Sir William Gordon. It is one of the best deep-water harbours in Europe and was an important commercial port and naval base. The distillery was commissioned in 1959 to create employment in the area, following the departure of the Royal Navy.

In 1966, Invergordon Distillers built Tamnavulin Distillery (*see* entry), using the same contractors that had built Tomintoul Distillery the year before. Three years later the company bought Bruichladdich Distillery and, in 1971, through its acquisition of Brodie Hepburn & Co, Tullibardine Distillery (*see* entry). In 1984, Ronald Morrison & Co (makers of Glayva) was acquired, and in 1985, Charles Mackinlay & Co (owner of Isle of Jura and Glenallachie Distilleries)

Following the acquisition of Charles Mackinlay & Co, Invergordon was able to claim that it was "the world's largest supplier of customer-specified whisky" (i.e. "own-brand whiskies"), exporting its products to well over 100 countries worldwide.

In 1988, the company was bought by its management. Profits rose sharply and Invergordon became liable to hostile takeover. This happened in 1993, through the Whyte & Mackay Group, with its ultimate owner American Brands. The latter company, which also owns the major bourbon brand Jim Beam, changed the operating name of the corporation to JBB (Worldwide) in 1996, with the Whyte & Mackay and Invergordon Distillers Groups falling under JBB (Greater Europe). In 2002, the management bought the Scotch whisky side of the company and former "Kyndal International", which (happily) reverted to its original name, Whyte & Mackay, in 2003. The Invergordon, one of only three single-grain whiskies that are bottled as such (the others are Cameron Brig and Black Barrel), was introduced in 1990 and targeted at first-time and occasional whisky drinkers. It is light and refreshing, and recommended over ice. Its creators describe it as "distilled sunlight". The brand won a gold medal at the 1993 International Wine and Spirit Competition awards.

Tasting notes: Light, cereal nose, with fresh grass and vanilla notes; very pale colour (the casks in which it is matured are selected for their lightness). Clean, slightly sweet with a dash of iodine; a pleasant, lingering finish. Overall, it has a positive and distinctive flavour that will confound anyone who maintains that grain whisky is tasteless.

Inverleven

Category: Lowland Distiller: George Ballantine & Son, Dumbarton
Owner: Allied Distillers, Dumbarton

This distillery originated in the early days of the Hiram Walker–Ballantine's relationship, which was marked by the building of the Dumbarton Grain Distillery on the site of the McMillan shipyard, where the River Leven meets the Clyde beneath Dumbarton Rock – the former capital of the

ancient British kingdom of Strathclyde. The distillery is
currently mothballed.

From the outset, Inverleven supplied fillings for Ballantine's
blends, and it has never been available as a single malt except
from specialist merchants. In about 1959, a new kind of still was
installed alongside the distillery's two conventional stills. The first
of its kind, it was named a "Lomond still" and its product was
occasionally bottled as a curiosity (known as "Lomond single
malt") by independent bottlers.

Hiram Walker later installed Lomond stills at Glenburgie
(producing Glencraig), Miltonduff (producing Mosstowie), and
Scapa (a wash still only). The first two have since been removed.
Loch Lomond Distillery, which produces Inchmurrin, also has
a pair of Lomond-style stills.

The idea behind the Lomond experiment was to produce a
lighter whisky (in terms of its specific gravity) which would appeal
to the American market. The stills themselves incorporated a cold-
water coil within the still-head, which increased the reflux and
acted as a kind of rectifier. Indeed, in some cases, including the
Inchmurrin stills, the coil was replaced by a small rectifying
column (*see* INTRODUCTION, GRAIN WHISKY PRODUCTION).

Tasting notes: An atypical Lowland with a highly perfumed
nose, with complex, fresh-fruit aromas: peaches, nectarines, citric
notes. The flavour is lightweight and sweetish, with traces of soft
fudge, and a catch of ginger in the finish.

Islebrae

Category: Lowland Distiller: dismantled

The small malt distillery installed by Inver House's American
owners within their grain distillery at Moffat on the outskirts of
Airdrie, Lanarkshire, produced three styles of malt, depending on
the degree to which the malt had been peated. Killyloch had a
Lowland style, Glen Flagler a Highland style (*see* entries), and
Islebrae an Islay character.

Isle of Arran

Category: Island (Arran) Distiller: Isle of Arran Distilling Co
Owner: Isle of Arran Distilling Co. Stirling

The Isle of Arran Distillery was opened in 1995 at Lochranza, a
pretty village and bay in the northeast of the island, with a ruined
castle in its midst. It was the brainchild of Harold Currie (former
managing director of Chivas Brothers and Campbell Distillers),
and the Isle of Arran Distilling Co is family owned.

Money was raised by an innovative "bondholders' scheme",
which investors could join for £450, receiving five cases of mature
malt in 2001, and five cases of Lochranza blended whisky in 1998
(all ex-duty). The distillery is purpose-built, with small, onion-
shaped stills similar to those at Macallan. It fits well into its setting
and is a popular tourist attraction, with an award-winning
restaurant. The distillery has not been in production 2002–4.

Tasting notes: The nose is sweetly floral, with just the slightest
hint of peat smoke. Complex and closer to Speyside than island in

style, it is pleasant and gentle, creamy and lightly toffeed, with some fresh citric notes and a hint of angelica. Dryish finish.

Isle of Jura

Category: Island (Jura) Distiller: The Invergordon Distillers, Leith Owner: JBB (Greater Europe)

The word *Jura* derives from the Norse for "deer", of which some 6,000 share the island with 225 people. The first distillery here was set up in the seventeenth century in its successor's grounds, which itself dates from 1810, although little remains since its roof was removed in 1901 to avoid paying rates (an odd feature of Scots law).

In 1958, the present distillery was conceived by two Jura landowners as a way of creating work on the island. They obtained the assistance of Scottish Brewers and employed the noted distillery designer, W. Delmé Evans. It was opened in 1963, and its first single malt came to market in 1974.

The distillery draws its water from Loch a' Bhaile-Mhargaidh (the market loch), a thousand feet (300 metres) above Craighouse, the island's only village. The water is dark with peat, but Jura whisky is surprisingly light, and not at all like some of its closest cousins neighbours on Islay.

The distillery was acquired by The Invergordon Group in 1985, and Invergordon was taken over by Whyte & MacKay in 1993. Its proprietor bottles at ten years old and the malt won a gold medal in the International Wine and Spirit Competition in 1991.

Tasting notes: This whisky is pale in colour, with a delicate nose – slightly oily, with a hint of peat. It has a light body, with a sweetish taste at first, and vanilla and walnut notes. The whole impression becomes drier on the finish, with a trace of saltiness, and very slight peatiness.

Killyloch

Category: Lowland Distiller: dismantled 1985 Owner: Inver House Distillers, Airdrie

Killyloch was produced in a pair of pot stills installed within Moffat grain whisky distillery in 1965. It was designed for blending only (*see* GLEN FLAGLER). It should have been named "Lillyloch", after the water source, but the cask stencil was misspelt! The malt whisky distillery was closed and dismantled in 1985. Extremely rare, the only known bottling was by Signatory in 1994 of a cask distilled in 1972.

Tasting notes: (*S 22 Years Old – 58.2%*) Mid-amber colour and a green, cereal nose with some oiliness. The flavour was soft, medium-bodied, and slightly tannic, the finish dry.

Kinclaith

Category: Lowland Distiller: distillery demolished 1982

The distillery was built in 1958 within the Strathclyde grain distillery complex constructed the same year by Long John International when this company was a subsidiary of Seager Evans.

It was the last malt distillery built in the City of Glasgow. Strathclyde incorporated vast storage, cooperage, and blending facilities, and it was natural to have a malt distillery close by, making use of the water available from Loch Katrine. The output was used for blending, and in 1975, after it was bought by Whitbread & Co, Kinclaith was dismantled to make way for the new distillery at Strathclyde.

Tasting notes: Highly perfumed for a Lowland, with light, grassy notes and a whiff of caramel. To taste – I cannot improve on Michael Jackson: "melon dusted with ginger".

Kininvie

Category: Speyside (Dufftown) Distiller: William Grant & Sons Owner: as above

A new distillery, built on the same site as Glenfiddich and Balvenie to provide additional fillings for William Grant's blends. Opened in 1991, it has not been bottled as a single.

Knockando

Category: Speyside (Strathpey) Distiller: Justerini & Brooks, London Owner: Diageo plc

Knockando Distillery is situated on a knoll overlooking the River Spey (hence the Gaelic name Cnoc-an-Dhu – "the dark hillock"), and draws its water from the Cardnach Spring, described as an especially good source of water and used only for Knockando. The distillery was built in 1898, and was acquired by Gilbey's in 1904 for £3,500 (*see* J&B RARE).

The distillery has long made a practice of bottling casks only when they are deemed to be "at their peak", and making an age declaration on the bottle, rather than automatically bottling at, say, 12 years old. Knockando was first exported in 1977–8 and is now sold in forty markets worldwide.

Tasting notes: Pale, even for a Speyside. Nose dry and cereal-like; mouth-feel smooth; complex flavour with layers of flowery, nutty, slightly smoky notes. A soft, clean, sweetish finish.

Ladyburn

Category: Lowland Distiller: distillery dismantled 1975 Owner: William Grant & Sons International, Dufftown

In the years following the Second World War, William Grant & Sons (*see* GRANT'S) underwent considerable expansion and quickly realized that it would need to secure its supplies of fillings for blending. In 1963, the company built the grain distillery at Girvan beside the Penwhapple Loch, followed, three years later, by the construction of a Lowland malt distillery called Ladyburn.

Ladyburn was once bottled in the late 1980s as a single malt for export to America; otherwise, the entire production was used in blending. Like many other Lowland distilleries, Ladyburn was shut down in 1975, when the whisky industry was suffering from over-supply. Only one other bottling is known: from Cadenheads at twenty years old.

Tasting notes: (*C 20 Years Old*) Pale-straw colour with bright highlights. Malty, full nose, with some oil and some peaty notes.

The flavour is smooth, soft, and slightly smoky; the overall impression, and the finish, is dry.

Lagavulin

Category: Island (Islay) **Distiller: *White Horse Distillers, Edinburgh*** **Owner:** *Diageo plc*

Lagavulin Distillery stands near the ruins of Dunyveg Castle, once a stronghold of the Lord of the Isles, in a little bay on the south coast of Islay. In Gaelic, the name means "the hollow where the mill is", and in the late 1700s there were known to have been up to ten illicit stills operating in the district. A century on, when he visited the island in 1887, Alfred Barnard remarked, "There are only a few of the Scotch distillers that can turn out spirit for use as single whiskies, and that made at Lagavulin can claim to be one of the most prominent."

By the 1830s, there were two remaining distilleries in the bay; these amalgamated in 1837 to form Lagavulin Distillery under the ownership of the Graham brothers and their partner, James Logan Mackie, uncle of Peter Mackie, who later became one of the "Big Five" in the whisky industry (*see* WHITE HORSE).

Indeed, it was at Lagavulin that the young Peter learned his trade as a distiller. Soon after succeeding his uncle, he earned the nickname "Restless Peter" at the distillery – a comment on the fact that he was always planning new enterprises and seeking new methods to improve efficiency. These initiatives included a "power flour" called "Bran, Bone & Muscle", the development of dark grains cattle-feed, tweed manufacturing, and the harvesting and distribution of Carragheen moss.

In 1908, Mackie instigated the restoration of two of the old buildings at Lagavulin, which had at one time been a small distillery called Malt Mill, built in 1816. He intended to distil a whisky according to the original techniques – only peat was burned in the kilns – and the final product was quite different to Lagavulin. This closed down in 1960, when it became necessary to build a larger still-house for the main distillery.

Sir Peter Mackie died in 1924, and Mackie & Co changed its name to White Horse Distillers. Three years later it joined DCL, and in 1930, when the malt whisky distilling activities of DCL were reorganized, Lagavulin was taken over by Scottish Malt Distillers.

Now Lagavulin is the best-selling of Diageo's Classic Malts. It won Best Single Malt and a gold medal at the 1994 International Wine and Spirit Competition, and gold medals in 1995 and 1996. The Distillers Edition won Best Single Malt Over 12 Years at the 1999 IWSC Awards. It is so popular that allocations to markets are rationed.

Tasting notes: Very dry nose; Lapsang Souchong tea – smoky, some toasted peat, but all in balance – nothing over-dominant. Big body. The flavour begins sweetish and malty, with some sherry, then becomes very dry and smoky. The finish is almost bitter, with lingering peat smoke and some salt. Lagavulin has been described as the aristocrat of Islays.

Laphroaig

Category: Island (Islay) Distiller: D. Johnston & Co (Laphroaig)
Owner: Allied Distillers, Dumbarton

The name is Gaelic for "the beautiful hollow by the broad bay",
and it was in this place on the south coast of the island of Islay
that two brothers, Donald and Alex Johnston, established a
distillery in 1815 that they built up during the 1820s. Many of the
original buildings remain, including the floor maltings. One of
the founding brothers died in unfortunate circumstances in 1847:
drowning in a vat of fermenting wash. Ownership passed through
the family, until between 1954 and 1972, the company was chaired
by Mrs Bessie Campbell.

Laphroaig has a reputation for being the most pungent of
all Scotch whiskies. It is very heavily peated – the distillery owns
its own peat banks, and malts around twenty per cent of its
requirement. The water in which the malt is mashed is dark with
peat (they say that Islay water tastes of whisky). Maturation takes
place close to the sea, which may account for the slightly salty
flavour that can be detected in Laphroaig.

Laphroaig's principal markets are the UK, the USA, France,
and Italy, and it is among the top five best-selling malts. The 15
Year Old won gold medals in the International Wine & Spirit
Competition in 1988 and 1993, and Best Single Malt up to 15 Years
Old in 1993.

Tasting notes: Nose is powerfully phenolic: smoky, medicinal,
seaweedy (fishing nets), peaty. The body is medium and oily. The
taste translates the smell element for element: peat smoke, tar,
diesel oil, seaweed, iodine, salt. The finish is dry and lingering.
The overall impression is clean and straightforward. Laphroaig
is an old tar, a salty dog, among whiskies, although it seems
to have been tamed somewhat in recent years, especially the
older expressions.

Ledaig

Category: Island (Mull) Distiller: Tobermory Distillers, Tobermory,
Isle of Mull Owner: Burn Stewart & Co, East Kilbride

Ledaig is the "safe haven" in Gaelic and well describes the cosy
anchorage of Tobermory on the Isle of Mull. The whisky is made
here, at Tobermory Distillery (*see* TOBERMORY), with more heavily
peated malt than the standard brew.

Tasting notes: (*Ledaig 18 Years Old* – 43%) A pale-gold whisky,
with a fresh, leathery, grassy note and some peat smoke. With
water, becomes sweeter, almost like cake-mix. The flavour is
surprisingly sweet and easy to drink, with a dryish finish and
continuing smoke.

Linkwood

Category: Speyside (Elgin) Distiller: John McEwan & Co
Owner: Diageo plc

Linkwood is the distillery closest to the sea on the River Lossie, just
south of Elgin. It was founded in 1821 by Peter Brown, an estate
factor (*i.e.* manager) and agricultural improver whose brother,

General Sir George Brown, commanded the ill-fated Light Brigade during the Crimean War. Little is known of the distillery in its early days, except to say that it passed to Brown's son, who completely demolished, then rebuilt it.

In 1898, at the height of the whisky boom, a public company was formed. With capacity doubled and access to railway transport, the whisky began to fetch a good price in the markets in the south.

In 1936, Scottish Malt Distillers took over the company and brought in a new manager, who, according to Professor McDowall, was "a Gaelic-speaking native of Wester Ross, who for many years supervised its making with unremitting vigilance. No equipment was replaced unless it was essential. Even the spiders' webs were not removed for fear of changing its character." Extensive rebuilding programmes were undertaken in 1963 and 1973. Linkwood has long been available from the independent bottler Gordon & MacPhail, and may be bought in small amounts from its owner.

Tasting notes: An initial cereal impression, quickly taken over by a strong, estery perfume: bananas and bubblegum (New World Chardonnay), with some nail-varnish remover and a trace of fino sherry. The flavour begins delicately sweet, and finishes dry, with bitter, appley flavours between.

Linlithgow (*see* ST MAGDALENE)

Littlemill

Category: Lowland Distiller: demolished 1997 Owner: Loch Lomond Distillery Co, Alexandria, Dumbartonshire

Situated at Bowling on the north bank of the Clyde close to Glasgow, Littlemill is possibly the oldest distillery in Scotland, claiming its foundation at least as early as 1772 (when accommodation for excise officers was erected). There was a brewery on the site, attached to nearby Dunglass Castle, which probably dates from a similar period (the fourteenth century), so it seems likely that distilling took place here from very early times.

The site had a good source of water in the Kilpatrick Hills and readily available barley from the fertile fields along the Clyde. When the first government survey on whisky was conducted in 1821, Littlemill was producing 20,000 proof gallons (over 90,000 litres) a year. During its long history, the distillery has changed hands several times, and periodically been out of production.

Littlemill was modernized in 1988 by its former owner, Gibson International, which went into receivership in 1994; the distillery was bought by Glen Catrine Bonded Warehouses, whose sister company now owns it. However, it did not resume production, and in 1966, the plant was dismantled. Part of the still-house was demolished to make way for a modified plant that was to be installed in the remaining warehouse buildings. Alas, this never happened, and these buildings were demolished in 1997.

Tasting notes: Littlemill is a typical Lowland malt: the colour of white wine with a light body; gentle, fresh, slightly sweet, malty (marshmallows?), with a dry, quick finish.

Loch Dhu (*see* MANNOCHMORE)

Loch Lomond

> *Category: South Highland* **Distiller:** *Loch Lomond Distillery Co, Alexandria, Dumbartonshire* **Owner:** *Loch Lomond Distillery*
>
> Loch Lomond Distillery is situated on a Victorian industrial estate at Alexandria, in a converted calico-dying factory. Calico dying requires a copious supply of (preferably soft) water and this was provided by the River Leven, which runs from Loch Lomond to Dumbarton (at its mouth is Ballantine's massive blending and bottling facility). The Leven's water is very soft, which made it eminently suitable for bleaching and dying calico; in 1768, there were four bleach fields and three print fields in the vicinity devoted to this important industry. Soft water is also favoured for the production of whisky, and the old calico factory was converted in 1965–6 by the owners of Littlemill Distillery (*see* LITTLEMILL), Barton Brands of the USA, to produce two malt whiskies, Inchmurrin and Old Rosdhu (*see* entries). In 1984, the distillery closed and was sold to Glen Catrine Bonded Warehouses of Ayrshire, the current owners under a different name. Under the chairmanship of one of the "grand old men" of the whisky industry, Sandy Bulloch, Loch Lomond proudly proclaims itself to be the largest independent whisky company, after William Grant & Sons. The distillery has two pairs of stills and produces seven styles of malt whisky (*see* INCHMURRIN, OLD ROSDHU, GLEN DOUGLAS, INCHMOAN, CROFTENGEA, CRAIGLODGE) and one blend (*see* LOCH LOMOND blend). It also has a continuous still for producing grain whisky. It is able to produce such a variety of malts because the still designs – not unlike the design of the Lomond stills installed at three of Hiram Walker's distilleries in the early 1960s (*see* INVERLEVEN, MOSSTOWIE, GLENCRAIG) – have twenty-foot rectifying columns attached to their necks. The rectifiers have up to fourteen plates in them, and by drawing off spirit at different plates you can obtain different styles, heavy or light. Furthermore, if distillate from the wash still is added to distillate from the spirit still, further variations are possible.
>
> Loch Lomond is the lightest of the malt whiskies made here, being drawn off at eighty-five per cent ABV.
>
> **Tasting Notes:** Very light, in colour and body. A vaporous, fruity-leafy nose. The flavour starts sweet and finishes somewhat pepperminty.

Lochside

> *Category: East Highland* **Distiller:** *Macnab Distillers – distillery closed 1992* **Owner:** *Macnab Distilleries, Montrose*
>
> Lochside Distillery was a brewery in the eighteenth century, and in the early nineteenth century, it was owned by William Ross, who sold it to James Deuchar & Sons, the Edinburgh brewer, which is now part of Scottish & Newcastle Breweries, although the very successful brand, Deuchars IPA (*i.e.* India Pale Ale) is made by the independent Caledonian Brewery. In 1957, the site

was bought by Joseph Hobbs, who converted it to a distillery and introduced a grain still alongside the traditional malt pot stills as he had at Ben Nevis. The managing company was Macnab Distilleries, and it produced a successful blend called Sandy Macnab's.

Lochside was sold in 1973 to Destilerias y Crianza del Whisky, a Spanish drinks company, which closed down the grain stills and successfully marketed the blend for many years. The distillery was mothballed in the mid-1980s and put up for sale. The plant has been dismantled.

Tasting notes: A lightly sherried nose with traces of toffee and rubber, then a deep, fruity note (blackcurrants). The flavour is innocuous – slightly sweet and sherried, becoming dry – then suddenly explodes into more sherry towards the end.

Lomond

*Category: Lowland **Distiller:** George Ballantine & Son, Dumbarton **Owner:** Allied Distillers, Dumbarton (part of Allied Domecq)*

Lomond was formerly produced at the Inverleven Distillery, Dumbarton, on Lomond stills. The enterprise is currently mothballed (*see* INVERLEVEN). Not to be confused with "Loch Lomond" (distillery, malt and blend).

Tasting notes: The sample I tasted had the sharp flavour associated with maturation in plain oak casks. The nose was initially reminiscent of fresh paint and oily, bourbon-like notes, then became mossy/dusty/fusty. The flavour was reminiscent of fresh lint bandages, with a sweetish start and a dry, even bitter, finish. The Scotch Malt Whisky Society unaccountably noted peaches, which is interesting in view of the tasting notes for Inverleven.

Longmorn

*Category: Speyside (Elgin) **Distiller:** Chivas Bros **Owner:** Chivas Bros, Paisley*

The name Longmorn comes from the early Gaelic *Lanmar-noch*, "the place [or church] of St Marnoch", and there was an ancient chapel here. A warehouse now stands on what was reputedly the chapel site, and long after the chapel itself had disappeared a water-driven meal mill was established there (in about 1600). John Duff, who built Glenlossie Distillery in 1876, purchased the site, which is about halfway between Rothes and Elgin, in 1893. He built two distilleries on it, Benriach and Longmorn, in order to take full advantage of the 1890s' whisky boom.

Longmorn Distillery opened in 1894, and has remained in continuous production. It has an ample supply of local peat and abundant spring water from the Mannoch Hill. In 1899, responsibility for its management passed to James R. Grant and later to his two sons, who became known as "The Longmorn Grants". Until 1970, the distillery remained with this family; then, the Longmorn Grants joined with the Grants of Glen Grant and the Smith-Grants of Glenlivet to form The Glenlivet Distillers, which later became a subsidiary of the Canadian giant Seagram (*see* THE GLENLIVET).

Longmorn retains the water wheel and steam engine that used to power the distillery and they can still be seen on the premises. Longmorn is highly prized by blenders (ranked "top class") and is generally regarded as one of the best Speysides. It won gold medals in the International Wine & Spirit Competition in 1993 and 1994.

Tasting notes: (*1963*) Highly sherried nose, slightly oily, buttery; a rich malty/fruity aroma; traces of shortbread (aromas tight and well-integrated). Full-bodied. Sherry on the palate; extremely smooth; malty and sweetish; slightly drier in the long finish, but no trace of bitterness.

Younger expressions are not so sherried: fresher and more flowery. An exceptionally well-made malt.

Longrow

Category: Campbeltown Distiller: J&A Mitchell & Co, Springbank Distillery, Campbeltown Owner: J&A Mitchell & Co, Campbeltown

Longrow has been distilled at Springbank Distillery in Campbeltown on the same stills as Springbank every year since 1990. The two whiskies are utterly different. The former is made from heavily peated malt (the distillery has its own floor maltings and uses local peat) and the resulting whisky is powerfully phenolic. In blind tastings it is usually mistaken for an Islay. From 2000, Longrow has been more widely available, bottled as a 10 Years Old; from 2014 there will also be a 14 Year Old expression. A cask of Longrow at nine years, re-racked into a fresh port pipe for the last four years of its maturation, was selected by the Scotch Malt Whisky Society as its millennium malt.

There was once a distillery called Longrow, established in 1824, and occupying part of the site on which Springbank now stands.

Tasting notes: Longrow has a pungent, earthy, peaty nose not unlike wet sheep. It is medium- to full-bodied and has an oily, creamy, malty palate, phenolic and very dry. Its finish is tenacious, salty, and intense.

The Macallan

Category: Speyside (Strathspey) Distiller: Macallan-Glenlivet, Craigellachie, Banffshire Owner: The Edrington Group, Glasgow

A farm distillery was established at Easter Elchies near Craigellachie in the early 18th century. Its product soon had a wide reputation even beyond Speyside, assisted by the fact that Macallan Farm was situated above one of the few fords across the Spey, one of the cattle-drove routes from the Laich o'Moray to the south.

The Macallan's popularity will have encouraged its owners to apply for a licence earlier than most (in 1824), but the distillery changed hands several times throughout the nineteenth century. In 1892, it was bought by an Elgin merchant, Roderick Kemp, who owned Talisker Distillery in Skye. The descendants of his two daughters (one of whom married a Shiach, the other a Harbinson) formed the largest shareholding group until they sold their shares to Highland Distilleries and Suntory in 1994. Allan Shiach was chairman of the company until 1996.

A programme of modernization and expansion was begun in the 1950s (trebling the output by 1959), but such was the demand that, in 1968, the directors decided to expand the distillery further and to follow a policy which, in time, would rely more on sales of single malt. New stills were installed, all built to the same pattern as the original stills (which are among the smallest in the industry), and bonded stores were built to house the maturing spirit. This includes what is currently the largest single-roofed whisky warehouse in Europe, built in 1990.

It is easy to forget that, in the early 1980s, there were relatively few single malts available beyond Scotland. The Macallan had long been considered a "top class" by blenders, so the decision to concentrate on selling the brand as a single malt was a bold one.

The Macallan's directors also determined at this time that all the whisky bottled as single should be matured in sherry wood. Within a few years, the availability of casks became a problem, so, in 1976, the company began to buy its own new wood in Spain, seasoning it in the bodegas of Jerez for three or four years before shipping and filling it. This is an expensive policy (the cost of a sherry butt is about ten times that of a bourbon barrel), but it makes a major contribution to The Macallan's flavour.

The first batch of The Macallan was not deemed to be ready for the market until 1980; since then, its popularity and success has been phenomenal. The brand currently stands at number three in the UK malt whisky market, number five in the world.

By 1994, Highland Distilleries and Suntory, the Japanese distiller, had acquired a majority shareholding. To the surprise of the management – but not of the industry – they decided to take the company over in July 1996.

Tasting notes: (*12 Years Old*) A deep amber colour and a bouquet as rich as fruitcake, with powerful sherry and butterscotch notes; round and deep. This is generally a full-bodied whisky and flavour is usually full and well-rounded, reminiscent of old Armagnac: sherry, fruit (currants, cherries), a hint of wood (more noticeable in the older expressions); clean, intense, and well-rounded. The finish is surprisingly dry, with a lingering sherry-wood aftertaste. A classic digestif.

Macduff (*see* GLEN DEVERON)

MacPhail's

Category: Speyside (district unknown) *Distiller: undisclosed*
Owner: Gordon & MacPhail, Elgin

In 1895, Gordon & MacPhail set up as "Italian warehousemen" in the Royal Burgh of Elgin, where many of the Speyside distillers had their offices. James Gordon was a whisky broker, and with his partner, John Alexander MacPhail, and a young assistant,

John Urquhart, they commenced trading as "Family Grocers, Tea, Wine & Spirit Merchants".

Initially, they were concerned with provisioning the local clientele, but quickly the firm made a speciality of whisky – blending and bottling under its own labels, as well as broking and dealing in mature whiskies. The latter was a pioneering move; indeed, Gordon & MacPhail can boast of being the first company to stress the virtues of aged single-malt whisky.

As early as 1896, the firm was advertising its Moray Brand Old Highland Liqueur Scotch Whisky in a London magazine; by 1914, its whiskies were being exported abroad. In the 1930s, ownership of the company passed to the Urquhart family. Today, the entire board is made up of children and grandchildren of the original John Urquhart.

The company's policy has always been to buy new whisky direct from the distillery, warehouse it, and bottle it when it is thought to be at its best. The "laying down" of malts has been going on for so long that some of the stock is now extremely rare, either because of its age or because the distilleries that supplied it have gone out of production. Several of the whiskies offered by Gordon & MacPhail would never have seen a bottle had it not been for the firm's commitment to invest in otherwise unknown malts. Apart from blending its own brands, Gordon & MacPhail has become best known for specializing in fine Highland malts. Unfortunately, legal injunctions prevent it from continuing to bottle certain prominent brands where the distillery proprietors wish to retain their exclusive right to do so. Gordon & MacPhail bought Benromach Distillery (*see* entry) in 1992.

The single malt which bears the founder's name is a case in point: its creator is kept a close secret, although apparently the distillery is very well known.

Tasting notes: (*10 Years Old – 60.5%*) Maturation in sherry wood is immediately apparent, but the nose also has a lot of fresh hay and barley, and a peppery top-note. Upon tasting, the sherry and malt lend a sweet smoothness, but the finish is dry. (*1973*) The aroma has developed into a profound fruitiness, incorporating elements of plums, stewed apples, *Rumtopf* (although there is a freshness to the fruit that suggests fruit salad to some noses); the sherry notes almost vanish in the fruitiness. The flavour is not as sweet as the nose would suggest, however; there is a faint sandalwood mustiness, and the finish is on the dry side, with cigar-box afterthoughts. The two expressions are utterly different.

McKillop's Choice

Category: a range of single malts **Distillers:** *undisclosed*
Owner: *Angus Dundee Ltd, London*

A changing range of single-cask bottlings from twelve to thirty years old.

Mannochmore

Category: Speyside (Elgin) **Distiller:** *John Haig & Co, Markinch, Fife*
Owner: *Diageo plc*

Mannochmore was built in 1971 by Scottish Malt Distillers a few miles south of Elgin, beside the company's distillery at Glenlossie; it has the capacity to produce a million proof gallons annually. All but a tiny amount of this goes for blending, and this small amount has only been available as a single malt since 1992. In 1996, more was made available as Loch Dhu, which has been very heavily coloured up.

Tasting notes: (*Loch Dhu 10 Years Old*) The colour of treacle with a dryish nose: fresh figs, dried fruit, mint toffee, polished leather, and over-ripe bananas. The flavour is flat and dryish, with a trace of burnt toast and liquorice-water. The finish is short and bitter.

Millburn

Category: North Highland Distiller: distillery closed 1985

Millburn was founded in 1807, which makes it one of the earliest distilleries. At that time, distilling was a difficult business in which to make a profit, owing to competition from illicit distillers, who paid no fees or taxes, and were more or less endemic throughout the Highlands. But Millburn survived, and, in 1853, it became the property of David Rose, an Inverness corn merchant, who largely rebuilt it in 1876.

In 1892, Millburn was acquired by two members of the Haig family (*see* HAIG), under whose ownership it was considerably expanded. In 1921, it was sold again, to Booth's, the famous London gin distiller. However, a fire in 1922 destroyed most of the essential buildings and it had to be completely rebuilt. Taken over by DCL in 1937, it was in continuous production from after the war until 1985, when it was dismantled.

Tasting notes: (*G&M 1971*) A robust nose: estery, malty, well-scented, clean. The flavour shows some sherry, smooth mouth-feel, pleasant malty notes, well-balanced. A good, slightly dry finish.

Miltonduff

Category: Speyside (Elgin) Distiller: George Ballantine & Son Owner: Allied Distillers, Dumbarton

Miltonduff Distillery is three miles outside Elgin ("The Whisky Capital"), close to Pluscarden Priory, which at one time was said to produce the finest ale in Scotland, so good that it "filled the abbey with unutterable bliss". The Benedictine monks of Pluscarden drew their water from the Black Burn, attributing its excellence to the fact that it had been blessed by a saintly abbot in the fifteenth century. Miltonduff uses the same source of water today. The distillery was licensed in 1824 as Miltonduff-Glenlivet.

It was renovated in the 1890s, at which time it was producing 300,000 proof gallons (over 1.3 million litres) a year, but suffered badly in the whisky crash of 1900.

It was sold to Hiram Walker in 1936, which licensed it to George Ballantine & Sons. Considerable modernization has taken place in recent years, including the installation of a pair of Lomond stills for a short period (*see* INVERLEVEN), with which a whisky named Mosstowie was produced.

However, apart from this experiment, every replaced still is identical to its predecessor, of which Alfred Barnard, visiting Miltonduff in 1877, wrote, "Some of the oldest fads and methods are in use [here], and the ancient style of stills and utensils, as carried on by the smugglers, have also been continued."

Miltonduff was bottled by its proprietor in the 1970s and 1980s: the owner now licenses Gordon & Macphail to bottle for them.

Tasting notes: (*12 Years Old*) Miltonduff is an elegant, fragrant, and complex malt. Its nose is flowery, with vanilla and almond notes; its taste lightly smoky, with faint almonds and a hint of honey. Its finish is long and aromatic, with some touches of nutty dryness.

Mortlach

Category: Speyside (Dufftown) Distiller: John Walker & Sons, Kilmarnock, Ayrshire Owner: Diageo plc

Until 1887, Mortlach was the only distillery in Dufftown; today, however, there are five (and once were seven). The site had been used by smugglers for many years, on account of its excellent spring, known as "Highlander John's Well". The distillery was licensed in 1823, following the changes introduced by the Excise Act of the same year.

Mortlach Distillery was established by three local men on a feu of land leased from the Earl of Macduff. By 1854, only one of the founders was still active, and he took one George Cowie into partnership. The latter, who became sole owner ten years later, sought markets beyond the immediate vicinity and Mortlach-Glenlivet became known as far afield as London.

By 1903, Cowie was able to refurbish the distillery, and brought in his son, Dr A.M. Cowie, who had studied medicine at Aberdeen University and was a senior medical officer in Hong Kong. He returned to Scotland to run the family business and became a much-respected local figure, eventually being appointed deputy lord lieutenant for Banffshire.

For many years, Mortlach was only available in independent bottlings, but it has long been regarded locally and by blenders (who rank it as "top class") as one of the best Speyside malts and is now bottled by its owners at sixteen years old.

Tasting notes: A rich, red colour in its proprietary bottling (this becomes paler and more tawny in most independent bottlings). It also has a deeply perfumed nose, like an oriental garden: full of mysterious scents, tropical fruits, and spices. This whisky offers a very smooth mouth-feel; with sweetish, nutty, dried-fruit and vanilla flavours, and an appealing dryish finish.

Mosstowie

Category: Speyside (Elgin) Distiller: George Ballantine & Son Owner: Allied Distillers, Dumbarton

This malt was produced at the Miltonduff-Glenlivet Distillery (*see*

MILTONDUFF) in Lomond stills fitted with rectifying columns within the still-head (*see* INVERLEVEN for a description). These have now been dismantled, and, although old stocks of their product can still be found, Mosstowie is not common.

Tasting notes: A pleasant, malty nose with fruity aromas quickly developing (figs, nectarines), with some sherry coming through. The flavour is sweet, smooth, and well-balanced (almost fruit-syrupy), but with a refreshing dryness and even a trace of wood in the finish.

North British

Category: Single Grain Distiller: The North British Distillery Co, Edinburgh Owner: Lothian Distillers Edinburgh

Built in 1886 in the Gorgie district of Edinburgh by a consortium of blenders and dealers, led by Andrew Usher, "The Father of Blending" (*see* USHER'S GREEN STRIPE), North British acted mainly as a bargaining token against DCL's monopoly of grain whisky production. It was the most modern distillery of its day, originally having one Coffey still and later expanding to four. The first Saladin maltings in Scotland were installed here in 1948.

The distillery was refurbished in 1992, and reduced to two stills; the following year, it was taken over by the current owners, Lothian Distillers, a consortium comprising the well-established whisky blenders Robertson & Baxter and IDV. The latter merged with UD to form Diageo in 1998. All of its make goes for blending. A single cask from 1964 was bottled by Signatory.

North Port

Category: East Highland Distiller: distillery closed 1983

The Royal Burgh of Brechin in Angus is of great antiquity. From early times, it was an important religious centre; it was sacked by the Danes in 1012, and its splendid little cathedral incorporates a Pictish "round tower". Its bishopric dates from 1150. The town was once walled, and traces of its gates – or "ports" – are still evident, hence the name of the distillery.

North Port was founded in 1820 by David Guthrie, who had established the first bank in the town and had served as provost (mayor). The Guthries were farmers in Angus, where some of the country's best barley is grown. Alfred Barnard wrote in 1887, "The district around Brechin being highly cultivated, barley of the finest quality is grown and carted by the farmers into the lofts of the distillery where nothing but the best barley is malted."

In 1892, the company changed its name to Guthrie, Martin & Co and became a limited company in the following year. DCL acquired the entire shareholding in 1922, in conjunction with W.H. Holt & Co, an independent wine and spirits merchant in Manchester. In 1922, it was licensed to Mitchell Brothers, Glasgow. It was closed down in 1983 and dismantled, and its product is now becoming very rare.

Tasting notes: The nose is dry and astringent, spirity, with some light smokiness, and sweet scents beneath the spirit: marzipan and

a trace of aniseed. The flavour is likewise dry and astringent, with
a brief blooming of sweet malt followed by a rapid finish.

Oban

Category: West Highland Distiller: John Hopkins & Co
Owner: Diageo plc

Situated on the west coast, midway between the Caledonian and
Crinan canals, Oban is known as the Gateway to the Isles.

Two brothers by the name of Stevenson settled in Oban in
1778, and were responsible for greatly enhancing the prosperity
of what had previously been no more than a hamlet. The brothers
were involved in slate quarrying, housebuilding, and
shipbuilding, and, in 1794, Hugh Stevenson built the Oban
Distillery, hiring an experienced Lowland distiller to manage the
whole operation. In effect the town grew up around the distillery.

The distillery remained in the hands of the family until 1866
and was eventually acquired by Walter Higgin in 1883. By this
time, Oban was a busy port, shipping wool, whisky, slate, and
kelp to Liverpool and Glasgow by steamship. The railway also
brought a new era of prosperity to the area in the form of
tourism, with the first scheduled passenger trains arriving from
Glasgow in 1880.

According to Alfred Barnard, in 1887, Higgin had made "vast
improvements in the machinery and appliances, and built two
new warehouses". While engaged in this renovation, rock was
blasted from the cliff behind the distillery to accommodate the
enlargements and a cave was discovered that contained human
bones and implements from the Mesolithic period (4500–3000BC).

In 1898, Alexander Edward, owner of Aultmore Distillery,
bought Higgin out. In its first year, the Oban & Aultmore
Distilleries suffered catastrophic losses, when the major blending
company Pattison's of Leith collapsed.

In 1923, Oban was sold to Dewar's and joined DCL with that
company in 1925. It was silent from 1931 to 1937 and from 1969 to
1972, when a new still-house was built. A good visitor centre was
installed in an old maltings in 1989, and the year after, Oban was
selected for promotion as a Classic Malt.

Tasting notes: Dryish nose, with a distinct seaside note, and
also a flowery/herbal hint of bog myrtle. The flavour begins sweet
and finishes dry with a whiff of smoke. Smooth, slightly viscous,
and fruity.

Octomore

Category: Islay Licensee: Bruichladdich Distillery Ltd
Owner: Murray McDavid, Port Charlotte,Islay

This will be a very heavily peated expression of Bruichladdich
(around seventy parts per million phenols). The first distillations
were done in 2002.

Old Pulteney

Category: North Highland Distiller: Inver House Distillers, East
Kilbride Owner: Inver House Distillers

Located at Wick in Caithness (only twelve and a half miles (twenty kilometres) south of Scotland's north coast), Pulteney is the most northerly distillery on mainland Scotland. In fact, much of the "modern" town of Wick is correctly called "Pulteneytown" after Sir William Pulteney, the director of the British Fisheries Society, which built it as a model fishing port in 1810.

The distillery was founded in 1826 by James Henderson and remained in the possession of his family until 1920, when it was sold to James Watson & Co. In 1923, it was bought by John Dewar & Sons. Later, the distillery came under the ownership of Hiram Walker, which completely rebuilt it in 1959. It was sold to Inver House in 1995, which began to bottle at twelve years old in 1997.

Tasting notes: Old Pulteney is known as the "manzanilla of the north", but its flavour is a complex balance of dry and sweet. The first impression is of almonds, almost marzipan, with pear-drop notes, and some traces of lemon sherbet. The almond/marzipan comes through when the whisky is tasted and there is even a sherbet "fizz" apparent. The texture is smooth and viscous, the finish long and dry.

Old Rosdhu

Category: South Highland Distiller: Loch Lomond Distillery Co, Alexandria, Dumbartonshire Owner: Glen Catrine Bonded Warehouse

Old Rosdhu is produced at the Loch Lomond distillery, which Glen Catrine has owned since 1985, and which also produces Inchmurrin on the same Lomond stills (see INVERLEVEN/ LOCH LOMOND).

One of the features of Lomond stills is that it is possible to produce whiskies of differing strengths and character from the same still. Rosdhu has a slightly lower specific gravity than its sister whisky, and a slightly different style of malt is used in its production so the flavour is also different. It is available in the UK and in export markets, but is not common.

Tasting notes: The nose is rich, heavy, and malty, with some heathery notes. The taste is succulently smooth: sweet, even on the roof of the mouth, but not in the slightest cloying. The heather traces remain, with some almonds.

Pittyvaich

Category: Speyside (Dufftown) Distiller: distillery closed 1993; part demolished 2003

Pittyvaich Distillery was built in 1974 as part of Bell's huge extension programme, close to the older, more traditional Dufftown Distillery, and part of the Dufftown complex. It was situated in the Dullan Glen, near to Mortlach Church (see MORTLACH), and drew its water from the Convalleys and Balliemore springs.

Bell sought to ensure that the new distillery was similar to the old one in every respect: its four stills were exact replicas of Dufftown's, and the storage and vatting facilities were matched one with the other. Yet its product was quite different, and, in my view, better. Most goes for blending, but since 1992 some has been bottled by United Distillers/Diageo as a single malt. The distillery was closed in 1993, and was largely demolished in 2003.

Tasting notes: Sweet, fruity-estery nose, lightweight, with the faintest trace of aniseed and pepper. Medium-bodied. It is sweet-tasting, with delicious caramel flavours; smooth and well-balanced. A fresh, dry, spicy finish.

Port Ellen

Category: Island (Islay) Distiller: distillery closed 1983

The distilleries of Islay are all built on the shore, where piers could be erected for convenient transportation. Port Ellen is no exception: the village which grew up around the distillery is now one of the largest on the island and its harbour has superseded Bowmore as the principal port.

The distillery was first established by A.K. Mackay in the 1820s, but he was soon involved in bankruptcy proceedings and Port Ellen passed into the hands of John Ramsay. Ramsay was a remarkable man. Liberal MP for Stirling and chairman of the Glasgow Chamber of Commerce, he was a leading figure of his day in the whisky industry. It was he who first saw the benefits of exporting whisky to America – which he did, direct from Port Ellen. He pioneered the spirit safe, which is now a standard item in every distillery. He assisted Aeneas Coffey and Robert Stein with their experiments which led to the invention of the Patent Still for the manufacture of grain whisky – much of their research was done at Port Ellen. He persuaded the government to allow Islay whisky to be bonded free of duty for many years. And he introduced the first regular cargo and passenger service from Islay to Glasgow by steamer.

Following his death, ownership passed to his wife and son, who sold their interest to the Port Ellen Distillery Co Ltd. in 1920. In 1925, the distillery was acquired by DCL and closed down. It reopened in 1967, following an extensive modernization programme, when it became licensed to Low Robertson & Co of Edinburgh. Port Ellen has been closed since 1983 and its plant removed. Most of the distillery buildings still stand, including the two original pagoda-roofed kilns (a later, third, kiln was demolished in 2003) and some of the oldest maturation warehouses in Scotland.

A substantial maltings was built adjacent to the distillery in 1973, with eight steeps and drums, and, in line with a concordat signed in 187 which was designed to preserve local employment, all the Islay distillery owners agreed to buy from the maltings.

Tasting notes: Port Ellen is unmistakably an Islay malt: lightly phenolic, with peat smoke and iodine, but also having gentler, spicy, mossy notes which lend interest and complexity. It is full-flavoured, sweet then dry, salty with a hint of bonfires, and boasts a good, lingering finish.

Pulteney (*see* OLD PULTENEY)
Rosebank
Category: Lowland **Distiller:** *distillery closed 1993*

The distillery is at Camelon, just north of Falkirk, on the bank
of the Forth-Clyde Canal, which was built by James Smeaton
in 1773. The first record of distilling activity here was in 1798
by Messrs Stark.

During the 1840s, the maltings of the Camelon distillery were
acquired by James Rankine, a local grocer and wine and spirit
merchant. He rebuilt the distillery and began to produce a whisky
of high quality. Such was the demand from the blenders that he
sold it on allocation, and was able to charge warehouse rent to his
customers (at the time he was the only distiller able to do so,
although this has since become universal practice). These were
the beginnings of the most well-known of the Lowland malts.

In 1894, Rosebank Distillery Ltd was formed, with Rankine
holding half the capital. A second issue of shares in 1897 was
fully subscribed. Unfortunately, Rosebank was hit by the collapse
of the market in 1900, and the ensuing slump – so much so that in
1914, it was among the companies that amalgamated to form the
Scottish Malt Distillers before this group became part of DCL.

Rosebank continued the Lowland tradition of triple
distillation, and maintained that the lightness of its product
is attributable to this practice.

Despite being widely regarded as the most distinguished
of the Lowland malts, Rosebank Distillery was closed in 1993.
Tasting notes: (*1979*) Amber colour, with a reddish hue. Sweet,
and very scented (Parma violets, Russian toffees, boiled apples),
very lightly sherried, traces of honey. Much drier flavour than one
would expect, still perfumed; perfectly balanced. Very elegant.

Royal Brackla
Category: North Highland **Distiller:** *John Bisset & Co, Leith* **Owner:**
John Dewar & Sons, Glasgow

The small Brackla Distillery was founded in 1812 on the Cawdor
Estate, near Nairn, a district made famous by Shakespeare's
Macbeth, who was Thane of Cawdor before he became king
of Scots. The distillery's founder, Captain William Fraser,
found it difficult to compete with the many illicit producers
in the neighbourhood and set about establishing a market in
the Lowlands and south of the Border.

In 1835, William IV granted Fraser a royal warrant as a sign
of his appreciation of the whisky; this was renewed by Queen
Victoria in the 1850s. After several changes of ownership, the
lease of the Brackla Distillery Co passed to two Aberdeen wine
and spirits merchants, who rebuilt it (1898). In 1926, it was sold
to John Bisset & Co, a blending firm. Royal Brackla became a key
ingredient of its two well-known blends, Bisset's Finest Old and
Gold Label. The firm joined DCL in 1943, and in 1965, the new
owner renovated Brackla Distillery and built new maltings. In
1980, it was again refurbished and extended from two to four

stills. In spite of this it closed in 1985 for six years. The distillery was sold to Bacardi Ltd, along with the John Dewar company, in 1998. At present, only a small amount of this malt is bottled as a single.

Tasting notes: Pale-gold in colour, with an aromatic, estery nose; some faint smoke, some fruit (bananas), and a trace of cereal. Sweet and malty, with a touch of salt. Bitter/dry finish, and a lingering fruity taste (bananas again).

Royal Lochnagar

Category: East Highland **Distiller:** *John Begg, Glasgow*
Owner: Diageo plc

> ... Oh, for the crags that are wild and majestic
> the steep frowning glories of dark Loch-na-gar.

These are the words of Lord Byron, himself a Scot, who spent much of his boyhood in this area of Deeside.

Lochnagar is a small distillery, founded in 1825, close to the Royal Family's summer residence at Balmoral Castle, in the shadow of the mountain of the same name. The founder was a local man, John Crathie, who took advantage of the 1822 Act that encouraged licensed distilling. The present buildings date from 1845, by which time the distillery was owned by John Begg.

In the same year, the Balmoral estate was bought by Queen Victoria, and in 1848, only three days after she and the Prince Consort arrived at Balmoral, Begg invited them to visit his establishment (he had heard how fascinated Prince Albert was with anything mechanical). The very next day he was honoured with a royal visit. In his diary, he recorded that after the tour, "I asked whether he [Prince Albert] would like to taste the spirit in its matured state, as we had cleared some that day from bond, which I thought was very fine." Some days later a letter arrived granting a royal warrant to supply the Royal Household.

John Begg was an innovative businessman. He was a close friend of William Sanderson, to whom most of the distillery's product went, chiefly for the blending of VAT 69. He also created his own brands, realizing that the future of whisky lay in blending (*see* JOHN BEGG BLUE CAP).

As late as 1967, Professor McDowall wrote, "It is a privilege to have tasted such a rich whisky. It is not generally available. Perhaps it is kept at the distillery in case the present Queen and her Consort pay a call, but there is enough of it made to justify a single bottling. At one time, it was the most expensive whisky in Scotland." John Begg & Co became part of DCL in 1916, and Diageo now bottles a small quantity of Royal Lochnagar as a single malt, lavishly packaged and distinctively labelled. It sells especially well in the Far East. The "Selected Reserve" is bottled from four butts (two ex-sherry, two ex-bourbon), chosen by experts during an annual ceremony. This bottling maintains the tradition of being the among the most expensive malts.

Tasting notes: Royal Lochnagar has a rich, toffee-gold colour. Aromas of butterscotch, rich fruit, and linseed oil notes crowd the nose, with a clear wisp of smoke. It is full-bodied and luscious; mouth-coating and very smooth. So the very clean, dry finish comes as something of a surprise when the whisky is tasted: it is balanced by an initial malty sweetness, and rounded off by a heathery fruitiness (raspberries).

St Magdalene (aka Linlithgow)

Category: Lowland Distiller: distillery closed 1983

The name derives from the lands near Linlithgow, known as St Magdalene's Cross, upon which the distillery was built in the late 18th century – once the site of a hospital of the same name, and of an annual fair. The distillery was also known as "Linlithgow". The town itself was once an important brewing and distilling centre, with five distilleries. The first recorded licensed distiller was Adam Dawson in 1797. Dawson was one of the loudest voices for the Lowland distillers against the exemptions granted to Highland distillers by the Board of Excise.

St Magdalene was well-placed for communications, especially after the opening of the Union Canal in 1822, upon which the distillery had its own wharf. Many of the buildings are now listed as being of historic interest, and have been turned into "residential appartments". The malt store predates the repeal of the malt duty and it still has iron bars on its windows.

In 1894, A&J Dawson was incorporated, and extended and modernized the distillery. But competition between the Lowland distillers was fierce, and in 1912, Dawson went into liquidation, all its assets being acquired by DCL. Here began the origins of Scottish Malt Distillers (SMD), the DCL subsidiary created by an amalgamation of five Lowland distillers. SMD made radical improvements at St Magdalene and, by 1927, most of the complex was electrified. The floor maltings were retained, and although the Depression of the 1930s caused most distilleries to close, the maltings at St Magdalene remained active throughout. The output from the distillery resumed after the war and production was maintained until 1983, when it was closed.

Tasting notes: *(1965)* The colour is that of amontillado sherry, shot through with red-gold. The aroma is dry, spicy, and strongly perfumed: attar of roses, fresh black pepper, dry hemp rope, dusky, oriental, and delightful. The flavour is very smooth and perfectly balanced, with a distinct smoky, artichoke flavour. Clean and dryish, with a perfect tapering finish. An experience!

Scapa

Category: Island (Orkney) Distiller: Taylor & Ferguson
Owner: Allied Distillers, Dumbarton

Scapa Distillery stands on the north shore of Scapa Flow in Orkney, where the German High Seas Fleet scuttled itself at the end of the First World War. For many years, the shadowy shapes of the giant battle cruisers *Hindenburg* and *Seidlitz* were visible beneath the waves, their masts above water at low tide.

An earlier fragment of Scapa history is recorded by the

Reverend John Brand in 1701, concerning a drinking custom
of the hamlet:

> "In Scapa, about a mile from Kirkwall to the southwest, it was
> said there was kept a large and ancient Cup, which they said
> belonged to St Magnus, King of Norway, who first instructed
> them in the principles of the Christian religion, and founded
> the church of Kirkwall, with which full of some strong drink
> their Bishops, at their first landing, were presented. If the
> Bishop drank it out, they highly praised him, and made
> themselves believe that they should have many good and
> fruitful years in his time."

"Orkney's other distillery" (the best-known being Highland Park)
was designed and built by J.T. Townsend, a prominent figure in
the Speyside distilling business, in 1885, and it was acclaimed
as one of the most up-to-date distilleries of its day. It is situated
beside, and draws its water from, the Lingro Burn. It uses
unpeated malt.

There have been continuous and extensive additions to the
distillery over the years as demand for the product increased; the
original site covered only an acre and a half, but today it covers
some seven acres as more warehouses have been needed.

During the Second World War, a fire threatened to destroy the
entire distillery, but Naval ratings who were billeted in the area
came to the rescue by the boatload and the buildings were saved.
After the war, the distillery underwent two changes of ownership
and was eventually acquired by Hiram Walker & Sons, which is
now Allied Distillers. Scapa was mothballed in 1994, but it is hoped
that production will resume. Allied Distillers allows Gordon &
MacPhail, the independent whisky merchant, to bottle a small
amount at ten years old.

Tasting notes: Scapa has an unusual nose: the first impression
is of old-fashioned oilskins; next comes a hint of heather-flowers
and a trace of bourbon. The flavour begins dryish, with a slight
tang, but finishes with caramel notes (even some chocolate). The
texture is silky-smooth (even at eight years old), the body medium
to full. Good, dry finish. A most interesting whisky, difficult to
locate in blind tasting if you had not sampled it before.

Speyburn

Category: Speyside (Rothes) **Distiller:** *Speyburn-Glenlivet Distillery
Co, Rothes, Morayshire* **Owner:** *Inver House Distillers, Airdrie,
Lanarkshire*

The distillery, which stands in a picturesque wooded glen just
outside Rothes, was built in 1897, from stones quarried from an
ancient river bed nearby, by a subsidiary of John Hopkins & Co.
That was also the year of Queen Victoria's Diamond Jubilee, and
the proprietors were keen that their first casks should bear the
historic date. As it happened, production only began during the
last week of the year and only one barrel was stencilled "1897"!
Hopkins & Co joined DCL in 1916, and Speyburn was licensed to
John Robertson & Son.

The distillery has two stills with worm-tubs and was the first in the industry to use drum maltings. These closed in 1968, and Speyburn was sold in 1990. It has been uncommon in the past, but is now being bottled by Inver House.

Tasting notes: Pale gold in colour, Speyburn has a closed, dryish nose, with a trace of heather. It is medium-bodied, and smooth-tasting. The flavour is malty, with heather-honey notes, but the overall impression is dry.

Springbank

Category: Campbeltown Distiller: J&A Mitchell & Co, Springbank Distillery, Campbeltown Owner: J&A Mitchell & Co

Springbank Distillery is still owned by the descendants of its founder, and is one of only a handful of privately owned distilleries remaining in Scotland. It produces a malt whisky that is acknowledged to be among the finest.

Kintyre, where Campbeltown is situated, and the town itself, were a haven of illicit whisky distilling from remote times. Indeed, some authorities maintain that the art of distilling arrived here from Ireland in the sixth century. It was one of the first centres of the commercial industry. Between the 1880s and the 1920s, there were thirty-four working distilleries here, producing at their height nearly two million gallons (over nine million litres) of whisky per annum. Today, only Springbank and Glen Scotia still operate. (The third Campbeltown malt, Longrow, is made at Springbank Distillery from different malt: *see* Longrow.) A fourth malt is made at Springbank's recently opened (2004) sister distillery, Glengyle (*see* entry).

Springbank Distillery was built about 1828 by the Mitchell family, who were local farmers, on the site of Archibald Mitchell's illicit operation. The original buildings are still in use, it has its own floor maltings, still uses worm-tubs, and its ancient wash still is riveted and direct-fired and accordingly equipped with a rummager (a length of copper chain mail) to scour the base of the still and prevent solid particles sticking there and scorching. Some maintain that this contributes to the flavour of the whisky.

Most unusually, Springbank has three stills and employs a form of triple distillation. The wash is distilled off in the usual way, and charges the low wines still, which is also distilled off, without taking a cut. This then charges the low wines still and is again distilled off, without taking a cut. This then charges the third still, called the doubler or spirit still, where the spirit cut is made – the foreshots and feints from this distillation being returned to the low wines still.

The spirit is matured in a mix of sherry and bourbon casks, and is manually filtered rather than chill-filtered. Since the 1970s, the common practice is to chill-filter: the temperature of the spirit is lowered so that microscopic particles which might make the whisky cloudy when ice and water are added are suspended and may be filtered out. Unfortunately these particles also contribute to the flavour.

The distillery is one of only two in Scotland that bottle their whiskies at source (the other being Glenfiddich). In 2000, Springbank was voted top malt by a panel of whisky experts for Whisky Magazine'

Tasting notes: Springbank is a very distinguished whisky, voted "best" by the readers of *Whisky magazine* in 1999. It is also very highly regarded by blenders, some of whom consider it indispensable for knitting together the many other components of a complex blend. It has a fresh, slightly salty nose with some sweetness; a smooth body; an even, centre-of-the-palate flavour, holding a delicate savoury/sweet balance (coconut, toffee, edible seaweed, some peat) and a long, slightly briny finish. Older expressions become raisiny and scented-waxy (like the altar of a High Church), with traces of pepper, allspice, and vanilla.

Strathisla

Category: Speyside (Keith) Distiller: Strathisla-Glenlivet Distillery Co, Keith, Banffshire Owner: Chivas Bros, Paisley

Flax dressing was an important industry in northeast Scotland in the early part of the eighteenth century, but by the latter half of the century, the industry was in decline and George Taylor, a wealthy Morayshire businessman, decided to reinvest his money. In 1785, he took a lease from the Earl of Seafield for an area of land near Keith on Speyside for the purpose of building a distillery.

Keith's connections with making alcohol are referred to as early as 1208, and the site itself was described in a charter of 1545 as having a brassina, or warehouse. The site had once belonged to Ogilvy of Milton, and the new distillery was named "Milton" or "Milltown" and opened in 1786. It is thus the oldest continuously operating distillery in Scotland.

The original still held only forty gallons (180 litres) of wash, in order to take advantage of the lower rate of duty provided for by the Wash Act, and Taylor supplemented his output with another (illicit) still. He was discovered by the Excise, however, and fined £500 – a huge sum in those days. Like most distillers, he ran a farm as well, and he was an early innovator in using the pot-ale as fertilizer.

In the 1820s, Taylor suffered a riding accident and, unable to work, sold the distillery to a local saddler, from whom it passed to William Longmore, a banker and grain merchant, in the early 1830s. Longmore was an important figure on Speyside; he had been instrumental in bringing the Great North of Scotland Railway to the district.

Production at Milton continued for many years without hindrance, until in 1876 and 1879, first a fire and then an explosion destroyed much of the machinery and caused considerable damage to the buildings. The equipment was replaced and a public company, William Longmore & Co, was formed with Longmore's son-in-law, J. Geddes Brown, as managing partner.

After Longmore's death in 1881, a bottling plant was installed at Milton, and by the end of the century the whisky produced was called Strathisla. It was well-known locally and was promoted further afield by Gordon & MacPhail of Elgin (*see* MACPHAIL'S), which had an agreement with the distillery that granted them a percentage of output, which G&M matured itself.

Shortly after the outbreak of the Second World War, a London financier, Jay Pomeroy, bought William Longmore & Co and began sending the entire production of the distillery direct to London. Customs and Excise became suspicious when it found that the companies buying the whisky were fictitious. Following a government inquiry, Pomeroy was discovered to be selling the whiskies, Strathisla included, under different names through the black market. He was charged and found guilty of tax evasion of £111,038.

Milton Distillery was in the hands of the receivers throughout the war, and in 1950, it was bought by Chivas Brothers, whose managing director was James Barclay, one of the foremost figures of the whisky industry of the day. He had been a director of George Ballantine & Son and had seen that company through its takeover by Seagram (*see* BALLANTINE'S), the Canadian distiller. Seagram had also acquired Chivas Brothers, to which company Barclay was appointed. Soon after this, the distillery took the name of its product, Strathisla. Until recently the malt was hard to find, but it is always worth looking for.

Tasting notes: Nosed straight, this is a rich, full-bodied malt, with toffee and nut aromas. When water is added, the nose is more sherried, with fruitcake notes. It is smooth and well-rounded to taste; sweet to start, dry to finish.

Strathmill

Category: Speyside (Keith) Distiller: Justerini & Brooks
Owner: Diageo plc

This distillery on the River Isla near Keith was originally built as a meal mill in 1823, converted into a distillery in 1891, and acquired by Gilbey's, the gin distiller, in 1895. The Gilbey brothers established their wine-merchant business in London in 1857. By the 1870s, the firm was distilling gin, and during the 1880s, it began to acquire malt whisky distilleries (*see* GLEN SPEY). In 1962, the company merged with Unwin's, which owned the old-established wine merchant, Justerini & Brooks (*see* J&B RARE), to become International Distillers & Vintners, and in 1997 IDV merged with United Distillers to become UDV/Diageo.

Strathmill is not bottled by the owners as a single malt, although it is available in merchant bottlings.

Tasting notes: The aroma is much richer than the pale colour would suggest; with water, the nose becomes typically Speyside, with some malty and feinty notes. The flavour starts sweet but immediately becomes sharp, even bitter; the finish is extraordinarily hot and peppery, reminiscent of chillis.

Talisker

Category: Island (Skye) Distiller: John Walker & Sons
Owner: Diageo plc

Talisker is the only distillery on the Isle of Skye. It stands on the shore of Loch Harport, near the village of Carbost, and takes its name from Talisker House, some miles away.

The distillery was started in 1830 by Hugh and Kenneth MacAskill from Eigg. Hugh was a tacksman (senior tenant farmer, who leased land to others) and acquired the lease of Talisker House and estate from MacLeod of MacLeod. Having cleared the land of people to make room for sheep, the MacAskills built a distillery at Carbost.

After the brothers' deaths, the distillery changed hands several times before being acquired by a partnership between Alexander Grigor Allan, procurator fiscal of Morayshire (who had an interest in Glenlossie Distillery), and Roderick Kemp, a wine and spirits merchant from Aberdeen. Substantial sums of money were invested in rebuilding and refitting Talisker Distillery, and the product itself was by now well-established. R.L. Stevenson mentioned it in a poem, "The Scotsman's Return from Abroad", in 1880:

The King o' drinks, as I conceive it,Talisker, Islay or Glenlivet.
In 1892, Kemp bought the Macallan-Glenlivet Distillery on Speyside and Allan took over the entire ownership of Talisker, merging it with Dailuaine to form the Dailuaine-Talisker Distilleries. This company extended the premises at Talisker, built a pier, a tramway to link it to the distillery, and houses to accommodate the employees and an excise officer. In 1925, through a previous merger with some of the founding members of the "Big Five", the distillery became fully owned by DCL.

Talisker was partly rebuilt in 1960 after a fire and its own floor maltings were demolished in 1972, but it has retained its traditional worm-tubs. A unique feature of the stills is that their lyne arms have a kink in them, like an inverted "U", before they enter and as a result, only a small amount of vapour passes over to be condensed; the remainder (perhaps eighty per cent) returns to be re-distilled. This is a major contribution to Talisker's flavour.

Talisker has long been available as a single, is highly regarded by connoisseurs, and won Best Single Malt under 12 Years Old at the 1999 International Wine and Spirit Competition. It is now part of Diageo's Classic Malts portfolio.

Tasting notes: Talisker has been called "the lava of the Cuillins", exploding off the palate and slipping down like liquid fire. Starting sweet, its flavour is distinctively peppery, sour, and oily.

Tamdhu

Category: Speyside (Strathspey) Distiller: Tamdhu Distillery, Knockando, Banffshire Owner: The Edrington Group ,Glasgow

The opening of the Strathspey railway line from Boat of Garten to Craigellachie encouraged distilling along the upper Spey Valley.

During the whisky boom of the 1890s, three distilleries were built in the parish of Knockando (Tamdhu, Knockando, and Imperial). The site for Tamdhu (pronounced "tam-doo") was known locally as "the smugglers' glen", and had been popular with illicit distillers on account of the excellence of its spring water.

The moving force behind Tamdhu's construction was William Grant, a director of Highland Distilleries and the agent for the Caledonian Bank in Elgin. When it went into production in 1897, the distillery was one of the most modern in the UK. It still has its own Saladin maltings, and today it is the only Speyside distillery to malt all its own barley. By 1903, it was producing 135,000 proof gallons (over 600,000 litres) of spirit, but with the downturn in demand in 1900, this was halved. Recovery was strong after the war, but the Depression followed and the distillery closed in 1928.

The distillery remained closed for twenty years, but by the early 1970s its make was in such demand from blenders that it was doubled in size. It is an important ingredient in The Famous Grouse and sells well as a single malt in France, Italy, Spain, Portugal, and the USA.

Tasting notes: Tamdhu is a mild malt, well-constructed with a clean, Speyside character. The nose is sweetish, slightly biscuity, and lightly malted, with a whiff of smoke; the flavour is very slightly toffee-like, but this develops into a dry, peaty/smoky finish.

Tamnavulin

Category: Speyside (Upper Spey) Distiller: The Invergordon Distillers, Leith, Edinburgh Owner: Whyte & Mackay Ltd, Glasgow

Glenlivet is known as "the longest glen in Scotland", so far spread are the distilleries that are entitled to attach the appellation. By the end of the last century, the designation was synonymous with Speyside. Although a latecomer to the tribe (the distillery was built in 1966), Tamnavulin is the only Glenlivet actually situated beside the fabled Livet Burn, although it draws its water from the surrounding hills.

The name is Gaelic for "the mill on the hill"; the carding mill referred to has been converted into an attractive visitor centre. However, both it and the distillery were closed in 1996 for an indefinite period.

Tasting notes: Unusually pale (no sherry wood is used during maturation); the lightest in body (not in taste) of the Glenlivets; sweetish, floral nose, with traces of peat and cereal; also sweetish taste, with cut-grass freshness, floral notes, and a trace of lemon.

Tantallon

Category: Speyside Distillery: not stated Owner: The Vintage Malt Whisky Co, Glasgow

Tantallon Castle stands on a promontory overlooking the Firth of Forth, west of Edinburgh, and was the ancient seat of the Earls of Douglas. It was deemed to be impregnable (the curtain wall is fifty (fifteen metres) feet high and twelve feet (three anda half metres) thick, beyond which are a ditch and a rampart) but it was ultimately made uninhabitable by General Monck's bombardment

in 1651. None of which has anything to do with Speyside, nor the
Speyside whisky that is bottled under the Tantallon label.

Teaninich

Category: North Highland Distiller: R.H. Thomson & Co (Distillers)
Owner: Diageo plc

Teaninich Distillery was built by Captain Hugh Munro on his land
near Alness in Ross-shire in 1817. At this time, illicit distilling was
endemic in the region, and most of the barley grown in the area
was being used by illegal producers. Despite encouragement from
the Excise, competition was fierce and several licensed distillers
were forced to close. Munro told a parliamentary inquiry that he
"continued to struggle on". After the Excise Act of 1823, Teaninich
(pronounced "chee-an-in-ick") was secured, and by 1830, Munro
was producing thirty times the original output.

The distillery passed on to General John Munro, who kept
production going, and eventually Teaninich was acquired in 1898
by Munro & Cameron, a spirits merchant and whisky broker in
Elgin, which invested a great deal of money in it.

In 1904, Innes Cameron became sole owner of Teaninich.
He already had many interests in Highland distilleries, including
Benrinnes, Linkwood, and Tamdhu, and later in his life he became
chairman of the Malt Distillers Association. He died in 1932, and
in 1934 his trustees sold the distillery to Scottish Malt Distillers.

In 1971, a new stillhouse was constructed to hold six additional
stills. Apart from the war years and some silent periods, Teaninich
has remained in operation, supplying fillings exclusively for
blending until 1992, when United Distillers began to bottle a small
amount at ten years old as a single malt. The older part of the
distillery (four stills) was mothballed in 1985, and its product
is rare.

Tasting notes: Pale, manzanilla colour. A pleasant, perfumed
nose (barber's shop), faintly citric, slightly salty, estery, fresh, and
cheerful. The flavour is reminiscent of Lapsang Souchong: a whiff
of scented smoke. It is sweetish and slightly salty, with a hint of
iodine. A perfect lunchtime whisky.

Tobermory (aka Ledaig)

*Category: Island (Mull) Distiller: Tobermory Distillers, Tobermory,
Isle of Mull Owner: Burn Stewart & Co, East Kilbride*

Tobermory Distillery – or Ledaig Distillery, as it is also known –
occupies the ground beside the Ledaig Burn on the foreshore of
the picturesque eighteenth-century harbour of Tobermory. In 1795,
John Sinclair took a lease of this land from the British Fisheries
Society, an offshoot of the Highland Society of London, which
was responsible for developing the port.

Sinclair was a well-established merchant with a fleet of ships
already sailing from the island to Glasgow and Liverpool with
cargoes of kelp. This made the transportation of barley from the
mainland easy, and in its first year, the distillery produced 292
proof gallons (1,327 litres) of whisky.

On Sinclair's death in 1863, the distillery ceased production and remained silent until 1890, when it was bought by John Hopkins & Co, which resumed distilling. In 1916, Hopkins & Co was bought by DCL, which kept open the distillery until June 1930, when it closed. It remained silent for forty years.

In 1972, it was reopened as Ledaig Distillery by a consortium representing some Liverpool shippers and the Domecq sherry group from Spain. The distillery was extensively reconstructed and the annual output raised to 800,000 proof gallons (over 3.6 million litres). However, this was a difficult time for the whisky trade and it proved to be too much for Ledaig's owners. In 1978, the distillery was bought by a Yorkshire family with wide business interests, who reopened it. Owing to depressed market conditions, operations ceased again between 1981 and 1990, until the industry stabilized. From time to time, the owners used the name Tobermory for a vatted malt, which is confusing, but after the distillery was sold to Burn Stewart in 1993, the labelling makes it clear that it is a single. The current owners produce two single malts: Tobermory (made from unpeated malt) and Ledaig (lightly peated malt). Both are now matured on the mainland, at Deanston Distillery, Perthshire.

Tasting Notes: A light-bodied malt, with a pale gold colour. The aroma is vaguely maritime, with a hint of peat. Somewhat thin in the mouth, but with pleasant malty sweetness to start, then a nutty-minty flavour and a dry finish.

Tomatin

Category: North Highland Distiller: The Tomatin Distillery Co, Tomatin, Inverness-shire Owner: Takara & Okura, Japan

Tomatin Distillery was built in 1897 by a consortium of Inverness businessmen, keen to take advantage of the phenomenal success the whisky industry was enjoying at this time. The chosen site was close to a fifteenth-century farmhouse called Old Lairds House, where drovers and travellers were wont to replenish their stocks of whisky at an illicit still before driving their beasts on to the southern markets. Close by is "the hill of parting", where the clans were disbanded after their defeat at the Battle of Culloden in 1746. The distillery draws its water from Alt-na-frith, "the free burn", which flows off the Monadhliath Mountains and down into the River Findhorn, passing through peat and over red granite – a passage that many claim makes for ideal distilling water.

Tomatin made steady progress until the war years, when grain shortages prevented distilleries working, and it was not until the 1950s that full production was resumed. Upgrading during the 1960s and 1970s made Tomatin one of the most modern, and certainly the largest malt distillery in Scotland, capable of producing five million gallons (over twenty-two million litres) of proof spirit each year from twenty-four stills, although it has never worked to full capacity.

During the cutbacks of the 1980s, the Tomatin Distillery Co was forced into voluntary liquidation, but in 1986 it was bought in a joint venture between Takara Shuzo Co and Okura & Co, two of

Japan's most important trading companies, which had long been customers of Tomatin.

The company bottles its single malt at ten and twelve years old and also produces a de luxe version and a standard blend, called "Big T".

Tasting notes: A fresh aroma, lightly smoky, slightly caramel, with some oak. Smooth flavour, but rather nondescript; neither sweet nor dry, with some peat and pepper.

Tomintoul

Category: Speyside (Strathspey) **Distiller:** *Angus Dundee Ltd, London*

The distillery was built in the 1960s by W&S Strong and Hay & MacLeod, two whisky-broking firms from Glasgow, which were later to merge with Whyte & Mackay. Tomintoul (pronounced "tomintowel") has been available as a single malt since 1974. The distillery was sold to Angus Dundee Ltd in 2000.

Tasting notes: A very light Speyside (perhaps the lightest in the district); grassy, spirity, some floral notes. The flavour is sweetish, with maltiness and cereal overtones. Surprisingly long finish with oaky, vanilla notes as it fades.

The Tormore

Category: Speyside (Strathspey) **Distiller:** *Allied Distillers, Dumbarton* **Owner:** *Allied Distillers*

The first new distillery to be commissioned in the Highlands in the twentieth century, Tormore began production in 1959. It was commissioned by Long John International and designed by Sir Albert Richardson, a past president of the Royal Academy, to be an architectural showpiece, complete with an ornamental lake and fountains. One writer has compared it (accurately) to a ,Bavarian spa. The Whisky Heritage Centre in Edinburgh has a fine working model.

Some connoisseurs claimed that a newly built distillery would not be able to produce a traditional Highland malt. They were confounded when the first batches were bottled at ten years old: not only is The Tormore a typical Speyside, it has a distinctive aftertaste. Its makers describe it as "a contemporary malt", "accessible" and "approachable", and it enjoys particular success among younger malt-whisky drinkers, especially in Europe.

Long John was taken over by Schenley Industries Inc. in 1956, and they sold the distillery (and the company) to Whitbread & Co in 1975. The company is now part of Allied Distillers.

Tasting notes: The nose is soft and lightly sherried with some dryness; faintly smoky. The body is medium and firm; the mouth-feel is smooth. An intriguing balance of malty sweetness and smoky dryness; the finish is well-rounded.

Tullibardine

Category: Central Highland **Distiller:** *Tullibardine Distillers Ltd* **Owner:** *Tullibardine Distillers Ltd*

The distillery is situated at Blackford, close to Gleneagles, on the northern slopes of the Ochil Hills in Perthshire, just above the

Highland Line. For a very long time, the village has been famous for its breweries: one produced a special brew by royal command for James IV's coronation in 1488. Tullibardine Distillery is on the site of the first public brewery in Scotland, drawing its water from the same source in the Ochils that made the brewery famous.

The distillery was designed by the noted distillery builder, W.L. Delmè Evans, in 1949, and passed into Invergordon's ownership in 1971. It is small and compact, with four stills. Invergordon became part of Whyte & Mackay in 1993 and the distillery was mothballed in 1995. It was bought by its current owners, a consortium of experienced whisky men, in 2003. It is intended to bring the distillery back in production by the end of 2004.

Tasting notes: A soft, malty, slightly sherried nose, richer than one might expect from so southerly a distillery; medium body; full flavour. Quite dry and spicy with a pleasant roundness. The finish is fragrant and peppery; bitterness in the aftertaste.

Directory

Blended Whiskies

KEY

Abbreviations: The following companies are abbreviated as follows: Distillers Company Limited: DCL; United Distillers & Vintners: UDV; Jim Beam Brands: JBB.

Category: There are no universally recognized categories of blended whisky. There are price differentials, however, and these tend to reflect a) the quantity of malt whisky in the blend, and b) the age of the malts used. The categories I have used are: Vatted Malt, Liqueur Whisky, Standard Blend, Premium Blend, and De Luxe Blend.

Licensee: In many cases, the original owner/proprietor or creator of the blend will have been taken over by another company; in others, the owning company will have licensed the brand to another. I have used the word "Licensee" loosely to cover either of these possibilities.

Owner: Where there are chains of holding companies, I have listed only the principal ones. The leading blenders and their ultimate owners are listed as follows: UDV is owned by Diageo (itself a merger of Guinness and Grand Metropolitan); Allied Distillers is the distilling arm of Allied Domecq; Chivas Brothers is owned by Pernod Ricard; Burn Stewart Distillers is a subsidiary of CL World Brands plc and Inver House Distillers of Pacific Spirits (UK) Ltd.

Information: The remarks in an entry reflect the amount of information brand-owners have been able to supply – not a great deal in some cases.

Abbot's Choice

Category: Standard Blend Licensee: John McEwan & Co, Leith Owner: Diageo plc

(*see* CHEQUERS) John McEwan was a successful farmer from Perthshire who occasionally brought his animals to market in Edinburgh. The story goes that on one such visit in the early 1860s, he lost his dogs and entered a tavern in order to look for them. Here he got into a conversation with some locals about blending whisky, and as a result, he resolved to enter the industry himself.

He bought Linkwood Distillery and several licensed premises, and eventually created Abbot's Choice, a blend that was once very popular in Scotland (the name refers to the tradition that whisky distilling was brought to Scotland by monks).

McEwan & Co was bought by DCL in 1933. The blend is now difficult to find.

Adelphi

Category: Premium Blend **Owner:** *The Adelphi Distillery, Edinburgh*

The Adelphi Distillery was built in the Gorbals district of Glasgow in 1826; in those days, the two-acre site was an orchard, fronted by a wharf. By the 1880s, it was one of the largest and most advanced distilleries in Scotland, producing both grain and malt spirit.

In 1880, the Adelphi was bought by Archibald Walker & Co, which had distilleries in Liverpool and Limerick. In 1902, it was bought by DCL and closed, and later demolished, although the warehouses were in existence until the 1960s.

The company name was revived by Archibald Walker's great-grandson, James, in 1993, with a view to selecting and bottling individual casks of aged malt whisky. The firm is now a leading independent bottler.

Demand from customers subsequently led the company to introduce a first-rate blended whisky in 1995 called The Adelphi Director's Reserve.

Ainslie's

Category: Standard and De Luxe Blends **Licensee:** *Ainslie & Heilbron (Distillers), Glasgow* **Owner:** *Diageo plc*

The firm of James Ainslie & Co started life as a wine and spirits merchant in 1868.

The company gradually became very successful, and in 1896 it bought Clynelish Distillery in Sutherland, which had been built by the first Duke of Sutherland in 1816. Following the terrible Sutherland Clearances, many farmers were moved to more fertile land on the coast, and thus there was an ample supply of local grain for the distillery.

After a series of takeovers in the early part of this century, and a merger with David Heilbron & Son, the company became a subsidiary of the DCL in 1926.

The Antiquary

Category: De Luxe Blend **Licensee:** *J&W Hardie, South Queensferry (subsidiary of William Sanderson)* **Owner:** *J&W Hardie Ltd, Glasgow, a subsidiary of The Tomatin Distillery Co, Inverness-shire*

The company was established in 1861, became a subsidiary of William Sanderson & Co (see VAT 69) some years later, and joined DCL in 1953.

The Antiquary (the moniker was chosen to commemorate Sir Walter Scott's novel of the same name) was formerly a very successful de luxe whisky that was packaged in a decanter-shaped bottle and backed by a national advertising and promotions campaign. In recent years, it has been allowed to decline into a single blend.

In 1996, however, The Antiquary – brand and formula – was sold by United Distillers (the successor to DCL) to Tomatin Distillers.

Argyll

Category: Standard Blend (also a range of single malts)
Owner: Beinn Buidhe Holdings, Inveraray, Argyll

These brands are available only from the shop at Inveraray Castle, home of the Duke of Argyll. I have not been able to ascertain where the malt whisky is distilled.

Inveraray Castle is one of Scotland's great houses. It was founded in 1746 to replace an older castle on a nearby site. The Dukes of Argyll are the chiefs of the mighty Clan Campbell, and the current Duke is a non-executive director of Chivas Brothers.

As We Get It

Category: Vatted Malt Owner: J.G. Thomson & Co, Glasgow
(parent: Tennent Caledonian Breweries, Glasgow)

As We Get It is bottled at cask strength (*i.e.* without the usual reduction to forty or forty-three per cent ABV). It is usually sold at about sixty per cent ABV (103° proof). The label states that it is distilled by Macallan-Glenlivet, Craigellachie, but the brand is apparently a vatting of several different malts. Each bottling is different from the last, so both the age and the strength of the finished product vary slightly.

As We Get It is only produced in small quantities, and is distributed only in Scotland, owing to the limitation on the supply of fillings. As a result, it is a something of a curiosity, sought out by enthusiasts.

J.G. Thomson & Co was once among Scotland's leading independent whisky blenders. The firm was founded as a wine merchant by Robert Thomson in the late 1600s, and moved to The Vaults, Leith (now the club premises of the Scotch Malt Whisky Society) in 1753. The company became known as JG Thomson & Co (after its senior partner) during the 1840s; by the time Thomson retired in 1876, it had become the pre-eminent wine merchant in Scotland.

The Usher brothers, Andrew and John (*see* USHER'S GREEN STRIPE), were partners of the firm, which began to blend whisky in the 1870s. It became a public company in 1905, and prospered until the Second World War, after which many private hotels (the company's principal customer base) amalgamated into chains or were acquired by breweries. J.G. Thomson had no alternative but to become the wine division of a brewery. It was bought by Charrington United Breweries in 1960, and in 1966 became a subsidiary of Tennent Caledonian. It moved into purpose-built premises in Glasgow in 1983, having operated from The Vaults for 230 years.

Avonside

Category: Premium Blend Licensee: James Gordon & Co, Elgin
Owner: Gordon & MacPhail, Elgin

(*see* MacPHAIL'S) The River Avon (pronounced "arn") rises near Tomintoul Distillery, runs past Glenlivet Distillery, and meets the Spey at Ballindalloch, close to Cragganmore Distillery. The

Junction Pool, where the two rivers meet, is one of the Spey's most famous stretches.

Bailie Nicol Jarvie

Category: Premium Blend Licensee: Nicol Anderson & Co, Leith
Owner: Glenmorangie plc, Broxburn

(*see* HIGHLAND QUEEN) Bailie Nicol Jarvie was a character in Sir Walter Scott's novel, *Rob Roy*. While journeying from Glasgow to visit his infamous cousin, he was resting at an inn in Aberfoyle when he was set upon by a fierce-looking Highlander. Finding that his sword had rusted into its sheath, the corpulent Bailie seized a red-hot poker and set the Highlander's plaid on fire! The Bailie's poker still hangs from a tree outside the Bailie Nicol Jarvie Hotel at Aberfoyle, and the incident is illustrated on the label of the blend which bears the Bailie's name.

The brand was introduced around the turn of the century, and it boasts a charming period label that was tastefully revamped in 1994.

Ballantine's

Category: various blends Licensee: George Ballantine & Son
Owner: Allied Distillers, Dumbarton

Ballantine's Finest consistently commands the third-largest annual sales of Scotch whisky in the world, and is number two in Europe. The 30 Years Old is among the most expensive blended whiskies in the world, and is available only in small quantities. The de luxe blends have established markets in the Far East, Southeast Asia, South America, and Europe. Ballantine's is a familiar name among whisky drinkers worldwide.

The eponymous George Ballantine (1807–91) was of Border farming stock, but served his apprenticeship with a grocer and spirit dealer, in which capacity he set up his own business in the Cowgate, Edinburgh, in 1827. In 1865, he delegated the running of his Edinburgh shop (by now situated on the more fashionable North Bridge, and soon to move to the even more fashionable Princes Street) to his son while he opened a larger establishment in Glasgow (Argyll Street, then Union Street). Here, he concentrated on the wine and spirit trade, bringing his second son, also named George, into the business. By the time he died, a contemporary booklet described the firm as "transacting an immense trade in supplying wines and spirits to families of distinction all over Scotland and in many parts of England and Ireland". Two years later, in 1903, the firm was granted a royal warrant.

In 1919, the Ballantine family capitalized on its success and sold the business to the junior partners, James Barclay and R.A. McKinlay, who incorporated the company under the Ballantine name and turned their considerable energies to exports, particularly in the USA. Throughout the Prohibition era (1920–33) James Barclay's efforts to obtain distribution in the USA were tireless and not without danger, but by the mid-1930s he had the best distribution network on the East Coast. David Niven, the actor, was an early salesman for the company.

Increasingly large resources were required to compete in the growing world market, and these were provided by another of James Barclay's contacts, Hiram Walker Gooderham & Worts, a major Canadian distiller which acquired George Ballantine & Son in 1937. The new owner's first task was to secure supplies of malt and grain whiskies – to which end the company purchased Miltonduff and Glenburgie malt distilleries and built a grain distillery, the largest in Europe, at Dumbarton.

During the Second World War (and for some years after) supplies of grain for whisky production were rationed, but once rationing was lifted, heavy brand promotion in North America could proceed. During the 1960s, the company turned its attention to Europe – at the time an unexplored market for Scotch – and by mid-decade it had secured a firm-enough foothold on the Continent to gear the home-trade operation to supporting the overseas business.

Between 1963 and 1975, Ballantine's sales in North America quadrupled (to 1.5 million cases), and during the same period Ballantine's Finest became the best-selling Scotch in the Eastern Bloc. Hiram Walker (Scotland) won the Queen's Award for Export Achievement in 1968, and again in 1986 – by which time nearly two bottles of Ballantine's whisky were being sold every second somewhere in the world. Royal Blue (12 Years Old) won Best Blended Whisky and a gold medal at the 1995 International Wine & Spirit Competition awards.

John Barr

Category: Standard Blend Licensee: John Walker & Co, Kilmarnock Owner: Whyte & Mackay Ltd, Glasgow

Until the practice was banned by an EC Commission Directive in December 1977, DCL's subsidiary companies operated a system of dual pricing for brands which sold well in export markets. Under the dual-pricing system, a UK trade customer was charged a higher in-bond price if brands were bought for resale within the EC rather than if they were bought for UK consumption (at that time, the difference was £5 on a case).

The reason for this was to compensate the appointed foreign distributors for the investments they had to make in promoting and distributing the brands within their markets, as well as to help them compete with local spirit brands which often enjoyed more favourable taxes. Without the price difference, it would also have been possible for UK trade customers to establish a profitable "parallel exports" business, based upon the lower price at which they could buy whisky intended for the home market, thus removing incentives for foreign distributors and ultimately destroying the export markets themselves, both within and without the EC.

Following the directive, DCL promptly withdrew a number of its leading brands from the UK market (notably Johnnie

Walker Red Label and Haig Dimple), offering them for export only.
The company also increased the price on other brands so as to
render them unattractive for parallel export (VAT 69 and Black &
White, for example). John Barr and The Buchanan Blend were
introduced to replace Red Label, and the former was sold to
Whyte & Mackay in 1986.

Baxter's Barley Bree

*Category: Standard Blend Licensee: James Watson & Co, Dundee
Owner: Diageo plc*

Founded in 1815, James Watson & Co was acquired by the
Buchanan-Dewar and Walker Group two years before it merged
with DCL in 1925. The acquisition brought some eight million
gallons (over thirty-six million litres) of whisky in bond, together
with Parkmore (defunct since 1930), Ord, and Pulteney distilleries.

Watson owned two blends, but their popularity declined after
1939; Baxter's Barley Bree enjoyed a recent revival, selling in South
Africa, the Lebanon, and Surinam, as well as in the UK (including a
specially made five-year-old variant) – but it has not been made
since 1998.

I have been unable to discover who the eponymous "Baxter"
refers to; *bree*, however, is Scots for "broth", "sauce", or "liquor",
and was once a colloquialism for whisky.

John Begg

*Category: Standard Blend Licensee: John Begg, Glasgow
Owner: Diageo plc*

In 1845, the eponymous John Begg took a long lease of 120 acres
(forty-eight hectares) in the parish of Crathie on Deeside in 1845
and built a small distillery there in the shadow of the mountain
Lochnagar (3,791 feet/1,156 metres), on a site which had been used
for distilling since 1825 (*see* ROYAL LOCHNAGAR).

Before he died in 1880, John Begg, realizing that the future
of the whisky industry lay with blends, acquired a bonded
warehouse, duty-paid cellar, and a bottling line in Aberdeen,
and proceeded to create and export John Begg Blue Cap and John
Begg Gold Cap (a de luxe version, now extinct).

Promoted by the internationally famous slogan "Take a Peg
of John Begg", the brands prospered under the direction of Begg's
son, Henry Farquharson Begg, and his son-in-law, William Reid.
The business became a limited company in 1902, and was sold to
DCL in 1916.

Today the brand's main market is in Germany, with a
substantial amount going to Madeira. A quantity is also exported
in bulk to the USA.

Bell's

*Category: Premium Blend; De Luxe Blend Licensee: Arthur Bell &
Sons, Perth Owner: Diageo plc*

In 1825, Thomas Sandeman, a member of the famous port family,
opened a wine and spirit shop in the Kirkgate, Perth. In 1845, he
employed Arthur Bell as his "traveller", and in 1851 Bell became
a partner in the firm.

Bell was a cautious, modest, highly moral man – a member of a religious sect whose motto was "work to the best of your light and play fair". He was one of the first to realize the potential of blended whisky. "Several fine whiskies blended together please the palates of a greater number of people than one whisky unmixed," he said. "I have long adopted that practice and allowed the qualities of my goods to speak for themselves."

Bell's firm belief in the quality and potential of his blends led him to appoint an agent in London in 1863 – the first-ever whisky company to do so, although at the time it was not a success – and he brought his sons, Arthur Kinmond and Robert, into the firm to look after the domestic and overseas markets, respectively. The elder Bell also interested himself in the whisky trade as a whole, successfully campaigning for (among other things) the introduction of standard bottle sizes for spirits.

By 1895, Bell's brands were selling in Australia, New Zealand, India, Ceylon, Italy, and France, but it was only in 1904, four years after the death of Arthur Sr, that the family name appeared on the label. A.K. Bell began to expand the business rapidly, first into Canada, then into almost every corner of the world with a potential market, including South Africa, where it quickly became the number-one brand. At this time, the company adopted the slogan "Afore Ye Go", which became known the world over; it was officially registered in 1925.

In 1933, Bell's purchased P. Mackenzie & Co, the owner of Blair Athol and Dufftown Distilleries (see THE REAL MACKENZIE, BLAIR ATHOL, DUFFTOWN); in 1936, Inchgower Distillery was also acquired. When A.K. and Robert Bell both died in 1942, this signalled the end of the family's connection with the company; William Govan Farquharson, who had joined the firm in 1942, became the next chairman. In 1956, Farquharson appointed a young "efficiency expert", Raymond Miquel; he joined the Board in 1962, became managing director in 1968, and succeeded Farquharson as chairman in 1973, on the latter's death.

By 1970, Bell's Finest was brand leader in Scotland (with a 9.9 per cent share of the UK market), and by 1980 a marketing effort which concentrated on the on-trade (pubs, etc.) had won a 22.9 per cent share and lifted the brand to best-selling Scotch in Britain. In 1980, Bell's lost its lead position of the Scottish market to Famous Grouse, but it retains its status in England. Growth in foreign markets was also steady, and this was recognized in 1983 by a Queen's Award for Export Achievement.

In 1985, Arthur Bell & Co was acquired by Guinness, and in 1987, Guinness took over DCL to form United Distillers, the world's largest (and most profitable) spirits company following a merger with Grand Metropolitan. In 1997, the company changed its name again, first to United Distillers and Vintners, then to Diageo plc.

In 1994, Bell's took the bold step of reblending "Extra Special" as an eight-year-old, backing the new whisky with a £15 million campaign. A year later, the company was the first to advertise its brand on television with a campaign aimed at attracting the twenty-five to thirty-five year-old market. Until then, there had been a "gentleman's agreement" among industry leaders not to use television advertising in the UK. "Extra Special" is now the ninth-biggest-selling whisky in the world.

Beltane

Category: Standard Blend Owner: The Beltane Whisky Co, Edinburgh

Beltane is the brainchild of the iconoclastic Phillip Hills, one of the founders of the Scotch Malt Whisky Society. The brand name is that of one of the most important Celtic festivals, which has been celebrated with fire on May 1 since time immemorial to signal the arrival of spring. In Edinburgh, some 2–3,000 people annually celebrate Beltane by watching the sun rise out of the North Sea from the top of Arthur's Seat, the mountain that reaches towards the sky from the centre of the city. The brand was launched at another annual Celtic festival, Samhain (one of the precursors of modern Halloween), in 1997.

Beltane is a mould-breaker. It is paler than other blends (no artificial colouring is used), it is made from young whiskies, and it is designed to be drunk very cold (like vodka or schnapps) or with mixers. Needless to say, it is designed to appeal to younger drinkers. Its makers claim that its youth and pale colour, and the fact that it is designed for mixing, is a return to the way blended Scotch was drunk before the 1890s.

Ben Aigen

Category: Standard Blend Licensee: Strathnairn Whisky, Inverness Owner: Gordon & MacPhail, Elgin

(*see* MacPHAIL's) Ben Aigen (more usually spelt *Benagen*) is a mountain seven miles west of Fochabers, between Moray and Banffshire, immediately east of the River Spey.

Ben Alder

Category: Standard Blend Owner: Gordon & MacPhail, Elgin

(*see* MacPHAIL's) Ben Alder (3,756 feet/1,145 metres) rises between Lochs Laggan and Ericht in Inverness-shire. Bonnie Prince Charlie lay concealed here between September 2 and 12, 1746, following his defeat at Culloden. The brand was introduced in 1900; it was originally called Dew of Ben Alder.

Beneagles

Category: Standard Blend Licensee: Waverly Vintners Owner: Peter Thomson (Agencies), Perth Proprietor: Scottish & Newcastle Breweries (Waverley Wines and Spirits)

At one time, the little yellow vans owned by Peter Thomson (Perth) which bore the motif of Beneagles whisky were to be seen all over Scotland. Today, although Beneagles is still available, it is no longer found in such quantities.

Peter Thomson started as a grocer and wine and spirit merchant in Perth in 1908. Drawing upon deep knowledge of Speyside malts and blending techniques, Thomson launched Beneagles in 1922, inspired by the newly built golfing resort of Gleneagles Hotel. The founder died in 1939, and ownership passed to his son David, who remained chairman until the company was sold in 1981. Following the Second World War, efforts were concentrated on wholesale distribution; by the 1970s, the firm's four retail shops had closed in favour of this area of the business.

The company enjoyed great success with a venture into miniature ceramic ornaments filled with whisky. In order to meet export requirements which restricted the sale of miniatures in North America, larger, more impressive ceramics were created; the "birds of prey" range of decanters is highly sought after by collectors.

The business remained under family ownership until it was sold to Stakis in 1981. Two years later, it was acquired by Waverly Vintners, the wine and spirit arm of Scottish & Newcastle Breweries, which sells Beneagles to the on-trade as well as through their own tied houses. A little also goes for export.

The brand's ceramics range is currently owned by Whyte & Mackay. Beneagles itself is blended and bottled by The Invergordon Distillers.

Benmore

Category: Standard Blend Licensee: Benmore Distilleries, Glasgow Owner: Diageo plc

Benmore Distilleries formerly owned Dallas Dhu, near Forres, Benmore and Lochead Distilleries in Campbeltown (both now defunct), and Lochindaal on Islay (also defunct). Benmore was acquired by DCL in 1929, and the brand now sells in Belgium, and is exported in bulk to Australia. The name in Gaelic literally means "the big hill".

Bennachie

Category: Vatted Malt Licensee: The Bennachie Whisky Co, Inverurie, Aberdeen Owner: International Multibrand Products, Keith, Aberdeenshire

Bennachie is the name of a conspicuous and isolated hill that rises in northern Aberdeenshire. Some say that the Battle of Mons Graupius – where the might of Rome was checked by the Picts – was fought on its slopes.

The brand name also recalls Bennachie Distillery (also known as Benachie or Jericho), which was established in 1824 at Insch in the shadow of the mountain, and closed in 1915. This was one of the first distilleries to issue its products in labelled bottles. A local saying had it that "there's nae sair heids in Bennachie"!

In 1992, the Shand family, which has long had connections with distilling, relaunched Bennachie as a vatted malt. The brand won a bronze medal at the International Wine & Spirit Competition awards in 1994, and the company went on to produce Scottish National Tartan (a single-malt), Murrayfield, Jock, Union Glen, and later a single malt expression of Bennachie. In January 1997, International Multibrands was established and the portfolio was extended to include other spirits, beer and wine.

Ben Roland

Category: Premium Blend **Proprietor:** *Ben Roland Scotch Whisky Co, Dartford, Kent (subsidiary of Unwin's)* **Owner:** *Phillips Newman & Co*

Ben Roland first appeared in a 1924 price list for Sordo Lopez & Son, wine shipper, and was registered in 1951. Sordo Lopez was owned by M.A. Wetz, whose grandson was until recently managing director of Unwin's, for whom this is an own-label brand sold through the Unwin's shops in the southeast of England. The blend employs Speyside and Highland malts of at least five years of age.

Berry's Best/Berry's All Malt

Category: Standard Blend; Vatted Malt **Owner:** *Berry Bros & Rudd, London*

(*see* CUTTY SARK) Berry Bros has occupied the same premises near St James's Palace since the late seventeenth century. The firm was originally described as "Italian warehousemen" – importers of such exotic groceries as tea, coffee, and spices – and the sign which still hangs above their door is that of a coffee-mill. This antique trademark decorates the labels of Berry's Best (a decent blend of eight-year-old [minimum] malts, predominantly from Speyside) and Berry's All Malt, which has a liberal dose of Islay malts, and considerable phenolic concentration.

Big T

Category: Standard and De Luxe Blends **Owner:** *The Tomatin Distillery Co Ltd (a subsidiary of Takara and Marubeni)*

The Takara & Okura Consortium (now Takara and Marubeni consortium) bought Tomatin Distillery in 1985. The "T" in Big T makes reference to the distillery, which no doubt supplies key fillings for the blends. Big T sells mainly in Japan.

Black & White

Category: Standard Blend **Licensee:** *James Buchanan & Co, London* **Owner:** *Diageo plc*

(*see* BUCHANAN'S) When the redoubtable James Buchanan managed to persuade the Members Bar of the House of Commons to stock his whisky in 1885, it quickly became the most popular blend. He changed its name first to House of Commons, then to Buchanan's Special, but everybody asked for it as "Black and White", on account of its bottle being very dark and its label very white.

Realizing the opportunity that this offered, the name was changed again in 1905 and reinforced by adopting black Scottish and white West Highland terriers as its symbol (Buchanan's own idea). It quickly became one of the most popular brands in the world, and currently stands at about twelfth-best-seller, its main markets being South Africa, Canada, and Italy.

Black Bottle

Category: Standard Blend **Licensee:** *Gordon Graham & Co* **Owner:** *Burn Stewart Distillers, East Kilbride*

Black Bottle is probably the fastest-growing brand in the most discriminating of the world's whisky markets, Scotland. And with good reason: it is a first-class blend. Its makers claim that it has many of the same attributes of a de luxe whisky (smooth, mellow, rich but not heavy, etc.), while selling at a premium price. Interestingly, the blend formula was altered and improved in the 1980s.

The brand was first registered in 1879 by Charles David and Gordon Graham, a company of tea importers and blenders in Aberdeen, for consumption by the partners and their friends. Initially it was known only in the northeast of Scotland (being especially favoured by the fishing community); Aberdonians, however, know what they like, and they took it with them around the world (*see* CATTO'S).

Gordon Graham & Co, as the company became known, abandoned tea to devote itself to its blended whisky. The company was taken over by the American giant Schenley Industries in 1959 (owner of Long John Distillers, Kinclaith, Tormore, and Glenugie distilleries), and subsequently became part of Whitbread & Co (1975), before being sold to Allied Lyons along with Whitbread's other Scotch whisky companies. The brand was sold to Highland Distilleries in 1995.

Black Bottle's unique bottle shape represents a pot still and dates from the 1890s. For many years, the brand was advertised with the slogan "Unchanged by Progress". The current slogan is "You live. You learn", which was the theme of the brand's second burst of television advertising in May 1997 (an earlier campaign in late 1996 had been very successful).

Black Bottle was sold to Burn Stewart Distillers (*see* DEANSTON) in 2002, along with Bunnahabhain Distillery.

Black Dog

*Category: De Luxe **Licensee:** The Invergordon Distillers, Leith*
***Owner:** Whyte & Mackay Ltd, Glasgow*

Among the Gaels "having the black dog on your shoulder" is a metaphor for depression.

This brand name, however, refers to a well-known traditional fishing fly. The whisky first became available in the 1890s, but it is now sold exclusively in export markets. It does especially well in India.

Black Prince

*Category: Premium and De Luxe Blends **Owner:** Burn Stewart Distillers, Glasgow*

Black Prince was first created before the Second World War by the Henkes Distillers Group of Holland, expressly for the US market. It was later acquired by Norden McCall of London, which later sold it to another Dutch company, Bols. Burn Stewart bought the brand in 1991, repackaged its three expressions, and is vigorously developing markets in the Far East. It is available in the UK and Europe, but is currently unusual (*see* BURN STEWART).

The Black Prince of Wales and Aquitaine (1330–76) was King

Edward III's eldest son. He was called "black" on account of his dark armour. He distinguished himself at the battle of Crécy.

Black Top

Category: Standard, 12, 15 and 18 Years Old Owner: Aberfoyle & Knight, Glasgow

Aberfoyle & Knight is an independent specialist spirits company based in Glasgow. Black Top was introduced in 1996, blended by Peter Russell & Co in Broxburn. It has already established a following in Venezuela, and was made available in Italy, Denmark, and the UK during 1997 (*see* DEERSTALKER).

Blairmhor

Category: Vatted Malt (8 Years Old) Licensee: R. Carmichael & Sons, Airdrie Owner: Inver House Distillers, Airdrie

(*see* INVER HOUSE) This is Inver House's vatted malt and completes the company's portfolio of brands.

Blue Hanger

Category: De Luxe Blend Owner: Berry Bros & Rudd, London

The name and the illustration on the label of this brand commemorates an eighteenth-century customer of Berry Brothers, one William Hanger. A dandy and a man of exquisite taste, he was known as "Blue" Hanger because he always dressed in shades of that colour (*see* CUTTY SARK).

Bonnie Scot

Category: Standard Blend Licensee: Judge, Craig & Pirrie, Edinburgh Owner: Whyte & Mackay, Ltd, Glasgow

Curiously, this brand was first registered by James J. Murphy & Co, a firm of wine and spirits merchants established in 1856 in Cork. History does not relate how it came to belong to Invergordon/JBB.

Braemar

Category: Standard Licensee: Grant, MacDonald & Co, Glasgow Owner Allied Distillers, Dumbarton

Braemar was first introduced by the well-known wine merchant, Stowells of Chelsea, as a "fighting brand" – priced lower than most. In the early 1980s) it was transferred to Long John International (at that time owned by Whitbread & Co) under the licence of its subsidiary, Grant, MacDonald & Co, and thence to Allied Distillers (*see* GLEN ROSSIE).

Breath of Angels

Category: Premium Blend Owner: Adelphi Distillery, Edinburgh

This distinguished blend modestly describes itself as "of no great distinction". Its label depicts an intoxicated cherub and the copy reads: "Think of Breath of Angels as a wing-ding whisky, a drink to celebrate with rather than concentrate on; an invitation to intoxication. And as you imbibe, remember the ancient Gaelic toast: 'I looks towards you and I gently smells your breath'."

The lines, which the brand-owner was later asked to adjust, do no justice to what is an excellent blend, and were penned by the current writer.

Brig O'Perth

Category: Premium Blend **Owner:** *Matthew Gloag & Sons, Perth, a subsidiary of The Edrington Group, Glasgow*

This excellent blend (forty-three per cent) has been around for as long as its more famous sister, The Famous Grouse, but is only rarely encountered. Its label has changed even less than The Famous Grouse's and depicts the ancient bridge across the River Tay at Perth.

Buchanan's

Category: De Luxe Blend **Licensee:** *James Buchanan & Co, London* **Owner:** *Diageo plc*

James Buchanan was born of Scottish parents in Canada in 1849. He was brought back to Scotland in his first year, but his parents swiftly removed to Northern Ireland, and he did not return until he was fifteen to become an office boy in a Glasgow shipping firm.

In 1879, Buchanan went to London as agent for Charles Mackinlay & Co (*see* MACKINLAY'S), and within five years he had set up a business on his own account with capital borrowed from a friend and stocks from W.P. Lowrie (*see* LOWRIE'S). He first sold whisky by the cask or jar to wine merchants, and then set about creating a blend which would be acceptable to the English palate and which could be sold by the bottle.

Having created The Buchanan Blend in 1880, he seduced or cajoled a number of leading London hotels into stocking it. Within a year, he had paid back the loan, and soon he was selling his blend, in its distinctive black and white livery, in both the Members' Bar of the House of Commons and in the majority of London music halls. For the former outlet, the brand was renamed House of Commons, then Buchanan's Special, then Black & White.

In spite of being dogged by ill health, James Buchanan was a tireless worker and self-publicist. He was among the first to advertise his brands in the newspapers, adopting the symbol of black Scottish and white West Highland terriers (his own idea; *see* BLACK & WHITE). He also bought the Black Swan Distillery in Holborn, London, a famous coaching inn, and from here despatched his whisky in a fleet of handsome drays, with uniformed coachmen (an operation which lasted until 1936). The company's first of several royal warrants was granted by Queen Victoria.

James Buchanan himself was something of a dandy – thin, tall (six fee three inches, 1.9 metres) and aristocratic in appearance (his is the portrait on the brand's label) – and he enjoyed the life of an English country gentleman. He loved horses, had his own racing stables, and twice won the Derby. In 1920, he was made a baronet, and in 1922, was raised to the peerage as Lord Woolavington of Lavington. He was a leading philanthropist and was much mourned when he died in 1935, aged eighty-six.

By the turn of the century, Buchanan's was firmly among the "Big Three" (with Dewar's and Walker's). In 1915, the first two companies created Scotch Whisky Brands (the name was changed four years later to Buchanan-Dewar) to protect their interests against DCL, but it was only a matter of time, and in 1925, the "Big Three" succumbed and joined DCL.

The brand's marketing proposition takes a leaf out of James Buchanan's own book and maintains that "Buchanan's De Luxe is enjoyed by dynamic, successful people. It is a reward for success in business"!

Buchanan's De Luxe is currently twenty-ninth best-seller in the world, selling mainly in Mexico, Venezuela, Brazil, Aruba, and Curaçao (in volume terms, ninety-three per cent sells in Central and South America).

Bulloch Lade (B&L Gold Label)

Category: Standard Blend **Licensee:** *Bulloch Lade & Co, Glasgow*
Owner: *Diageo plc*

Bulloch & Co merged with Lade & Co in the 1830s, and traded successfully until 1920, when the company went into voluntary liquidation and was taken over by a group of distillers and blenders led by DCL. Seven years later, DCL bought the entire share capital and whisky stocks for half a million pounds.

The company owned Caol Isla Distillery between 1880 and 1920. Following the distillery's acquisition by DCL in 1927, it was again licensed to Bulloch Lade. Caol Isla is a constituent of B&L Gold Label, and the blend was apparently first produced at the distillery in 1857. Today, a small amount is bottled in Scotland and sold in Canada, but the largest volume is shipped in bulk to the USA and New Zealand, where it is bottled.

Burberry's

Category: Standard and De Luxe Blends **Owner:** *Burn Stewart Distillers, East Kilbride*

Burn Stewart retains the exclusive right to blend and distribute this whisky brand for the world-famous London fashion house (*see* BURN STEWART)

Burn's Heritage

Category: Standard Blend **Owner:** *Morrison Bowmore Distillers, Glasgow*

(*see* ROB ROY)

Burn Stewart

Category: Standard and De Luxe Blends **Proprietor:** *Burn Stewart Distillers, East Kilbride*

Burn Stewart Distillers has its origins in the 1940s, but owes its present incarnation to a management buy-out in 1998. The firm's distilling base was achieved by the acquisition in 1991 of Deanston Distillery; the same year, it became a public company, was granted the Queen's Award for Export Achievement, and the British Venture Capital Association's prize for the Best Company Turnaround. In 1992, Burn Stewart bought Tobermory Distillery (*see* LEDAIG) and built bottling facilities at East Kilbride. In

December 2002, Burn Stewart was acquired by CL World Brands plc. The brand/company name came from Burn Stewart & Co, a well-established firm of blenders, exporters, and brokers in Dumbarton and London, with a portfolio of five companies and about twenty brands.

Burn Stewart 12 Years Old has a noticeable trace of Islay in its flavour. The principal markets for Burn Stewart are France, South Africa, Japan, and Taiwan.

Campbeltown Loch

Category: Standard and De Luxe Blend **Licensee:** *Eaglesome* **Owner:** *J&A Mitchell & Co, Campbeltown*

(*see* SPRINGBANK) J&A Mitchell & Co is still a family company. Its blend, Campbeltown Loch, can be relied upon to have the excellent Springbank at its heart. A twenty-five-year-old expression was labelled in January 2002.

Carlton Blend

Category: Standard Blend **Owner:** *Charles H. Julian and Co*

It was to Charles Julian that Justerini & Brooks turned in the 1930s to reblend J&B Rare. He had formerly blended Cutty Sark for Berry Brothers & Rudd and Chivas Regal for Seagrams. Later he became master blender for Justerini & Brooks. Charles H. Julian Ltd was established by his sons.

Catto's

Category: Premium and De Luxe Blends **Licensee:** *James Catto & Co* **Owner:** *Inver House Distillers, Airdrie, Lanarkshire*

James Catto established his firm of whisky blenders at Aberdeen in 1861, and soon built up a loyal local following. Before the end of the century, this had become an international following through the enthusiasm of Aberdonian emigrants – in particular, the support of two schoolfriends who founded famous shipping lines (P&O and White Star) and carried the whisky to destinations far and wide.

James Catto's son Robert opened up the English market, but he was killed in France in 1916. After the First World War, the company became part of Gilbeys, and recently it was bought by Inver House.

Century

Category: Vatted Malt **Owner:** *Chivas Bros, Paisley*

This extraordinary vatting of 100 different malt whiskies was introduced by Chivas Glenlivet around the time of the 500th anniversary (in 1994) of the first written mention of Scotch. The only filling not listed in the "Malts" section of this book is Craigduff, an experimental malt whisky produced at Strathisla Distillery in the 1970s, using heavily peated malt in a (presumably unsuccessful) attempt to replicate the Islay style. It has never been bottled as a single, to my knowledge.

The label of "The Century of Malts" (to give the brand its full name), is embossed with Chivas Brothers' seal: a mounted medieval knight with the Gaelic motto "Treibhireas, Bunaiteachd Bho 1801" – "Faithful (and) Steadfast from 1801" (*see also* ULTIMA).

Chairman's

Category: Standard Blend **Owner:** *Eldridge Pope & Co, Dorchester, Dorset*

This is a comparatively new blend, created by the company's wines and spirits director, Mr Naughtie, who is also a Master of Wine. The label is a picture of the current chairman's fireplace painted by Sir Hugh Casson, past president of the Royal Academy (*see also* OLD HIGHLAND BLEND).

Chalié Richards

Category: Standard and De Luxe Blends; Vatted Malt; Single Malt **Licensee:** *Chalié Richards & Co, Horsham, West Sussex* **Owner:** *Halewood International, Robertown, West Yorkshire*

Chalié Richards, wine merchant, was established in 1685 by the French Huguenot, Pierre Chalié, who had fled to England to avoid the persecution of Louis IX. Although the company doesn't currently possess one, it has held various royal warrants under six monarchs. It was acquired by Halewood International in the early 1990s. The latter company was established in 1978, and now describes itself as "Britain's most important independent wine and spirit company".

The company's founder, owner and chief executive is John Halewood, who learned his trade with González Byass, the well-known sherry house.

Chequers

Category: Standard Blend **Licensee:** *John McEwan & Co, Elgin* **Owner:** *Diageo plc*

The brand name refers to the *ex officio* country residence of the Prime Minister of the United Kingdom. John McEwan & Co was established in 1863, and acquired Linkwood Distillery near Elgin through its membership of DCL in 1932.

Chequers is a big brand in Venezuela, Paraguay, and Aruba.

Chieftain's Choice

Category: A range of blends and malts **Licensee:** *Scottish Independent Distillers Co* **Owner:** *Peter J. Russell Group*

Leonard Russell, father of the eponymous Peter J. (currently chairman of the group), commenced business as a whisky broker in 1936, and soon expanded into blending and exporting. Today, the group sells annually over ten million bottles worldwide and is one of the largest independent companies in the whisky industry.

The group acquired the Scottish Independent Distillers Company in 1985. This company had been formed in 1928 by a number of independent blenders and distillers with the primary intention of pooling their knowledge and skills to produce prestige whiskies. In 2003, Peter Russell and Co acquired Glengoyne Distillery (*see* entry).

The Chieftain's Choice range sells through specialist outlets in the UK, Japan, the USA and France. A de luxe expression (blended Scotch) at 32 Years Old won a gold medal at the 1995 International Wine & Spirit Competition awards.

Chivas Regal
Category: De Luxe Blend Licensee: Chivas Brothers, Paisley

In 1801, William Edward established himself as a wine merchant and grocer at 49 Castle Street, Aberdeen. The small shop was close to the busy harbour, where cargoes of tea, coffee, sugar, spices, and dried fruits were continually being landed, as well as kegs of gin, brandy, and rum. Edward's business grew steadily, and before long he was looking for a partner.

A friend – the well-known Aberdeen advocate Alexander Chivas – suggested his young cousin, James Chivas, who joined the firm in 1837. The same year, the business was moved to a grander site at the head of King Street, where it remained for over 100 years.

The Chivas family came from Tarves in Aberdeenshire and took their name from the ancient barony of Schivas. Four years after James Chivas joined the firm, William Edward died and Chivas formed a new partnership with another wine merchant, but this was not a success, and the relationship was dissolved in 1857.

The business prospered, however. Queen Victoria regularly had provisions sent down from Chivas' shop to her summer home at Balmoral, and granted a royal warrant to the firm in 1843. Its reputation travelled far and wide, and soon, orders were arriving from all over Britain and abroad; the shop supplied whisky, among other items, to the Austrian emperor.

In 1858, James Chivas took his brother John as a partner, and the firm became Chivas Brothers; however, John died five years later. Driven by James' energy, commercial flair, and good taste, the firm continued to expand, both physically (along King Street) and economically. The range of services and goods offered included, for example, a staff agency for shooting parties, and a new department selling household goods. By the time of James' death in 1886, whisky had become a key part of the business.

Chivas Brothers began to sell its own blend, Glen Dee, in the early 1870s. It was eagerly bought by the company's existing customers, both locally and abroad: order books from the 1880s list princes and peers, admirals and generals, bishops and professors. James was succeeded by his son, Alexander, but the latter died in 1893 of a "quinsy throat" (followed by his wife, three days later), and control passed to his assistant, Alexander Smith, who managed the firm on behalf of Chivas' trustees and brought Charles Stewart Howard, an Edinburgh man, into the business.

Howard had worked for J&G Stewart & Co and was experienced in the whisky trade. By this time, the company had built up a good name abroad for its two export blends, Royal Glen-Dee and Royal Strathythan (the Queensland *Licensed Victualler's Gazette* of 1889 states that "in every well-conducted hotel Glen-Dee is as well-known as Guinness or Pommery"), and other brands were available locally. The retail side of the business continued, but was now secondary to whisky. The firm had built up a good stock of well-matured malt whiskies, and under Howard's guidance, new blends were created and exported all over the world, especially to the new and burgeoning market in North America. In 1909, Chivas Regal was introduced to both Canada and the USA.

A fire at the King Street premises in 1929 destroyed much of the administrative and accounts departments, and the deaths of both Smith and Howard in 1935 resulted in Chivas Brothers becoming a limited liability company. In 1949, this company became a wholly owned subsidiary of Seagram, the Canadian distilling giant. By this time, Chivas Regal was one of the most successful brands in the world.

In 1950, Chivas Brothers/Seagram bought Strathisla Distillery; seven years later, the company began construction of a new distillery at Glen Keith, which incorporated parts of an old flour and meal mill – the first new malt whisky distillery built in Scotland since the Victorian era. Soon afterwards, the Keith Bond was built nearby to accommodate the output of both distilleries; at the time, it was the largest complex of its kind in the world, and it is still among the biggest.

In 1958, with growing stocks of whisky reducing the space available at Keith, it was decided to build a separate blending and bottling plant with further warehousing.

Since most of the company's exports went through Glasgow, a suitable site was found on Clydeside, at Paisley, which remains the company's base in Scotland. The original Chivas Brothers shop in Aberdeen continued until 1981.

In 2000, Pernod Ricard, the French drinks giant, acquired Seagram's Scotch whisky interests. Some would argue that, along with J&B Rare and Johnnie Walker, Chivas Regal is the only truly global brand of Scotch whisky. It sells in over 150 countries, is the top premium brand, and is the seventh-best-selling whisky in the world.

Clan Ardroch

Category: Standard Blend **Owner:** *Hall & Bramley, Liverpool*
(*see* GLEN GHOIL) Curiously, *ardroch* (more usually *ardrach*) is the Gaelic term for a ferry-boat. The word is actually Middle Irish, so – given its owner's origin – perhaps it refers to the large number of Gaelic-speaking Irish people who came over to Liverpool on the ferry. Or perhaps the ferry is that across the Mersey...

Clan Campbell

Category: Standard and De Luxe Blends **Licensee:** *Campbell Distillers* **Owner:** *Chivas Bros, Paisley*
Clan Campbell is something of a phenomenon. Although the brand was only launched in 1984, it trebled its sales to 800,000 cases by 1991, and won the accolade of being the fastest-growing brand of blended whisky in Europe. Currently, it sells just over a million cases worldwide.

The House of Campbell (S. Campbell & Son) dates from 1879 and was originally based in Glasgow, then at Kilwinning, Ayrshire.

The Aberlour-Glenlivet Distillery was bought in 1945, and the tiny Edradour Distillery in 1982.

In 1988, Campbell Distillers was created by the merger of the House of Campbell and J.R. Parkington, a long-established wine and spirits distributor. The same year, Campbell Distillers became the UK subsidiary of the Pernod Ricard Group, the third-largest wine and spirits firm in the world (and the largest in Europe before Diageo was incorporated). In 1989, the company bought Glenallachie Distillery on Speyside, which doubled its capacity.

Naturally, the marketing tactic focused first on France, with the help of its mighty partner; Clan Campbell is now number three in this market. It also sells well in Italy and Spain, and significant progress has been made in Argentina, Australia, China, and Taiwan. It is not available in the UK, but was recently launched in the USA.

In late 1991 and early 1992, Campbell Distillers launched two de luxe expressions of Clan Campbell: 12 and 21 Years Old. The latter was changed to 18 Years Old in 1997.

Clan MacGregor
Category: Standard Blend Licensee: J.G. Thomson & Co, Glasgow Owner: William Grant & Sons, Dufftown

This secondary (*i.e.* price-competitive) brand was introduced by William Grant to North America in the 1970s. By 1990, it was selling over 500,000 cases in export markets, and in 1997, it achieved a million cases. It currently stands just within the top twenty best-sellers. Although available in the UK, it is principally an export whisky.

The war-like MacGregor clan fell foul of the politically powerful Clan Campbell and was outlawed in 1603. It became illegal to bear the name MacGregor; anyone was at liberty to murder a MacGregor and claim a reward. This brutal order was only repealed by Act of Parliament in 1774.

Clan Murdoch
Category: Standard Blend Licensee: Murdoch McLennan, Edinburgh Owner: Glenmorangie plc, Broxburn

Murdoch McLennan was an agricultural experimenter as well as a whisky merchant, and specialized in ways of increasing barley yield for whisky production (*see* HIGHLAND QUEEN, JAMES MARTIN'S).

Clan Roy
Category: Standard Blend Owner: Morrison Bowmore Distillers, Glasgow

The markets for this blend are Spain, Portugal, and North America (*see* ROB ROY).

Clansman
Category: Standard Blend Owner: Glen Catrine Bonded Warehouse, Ayrshire

This blend is produced mainly for export to South America (*see* GLEN CATRINE).

(The) Claymore

Category: Standard Blend Owner: Whyte & Mackay Ltd, Glasgow

The Claymore was launched by DCL during the summer of 1977 as a low-priced or "secondary" brand, taking the company into a sector of the market it had hitherto shunned. This was an attempt to secure market share following the withdrawal of Johnnie Walker in the same year. The brand immediately became the leader in its sector, winning a 5.6 per cent share of the market in the UK.

During the titanic take-over battle for DCL in 1987, one of the objections was the company's share of the UK market, and in order to avoid protracted investigation by the Office of Fair Trading, a number of brands were sold to Whyte & Mackay. The new owner has continued to develop The Claymore's market, especially in the UK, where it now ranks number four.

Club

Category: Premium Blend Licensee: Justerini & Brooks, London Owner: Diageo plc

In the 1880s, J&B became one of the first London wine and spirits merchants to buy up stocks of old whisky in Scotland in order to create a house blend of consistent quality. The first brand was Club, which today is available only from J&B's shops in London (*see* J&B RARE AND RESERVE).

Cluny

Category: Standard and De Luxe Blends Licensee: John E McPherson & Sons Owner: Whyte & Mackay Ltd, Glasgow

John E. McPherson, Edinburgh, established his wine and spirits company at Newcastle upon Tyne in 1849. The brand takes its name from the MacPhersons of Cluny, the chiefs of Clan MacPherson, one of whom escaped with Bonnie Prince Charlie after the battle of Culloden (1746), and was hidden by his clan for nine years in a specially adapted cave known as "Cluny's Cage".

In 1857, when the brand was introduced, the Macpherson of Cluny was John McPherson's cousin, and his arms – complete with supporters (two clansmen) and motto ("Touch Not The Cat Bot [sic] A Glove") – adorn the label to this day. Clan MacPherson originated in Badenoch on Speyside.

Cluny quickly accumulated awards (and a royal warrant in 1931), but it is not sold in the UK today. Its main markets are in the US, Canada, Australia, Sweden, Norway, and Italy. In 1990, it stood at thirty-one in the league table of export brands.

Cock o'the North

Category: Whisky Liqueur Owner: The Cock o'the North Liqueur Company, Aboyne, Aberdeenshire (made by Spayside Distillery)

Cock o'the North is a mixture of malt whisky, blaeberries (mountain blueberries), honey, and "a special ingredient known only to the Marquis of Huntly and his son the Earl of Aboyne". The "Cock o'the North" is the nickname of the Chiefs of Clan Gordon, and the current "Cock" is the Marquis of Huntly, who began to produce this malt whisky-based liqueur from a family recipe in

1998. The soubriquet was first bestowed upon his ancestor, George
Gordon, Fourth Earl of Huntly and Chancellor of Scotland, in 1550.

The Gordon estates once stretched from Deeside to Speyside
and included much of what is now the malt whisky heartland. The
present Marquis's forbear was the fourth Duke of Gordon who
sponsored the Act of Parliament in 1823 which heralded the
modern era of whisky-making.

The malt whisky base comes from Speyside Distillery, a site
which had formerly been part of the Gordon estates.

Compass Box
Category: Vatted Malts Owner: Compass Box Ltd, London

Compass Box is the creation of the innovative free-thinker John
Glaser, who learned his trade with Johnnie Walker in America.
The company produces small batch whiskies that break bravely
with traditional blending methods. His range includes the unique
"Hedonism", the only "vatted grain" (a blend of grain whiskies
from different distilleries) ever produced in Scotland, and the
grain and malt blend "Asyla" (plural of Asylum), which won a
gold medal for blended whisky at the International Wine and Spirit
Competition 2003. Glaser's most recent release is "Juveniles", a
vatted malt created, strangely enough, in collaboration with the
Scottish ex-pat owner of a Parisian wine bar.

Corney & Barrow
*Category: Standard and De Luxe Blends Owner: Corney &
Barrow, London*

Established in 1780, Corney & Barrow is one of the top UK
specialist wine and spirits retailers and currently holds three royal
warrants. In addition to its two shops in London, it also operates
one each in Edinburgh, Ayr, and Newmarket. These outlets
notwithstanding, the majority of its business is conducted by
mail order.

Between the wars, the firm held a controlling interest in James
Catto & Co (*see* CATTO'S), and once did its own blending and filling.
A range of high-quality own-label whiskies was launched in
Britain during the 1940s, and several brands are now becoming
established in the Japanese market. The whiskies are blended for
Corney & Barrow by Peter J. Russell & Co, Edinburgh (*see*
CHIEFTAIN'S CHOICE).

The Country Gentlemen's
*Category: Standard Blend Licensee: William Maxwell Owner:
The Country Gentlemen's Association, Baldock, Herts*

This blend is available exclusively to members of the Country
Gentlemen's Association, and to customers of Hedley Wright &
Co (Bishop's Stortford-based wine merchants), which supplies
it to the Association. Hedley Wright himself owns the
Springbank Distillery.

Crabbie's
*Category: Standard Blend Licensee: John Crabbie & Co, Leith
Owner: Diageo plc*

Crabbie & Co was a family blending firm until it joined DCL, via amalgamation with Macdonald Greenlees and others, in 1922 (*see* OLD PARR). The firm traces its origins to 1801, and is especially well-known for its Green Ginger cordial (mixed with whisky to make what is known as a Whisky Mac, a deliciously warming cold-weather drink).

At one time, the firm held the licence for the historic Balmenach Distillery near Cromdale (*see* BALMENACH). Crabbie's premises in Leith have now been turned into flats.

Crawford's 3 Star

*Category: Standard Blend **Licensee:** (domestic market) Whyte & Mackay, Glasgow; (other markets) A&A Crawford, Edinburgh **Owner:** Diageo plc*

The brothers Archibald and Aikman Crawford went into business as whisky blenders and merchants at Leith in 1860. The company was incorporated in 1942, by which time Crawford's 3 Star was a leading brand in Scotland. In 1944, its owners joined DCL.

In 1981, A&A Crawford & Associates was formed to handle the Scottish domestic sales of ten of DCL's smaller companies. The UK rights to the Crawford's brands were licensed to Whyte & Mackay in 1986 (*see* WHYTE & MACKAY). 3 Star currently stands at number five in the Scottish market (with a 30% market-share) and number twelve on the UK best-selling list. It is exported to France, Italy, the Netherlands, Japan, French Guiana, Costa Rica, Qatar, and South Africa. The brand's label derives from a design that was originated in 1900.

Crinan Canal Water

*Category: Premium Blend **Owner:** Cockburn & Co (Leith), Edinburgh*

The Crinan Canal was built in the late-eighteenth century, at the head of the peninsula of Kintyre in Argyll, in order to allow direct access from the Firth of Clyde to the Sea of the Hebrides, and thus to the Atlantic. Before the canal was built, vessels had an extra seventy-mile journey around the treacherous Mull of Kintyre (*see* THE DOMINIE).

Cumbrae Castle

*Category: Standard Blend **Proprietor:** Macduff International, Glasgow*

This is a new brand recently launched by Macduff International (*see* MACDUFF). The islands of Little and Great Cumbrae are situated in the Firth of Clyde. The "castle" is a ruined tower of indeterminate date, surrounded by a ditch and rampart, and was destroyed by Oliver Cromwell.

The brand takes its name, however, from a four-masted clipper ship which bore emigrants and pioneers from Scotland to the New World in the nineteenth century. In the export markets at which the brand is directed, the slogan is that it will provide a "taste of home"! It does well in the Far East and in South America.

Custodian

*Category: Standard Blend **Licensee:** Douglas Denham **Owner:** Red Lion Blending Co, London*

This blend is chiefly exported to Venezuela (*see* DINER'S).

Cutty Sark

*Category: Premium and De Luxe Blends **Owner:** Berry Brothers & Rudd, London*

Number 3 St James's Street has been occupied by the Berry family, or their close associates, since the 1690s. The firm remains essentially a family concern: the current chairman is John R.Rudd and a current non-executive director is Anthony Berry. The original business conducted from St James's Street was that of "Italian warehousemen" (*i.e.* grocers and, later, wine merchants). The present building was erected in the 1730s, and the shop has changed very little since that time.

Cutty Sark originated over a luncheon in the "parlour" of Number 3 St James's Street on March 23, 1923. Present were the partners – Anthony Berry's grandfather Francis, great uncle Walter, and Hugh Rudd – and the well-known Scottish artist, James McBey. Francis Berry wanted to augment the firm's existing list of blended Scotch whiskies with a new brand with a light character and colour (without the traditional addition of caramel colouring).

They required a name and McBey suggested "Cutty Sark", since the famous Dumbarton-built clipper had newly returned to England after years of serving under the Portuguese flag. The *Cutty Sark* – which was the fastest ship of her day (and still holds the record for the run from Australia to England) – was herself named after the fleet-footed young witch in Robert Burns' great poem, *Tam O'Shanter* (the name literally means "short shirt"). Interestingly, Burns' inspiration for the character "Cutty Sark" was a friend called Katie Stein, who lived at Kirkoswald, and was a scion of the great distilling family (*see* HISTORY).

McBey also volunteered to design the label, which remains exactly the same today as when he drew it, right down to the hand-drawn lettering and the uncommon description "Scots Whisky". Only the colour of the label is different: McBey wanted a shade of cream, but the printers accidentally used canary yellow. The mistake was so striking that it was retained.

Like several other firms, Berry Bros consolidated its "offshore" contacts in the Caribbean during the years of Prohibition, to build a springboard into the American market when the antidrink laws were repealed. One of their "agents" was Captain William McCoy, a rum-runner of proverbial integrity, whose name was to become synonymous with good whisky – *i.e.* "The Real McCoy". After 1933, the brand made rapid progress in the USA (even throughout the war years) and it remains one of the leaders in this market.

Today, Cutty Sark ranks among the top ten international Scotch whisky brands. It is brand leader in Greece and Portugal, and the fastest-growing brand in Spain and Japan. In the UK, it is available only through a limited number of outlets.

Dalmeny

Category: Standard Blend Owner: J. Townend & Sons, Hull

This company of wine and spirit merchants, which has been well-established in the north of England for over a century, acquired the business of J.J. Rippon in the 1930s. With it came the Dalmeny brand, which has been available since at least 1893.

Dalmeny House, on the southern shore of the Firth of Forth, near Edinburgh, is the seat of the Earl of Rosebery.

Peter Dawson

Category: Standard Blend Licensee: Peter Dawson, Glasgow
Owner: Diageo plc

Peter Dawson was a family company established in 1882, which owned distilleries at Auchnagie and Towiemore (both are now long extinct) and partially owned Balmenach Distillery. The company was licensed to operate Ord Distillery (by John Dewar & Sons) until 1982, and sold Ord as a single malt.

Peter Dawson joined DCL in 1925, by which time the brand Peter Dawson was popular enough for the company to introduce special mallet-shaped bottles covered in "blisters" as a protection against counterfeiting (*see* VAT 69). Today, the brand sells in such far-flung markets as Chile and Canada, Grenada and Norway, Belgium and Aruba.

Derby Special

Category: Standard and De Luxe Blends Owner: Kinross Whisky Co, Haywards Heath, Sussex

(*see* GOLD BLEND)

Dewar's White Label

Category: Standard Blend Licensee: John Dewar & Sons, Glasgow
Owner: John Dewar & Sons, Glasgow

Dewar's White Label has been, for many years, the best-selling Scotch in the USA, and is among the top five best-sellers worldwide.

The brand's story begins in 1828, when John Dewar, aged twenty-three, walked the twenty-five miles from his home village of Moneydie to Perth to take up employment in a relative's wine and spirits shop. Nine years later, he became a partner, but in 1846, he set up in business on his own and opened a shop in the High Street of Perth, selling, among other items, his own blended whiskies. In the late 1860s, Dewar began offering his blends in branded bottles, rather than by the keg or in plain stone jars as was the usual custom. He was probably the first person to sell branded bottles.

John Dewar died in 1880, and was succeeded by his son, John Alexander, who brought his brother, Thomas Robert, into the partnership five years later, when the latter reached the age of twenty-one.

The Dewar brothers were men of outstanding ability, and they began immediately to expand their business. Tommy went to London in 1885 to establish the firm's brands, and it has been said that he was probably more responsible than anyone else for the success of Scotch whisky in London. By 1890, Dewar's whiskies were in the bars of most of London's fashionable hotels, and in 1893, the firm was granted a royal warrant. Between 1892 and 1894, Tommy Dewar toured the world, visiting twenty-six countries and appointing thirty-two agents. A New York office was opened in 1895, and bottling plants were built in London and Manchester in 1897 and 1898. In 1896, the firm commenced the construction of Aberfeldy Distillery to secure supplies of malt whisky (by 1923, the company also owned Lochnagar, Ord, Pulteney, Aultmore, Parkmore, and Benrinnes distilleries).

At the Brewer's Show in 1896, he employed pipers to draw attention to his wares and drown out any opposition! Even today, Dewar's retains the services of a piper for promotional purposes – echoing the image on the brand's label. The company pulled off something of a coup in this connection when it sponsored the "Beating of the Retreat from the 20th Century" on December 30, 1999, with 1,200 pipers processing down the ancient Royal Mile in Edinburgh to join the Scottish Fiddle Orchestra for an evening of massed pipes and fiddles which was televised all over the world.

One of Tommy Dewar's mottos was, "If you don't advertise, you fossilize", and the company pioneered several advertising innovations. In 1898, the firm made the first ever film commercial, based on their print advertising campaign, "The Drink of your Ancestors", in which the "ancestors" climb out of their portrait frames and dance crazily around for a minute or so. A few years later Dewar's erected the largest electrically lit sign ever, on a tower on the south bank of the river Thames: a kilted Highlander, drinking copious glasses of whisky.

John Alexander Dewar was very different from his extrovert brother. He became treasurer of the City of Perth (for six years he was Lord Provost, *i.e.* Mayor) and was a Liberal MP for Inverness-shire. He was made a baronet in 1907 (the first of the "whisky barons"), and was elevated to the peerage as Lord Forteviot in 1917.

Tommy Dewar became Baron Dewar of Homestall in Sussex in 1919, having been knighted in 1902. He was a sheriff of the City of London and a Conservative Member of Parliament. Three times he was chairman of the Worshipful Company of Distillers.

The brothers died within a year of each other (in 1929 and 1930). Peter Dewar (no relation) became chairman, but after 1946, the family again assumed the mantle of leadership, with John Arthur Dewar becoming chairman and being succeeded by his cousin, Evelyn Dewar, third Lord Forteviot, whose son and heir is still a director.

Control of the company had long since passed into other hands, however. In 1915, Dewar's entered into "close and permanent association" with James Buchanan & Co, setting up Scotch Whisky Brands to pool profits and stocks (which included the largest holding of mature whisky in Scotland), and to draw on their joint resources under a management arrangement. Ten years later, both companies joined DCL.

Dewar's benefited greatly from the lifting of Prohibition in the US in 1933, and further dramatic growth continued throughout the 1950s, 1960s, and 1970s (the company won six Queen's Awards for Export Achievement between 1966 and 1979). Today, Dewar's White Label sells in 172 countries, its main markets being the USA, Greece, Venezuela, Spain, Dominican Republic, Puerto Rico, and Lebanon. When Diageo, and its spirits arm UDV, were formed by the merger of Guinness and Grand Metropolitan, the new company was obliged by the U.S. Foreign Trade Convention to sell two of its leading brands if it was to continue to trade in the USA. Dewar's was bought by Bacardi Ltd, through their subsidiary William Lawson & Sons, together with Aberfeldy, Royal Brackla, Aultmore, and Craigellachie Distilleries. William Lawson changed its name to John Dewar & Sons. "Dewar's World of Whisky", an interactive exhibition and celebration of the brothers' achievement and the continuing success of their brand, opened at Aberfeldy Distillery in April 2000, and has since won much accolade.

Dew of Ben Nevis

Category: Standard Blend Licensee: Long John Distillers
Owner: Nikka Whisky Company

(see LONG JOHN, BEN NEVIS) As early as the 1840s, Long John's Dew of Ben Nevis was the single malt from Ben Nevis Distillery. In 1911, the name "Long John" was sold to W.H. Chaplin & Co, by which time the whisky had become a blend. The firm D.P. Macdonald continued to market Dew of Ben Nevis for a time, enjoying some success in Europe and Egypt, but the brand lapsed. Happily, with the building of a visitors centre at Ben Nevis Distillery in 1993, "The Dew" is now available again, from there and limited outlets.

Dimple

Category: De Luxe Blend Licensee: John Haig & Co, Markinch
Owner: Diageo plc

(see HAIG) The five sons of John Haig (who died in 1773) all learned distilling at Kilbagie in Kincardineshire, in the distillery of their uncle, Robert Stein. The eldest son, James, moved to Edinburgh aged twenty-seven, and with help from his uncle opened a distillery at Canonmills in 1782, and later at Sunbury and Lochrin. His sons continued to run the latter two, while their cousin, John, built Cameronbridge Distillery, and later went on to develop a massive blending and bottling plant at Markinch close by. Dimple and the other Haig blends originated and are still made here.

John's son, John Alicius, established the firm of Haig & Haig in 1888 to market the family's products in the USA. Between 1909 and 1925, this company was controlled by Robertson & Baxter (see LANG'S), before it became a subsidiary of John Haig & Co and part of DCL. Haig & Co was appointed purveyor to the

House of Lords in 1906, and was granted a royal warrant by King Edward VII.

Following a ruling by the EC Commission in 1977 concerning "parallel exports", Dimple was withdrawn from the UK market for some years (*see* JOHN BARR). It has since been restored.

Dimple/Pinch's trademark is its distinctive bottle, introduced in 1893 by George Ogilvy Haig. It has long been popular among sailors for displaying their "ship-in-a-bottle" models, and among small boys for holding silver sixpences (when such were minted). It was the first-ever bottle to be patented in the US, as late as 1958.

The other distinctive feature of the packaging is the wire net around the bottle. This was introduced to prevent the cork stopper from coming out during a sea voyage. The nets were specially made in France and applied by hand – expensive exercises, and indicative of the value Haig's placed upon its de luxe blends. In 1987, Dimple won a gold medal and "Best Blended Whisky" at the International Wine & Spirit Competition.

Diner's

Category: Standard and De Luxe Blends and Vatted Malt
Licensee: Douglas Denham **Owner:** *Red Lion Blending Co, London*

The Red Lion Blending Company was established by Robert Mendelson and David Hallgarten, men well experienced in the wine and spirit trade.

The company began as specialist bottlers and blenders for various firms around the world. The associate company, Douglas Denham, is responsible for the own-label whiskies sold by Diners Club, the international credit card company.

The 12 Year Old won prizes at the International Wine & Spirit Competition in 1979 and 1980. Red Lion Blending Company's main business is now bulk and case export.

Doctor's Special

Category: Standard Blend **Licensee:** *Hiram Walker & Sons* **Owner:** *Allied Distillers, Dumbarton*

This brand was established by Robert McNish & Co (*see* GRAND MACNISH) in the 1920s. It is currently only available in the Scandinavian market.

The Dominie

Category: Standard Blend licensee **Owner:** *Cockburn & Corleith, Edinburgh*

Cockburn & Co was established in 1796 in the prosperous port of Leith. Robert and John were the enterprising brothers who founded the business, although in the early days, their names were less well known than that of their brother Henry, Lord Cockburn, the famous Scottish judge, and author of *Memorials of My Time*.

The two brothers prospered, and soon built up a large and prestigious client list. Upon his death in 1870, the inventory of Charles Dickens' cellar included "17 dozen vey [sic] fine old whiskey Cockburn & Company, Leith". Other clients included Sir Walter Scott, many aristocrats, and even the Royal Household.

Cockburn is better known for its port than for its whisky: one of the brothers went to Oporto and established this side of the business. The company was acquired by Drambuie in 1980, which sold it to The Wine Company (Scotland) in 1993. The latter had been set up to take over the Wine Emporium, Edinburgh (established 1986). In April 2004, it was subject to a management buy-out by its principal directors, Ian Macphail and David Forbes, who plan to develop the brand.

The Douglas

Category: Deluxe Blend (also single malt) **Owner:** *Douglas Laing & Co, Glasgow*

Presumably, The Douglas refers to "the good Sir James", friend of King Robert the Bruce – he died in battle in Spain carrying the heart of Robert the Bruce to the Holy Land in 1330.

His descendants were Earls of Douglas, Angus and Morton, Marquesses of Douglas and Queensberry, and Dukes of Hamilton and Buccleuch in other words, some of Scotland's greatest families. This whisky is the house choice of the current Duke of Buccleuch (whose family name is Montague *Douglas* Scott). The label refers to Douglas of Drumlanrig, the Duke's direct ancestor. Drumlanrig castle is the principal seat of the Dukes of Buccleuch. As a single malt it is mainly sold in Scandanavia and Japan (*see* King of Scots).

Drambuie

Category: Whisky Liqueur **Owner:** *The Drambuie Liqueur Co, Edinburgh*

After fleeing from his ruinous defeat at Culloden in 1746, Prince Charles Edward Stuart made his way to the Isle of Skye, where he was sheltered by, among others, Captain John Mackinnon of Elgol.

The prince arrived at Mackinnon's house disguised as a maidservant, and spent the evening playing with his son, "carrying him in his arms and singing to him, saying, 'I hope this child may be a captain in my service yet'". The story goes that, on parting, the prince had nothing to offer his host for his hospitality other than the recipe for a liqueur, presumably brandy-based in its original form. The secret was kept by the Mackinnons of Corrie for many generations (they were related to the Elgol branch). Dr Johnson and James Boswell visited in 1773, and their journals recount how Boswell suffered a terrible hangover after sitting up with Lachlan Mackinnon of Corrie until 5am, drinking five bowls of "punch". Might this have been "the secret brew"?

In 1871, Mackinnon gave the recipe to his friend James Ross, who owned the inn at Broadford, Skye. His son, also named James, began to produce the liqueur and sell it locally.

The name was bestowed by a local man, a Mr Maclean, who was a Crimean War veteran and who came to Broadford once a week to collect his pension, then went to the pub. When offered a glass to try, he pronounced it to be *dram buidhe*, "the drink which satisfies". James Ross registered the shortened name "Drambuie" in 1875.

Upon Ross' death in 1902, the rights to the brand passed to his widow, who moved to Edinburgh and sold the recipe to Malcolm MacKinnon in 1912. MacKinnon was employed by a blending firm called W. Macbeth & Sons; when this failed in 1914, he kept the secret recipe and successfully established the Drambuie Liqueur Company. When he died in 1945, the secret passed to his widow, Gina, who continued to run the company with her brother, W.A. Davidson. Today it is owned and managed by her son and grandsons, who are still the custodians of the secret recipe.

The demand for the liqueur grew steadily after the war, and it is now one of the most successful brands of spirit in the world, available in 100 countries.

Angus Dundee

Category: De Luxe Blend Owner: Angus Dundee Distillers Ltd

Terry Hillman, the founder of the family company Angus Dundee Ltd, was a director of Burn Stewart prior to the management buy-out in 1998. The discreet, London-based company is now managed by the second generation of the Hillman family, supported by the third generation. The company sells its whiskies in export markets. In 2000, the company bought Tomintoul Distillery from Whyte & Mackay (JBB), and in 2004, Glencadam from Allied Distillers. The Angus Dundee range currently includes twelve, twenty-one, twenty-five, thirty and thirty-five-year-old blends. The company also produces a standard blend called "Dundee" and a de luxe blend called "Old Dundee".

Dunkeld Atholl Brose

Category: Whisky Liqueur Owner: Gordon & MacPhail, Elgin

"Atholl Brose is a giant's drink," wrote Sir Robert Bruce Lockhart in his seminal book on whisky, *Scotch*, published in 1951. However, he was not referring to the brand, for "brose" has been drunk in the Highlands for centuries and can be used to describe any drink.

There is, however, a curious tradition behind "Atholl Brose". Late in 1475, a sentence of death and forfeiture was passed on John, last Lord of the Isles. The Earls of Atholl and Crawford commanded a formidable sea-borne expedition into the Western Isles to enforce the sentence, and the rebellious lord took to the hills. The story goes that when the Earl of Atholl discovered where the fugitive was drawing water, he ordered that the well be filled with a mixture of whisky, honey, herbs, and oatmeal, so as to encourage him to stay put while reinforcements were brought up. Alas, the Lord of the Isles was beguiled, and "Atholl Brose" was invented.

Described as "a whisky liqueur of rare distinction", Dunkeld Atholl Brose is made to a secret recipe which dispenses with the oatmeal and uses only twelve-year-old malt whisky. Gordon & MacPhail won a silver award in 1985 for it and a gold in 1987 at the International Wine & Spirit Competition; on the latter occasion it was named "The Best Liqueur in the World".

Dunhill

Category: Deluxe Blends Licensee: The Edrington Group, Glasgow Owner: Alfred Dunhill Scotch Whisky

The distinguished London tobacconists Alfred Dunhill have offered their own brand of whisky since 1982. The whiskies are blended for the company by Robertson and Baxter, Glasgow, a subsidiary of the Edrington Group (*see* THE FAMOUS GROUSE).

Alexander Dunn

Category: Standard, Premium and De Luxe Blends; and Vatted Malt Owner: Alexander Dunn & Co (whisky blenders), Bracknell, Berks

Alexander Dunn & Co specializes in quality bottlings of wines and spirits as "executive gifts" (*see* SLAINTHEVA). This range was originally produced in 1987 for a French supermarket, and is now also available in Japan.

Since each expression is made to order, there is a certain amount of variation in strengths and contents.

Easy Drinking Whisky

Category: Vatted Malts Owner: Jon, Mark & Robbo's Easy Drinking Whisky Company Ltd, Perthshire

The Easy Drinking Whisky Company was established in 2003 by three friends – Jon Geary and his brother Mark, and David Robertson – all of whom had worked in the whisky industry. David Robertson was Master Distiller of the Macallan at the time, and their project has been supported by Edrington.

Their plan was to produce a range of whiskies which would have broad appeal, particularly to younger consumers. Their first three bottlings are named simply "The Rich Spicy One", "The Smooth Sweeter One", and "Smokey Peaty" (an Irish malt from Cooley Distillery). Unusually, they list all the filling malts that go into these blends with age, proportion, and cask type. The whiskies have been well received and the company is now seeking export markets.

El Vino

Category: De Luxe Blend Owner: El Vino Co, London

El Vino's wine bars have been a feature of the City of London since the company's foundation in 1879. They have always been wine and spirit merchants, and this distinguished blend was originally created for the company's founder, Sir Alfred Bower, in the 1880s. It was well known in London in the 1920s, when Sir Alfred was Lord Mayor and it was served at official functions.

The formula was lost soon after Bower's death in 1948, and for a time the blend was unavailable. Happily, however, the original recipe was discovered in a notebook deep in Sir Alfred's desk by his grandson, David Mitchell, who is currently El Vino's chairman.

Connoisseur's Blend is available from El Vino's shops in the City, and also by mail order from the company's head office. The blend has a high malt content (about fifty per cent), and is married in the sherry casks used to ship El Vino sherry.

The Famous Grouse

Category: Premium Blend, De Luxe Blend, Vatted Malt Licensee: Matthew Gloag & Sons, Perth Owner: The Edrington Group, Glasgow

Matthew Gloag (died 1860), the grandfather of the creator of The Famous Grouse, began life as a butler on a sporting estate near Perth in the house of the Sheriff Clerk of Perth (an important lawyer). In 1797, he married the daughter of a grocer and wine merchant in Athole Street, and by 1820 had taken over the running of the business, supplying the gentry of Perthshire with provisions. When Queen Victoria visited the town in 1842, Gloag was invited to supply the wines.

Matthew's grandson, also named Matthew, worked in the wine and spirit trade in France (with Octave Calvet of the famous family of wine *négociants* in Bordeaux) before returning to Perth in 1896 to take over the family business. The following year he created a new blend of house whisky which he named The Grouse Brand in the hope of attracting the many sportsmen who came through Perth during the shooting season. His daughter Philippa was responsible for the label which is still the brand's trademark, and it proved so successful that within only a few years "The Famous" was added and "Brand" dropped.

Until 1998, Matthew's great-grandson represented the family on the board – the sixth generation to do so.

By the 1920s, The Famous Grouse was dominating Gloag's business. Markets were opened up in the West Indies, and after the repeal of Prohibition in 1933, the brand was poised to sell in the USA. In 1936, a bonded warehouse and bottling plant opened in Perth, and further export markets were opened up during the late 1930s. Gloag's agents in the Caribbean during the 1930s sold the whisky with the memorable line: "Mellow as a night of love . . . One Grouse and you want no other."

The Gloag family still held all the equity in the company, but after the death of Matthew Frederick Gloag in 1970, followed within days by that of his wife, punitive death duties obliged them to sell the company to Robertson & Baxter and Highland Distilleries, from whom they had long bought the key fillings for The Famous Grouse: Glen Rothes, Highland Park, and Tamdhu.

This provided the company with a much-needed injection of capital with which to build up stocks. At the same time, retail price maintenance was abolished, which offered great opportunities to those companies that could afford to seize them.

The new owner immediately embarked on a marketing campaign for the brand which was so successful that Grouse became the fastest-growing brand in Britain, with its sales rising from 90,000 cases in 1970 to over one million cases in 1979. It has been brand leader in the discriminating Scottish market since 1980, currently stands at number two in the UK, and is the eighth-biggest-seller worldwide. Its main export markets include France, Holland, Spain, Greece, the USA, South Africa, Australasia, and Japan.

The Famous Grouse was granted a royal warrant in 1984, and is currently (1997) the only major blended whisky that is increasing its market share in the home market. A de luxe expression, named "The Famous Grouse Gold Reserve", was introduced in 1996 and is already doing well in China and the Pacific Rim. "The Famous Grouse Vintage Malt" (a vatted malt) was introduced in 2002.

Findlater's Finest

Category: Standard Blend **Licensee:** *Findlater Scotch Whisky (sole agent for Findlater, Mackie, Todd & Co)* **Owner:** *The Invergordon Distillers, Leith, Edinburgh (a subsidiary of Whyte & Mackay Ltd, Glasgow)*

In Dublin in 1823, Alexander Findlater went into business as a wine and spirit merchant at the age of twenty-six. He had learned about Scotch from his father, an excise officer who had once worked with Robert Burns. The family came originally from the shore of the Moray Firth. Alexander's firm prospered and he established partnerships in various English cities, including Findlater, Mackie, Todd & Co in London (in 1863).

Findlater's Finest is reputed to be the first brand of blended whisky to carry the name of the supplier, and the company has received several royal warrants. It also won a gold medal at the 1993 International Wine & Spirit Competition awards.

Findlater, Mackie, Todd and Co became part of the John Lewis Partnership in February 1993; the brand was sold to Invergordon, and became the house whisky of John Lewis' wines and spirits arm, Waitrose. The trading name of the company is now Waitrose Wine Direct (a mail-order company, publishing a monthly magazine). The original name is perpetuated as a supplier of clubs, restaurants, and businesses.

Fine Old Special

Category: Standard Blend **Owner:** *Joseph Holt, Manchester*

The company was founded in 1849 and has been selling a blended whisky since very early in its history. This blend is available through the firm's tied houses and free-trade outlets within twenty miles of Greater Manchester.

First Lord

Category: De Luxe Blend; Vatted Malt **Owner:** *Edwin Cheshire, Stansted, Essex*

Edwin Cheshire is a private company, and the device on the label of its brand depicts part of the coat of arms of the county of the same name: three sheaves of corn. The title "First Lord" (now defunct) was that of the senior officer in the Royal Navy. The title persists in the First Lord of the Treasury (the British Prime Minister). The brands sell mainly in the export market.

Five Millionaires

Category: Standard Blends **Owner:** *Macduff International, Glasgow*

This intriguingly named range of whiskies comes in three expressions: Blue, Red, and Black, all of them standard blends. They were created in 1997 by Macduff International for a customer, who supplied the name as well as the specification and has the licence to sell them. So far, I have not been able to ascertain who the five millionaires are.

Fortnum & Mason

Category: Premium and De Luxe Blends; Old Malt **Owner:**
Fortnum & Mason, London

Fortnum & Mason (established 1707) is probably the most famous food store in the world, with a distinguished reputation for the high quality of its products. Fortnum & Mason's Choice Old has been available for many years exclusively from the shop in Piccadilly.

Fraser's Supreme

Category: Standard Blend **Licensee:** *Strathnairn Whisky, Inverness*
Owner: *Gordon & MacPhail, Elgin (see* MACPHAIL'S)

Gairloch

Category: Standard Blend **Owner:** *McMullen & Sons,*
Hertford, Herts

McMullen & Sons is an established firm of independent brewers and wine and spirit merchants which used to buy in single malts and blend Gairloch itself. This is now done to specifications by a blender in Scotland. First created in 1904, Gairloch is named after the port in Easter Ross, on the loch of the same name. It sells mainly in the on-trade in the northern Home Counties.

A number of first-division malts are used in Gairloch, mainly from the Highland Distilleries/Robertson & Baxter stable, including Glengoyne, Glen Rothes, Highland Park, Tamdhu, and The Macallan (at three to four years old).

Gale's

Category: Premium Blend **Owner:** *George Gale & Co,*
Horndean, Hants

George Gale & Co traces its origins to the 1730s and the purchase of the Ship and Bell Public House in Horndean, near Portsmouth. Today, the company's principal activity is brewing, with a tied estate of 154 pubs and about 300 free-trade customers, mainly in Hampshire, West and East Sussex, Wiltshire, Surrey, Berkshire, and the Isle of Wight. The firm's own-label whisky is sold through these outlets.

Gale's Blended Glenlivet, as it was originally named, was first created over 100 years ago; the name was borrowed by verbal agreement with George & J.G. Smith (*see* THE GLENLIVET). When The Glenlivet Distillery became part of the Seagram empire, it was thought wise to drop the appellation. Unlike many brand-owners (and to its credit), George Gale & Co is happy to declare the fillings for its blend: Glenlivet, Ben Nevis, Dufftown, Glen Grant, Bunnahabhain, Highland Park, and Dalmore. Grains are: Strathclyde, Dumbarton, Cameron Brig and North British.

Galloway Pride

Category: Secondary Blend **Owner:** *Andrew McMillan, Stranraer*

This unusual blend is found only in the extreme southwest of Scotland and depicts a "Belty" (*i.e.* a Belted Galloway cow) on its label. It is described as being "true to the heart of Bonnie Gallowa".

Gamefair

Category: Vatted Malt Owner: Hynard Hughes, Leicester

Hynard Hughes, wine merchant, was established in Leicester in 1926. It is still a family company, directed by Messrs M.W., J.M. and I.C. Hynard. The brand is popular locally.

Ghillie

Category: Standard Blend Licensee: C.C. George & Co Owner: Campbell Distillers, Brentford, Middlesex

George & Co was a subsidiary of the well-known firm of distillers and blenders, William Whiteley & Company (*see* EDRADOUR, GLENFORRES). Ghillie is uncommon; indeed, it is doubtful whether it is still bottled today.

Gillon's

Category: Standard Blend Licensee: John Gillon & Co, Glasgow and Stonehaven Owner: Diageo plc

The firm, established in 1817 by Sir John Gillon of Linlithgow, was acquired by Ainslie & Heilbron (*see* AINSLIE'S), became part of Macdonald, Greenlees & Co (*see* OLD PARR), and joined DCL in 1925. For many years, Glenury Distillery was licensed to Gillon & Co (*see* GLENURY ROYAL). Italy is currently its only market.

Glayva

Category: Whisky Liqueur Licensee: Glayva Liqueur Co, Edinburgh Owner: Whyte & Mackay Ltd, Glasgow

This whisky liqueur is popular with expatriate Scots worldwide, and is available in most whisky markets, doing especially well in Australia, Canada, South Africa, New Zealand, and Portugal.

It was introduced many years ago by Ronald Morrison & Co of Leith, a well-known firm of wine merchants and whisky blenders, and was the invention of Ronald Morrison himself and George Petrie, a flavour expert and rectifier, who spent months blending malt and grain whiskies with heather-honey, herbs, and botanicals (even some tangerine) before their Gaelic-speaking warehouseman pronounced the blend to be gle mhath – "very good".

Glayva is a sponsor of the world-famous Edinburgh Military Tattoo, and also supports curling throughout Scotland. Sales are currently growing at around ten per cent per annum in the UK off-trade. It is a versatile drink, and may be enjoyed long or short (best over ice). It is also used successfully in cooking.

Glenalmond

Category: Vatted Malt Owner: Vintage Malt Whisky Company

Glenalmond is both an attractive Perthshire blend and a famous public school. The fillings for this vatted malt change from bottling to bottling. The brand won a silver award at the 1994 International Wine and Spirit Competition. (*see* FINLAGGAN).

Glen Baren

Category: Vatted Malt Owner: Kinross Whisky Co, Haywards Heath, Sussex

(*see* GOLD BLEND)

Glen Calder

Category: Standard Blend Owner: Gordon & MacPhail, Elgin
(*see* MacPHAIL'S) The name suggests not a place but a person:
Sir James Calder, seventeenth-century MP for the Royal Burgh
of Elgin. He built a mansion in North Street, not far from Gordon
& MacPhail's shop; the mansion later acquired a reputation for
being haunted.

Glen Carren

Category: Vatted Malt Owner: Hall & Bramley, Liverpool
(*see* GLEN GHOIL)

Glen Catrine

*Category: Standard Blend Licensee: Glen Catrine Bonded
Warehouse, Ayrshire Owner: Loch Lomond Distillery Co Ltd,
Alexandria, Dumbartonshire*

This independent company has its origins in A. Bulloch &
Co, established in 1856, a wine and spirits merchant based in
Glasgow. From the outset, the company blended and bottled its
own whisky brands, of which High Commissioner is the oldest.
In 1973, the business was moved to a bonded warehouse in
Catrine, Ayrshire, to allow for the expansion of the blending and
bottling facilities.

In 1985, Loch Lomond Distillery was acquired from Inver
House Distillers (*see* INCHMURRIN). It resumed operation in 1987,
and in 1993, the company opened a grain distillery adjacent to it
in Alexandria. Glen Catrine's production activities, both here and
at Glen Scotia Distillery, are now managed by the Loch Lomond
Distillery Company.

After the liquidation of Gibson International in 1994, Glen
Catrine bought the firm's brands and distilleries (the aforesaid
Littlemill and Glen Scotia. Glen Catrine's chairman is Alexander
Bulloch, a direct descendant of the founder.

Glen Clova

*Category: Standard Blend Licensee: Ewen & Co, Leith
Owner: Whyte & Mackay Ltd, Glasgow*

Named after one of the "Angus Glens", this is one of Whyte &
Mackay's off-the-peg secondary brands. Ewen & Co was part of
The Waverley Group of companies, the wine and spirits arm of
Scottish Newcastle Breweries.

Glencoe

*Category: Vatted Malt Licensee: R.N. MacDonald & Co
Owner: Red Lion Blending Co, London*

(*see* DINER'S) Glencoe is one of the most dramatic places in all of
Scotland. Narrow and set about with high peaks, it is reputed to
be the birthplace of Ossian, son of Fingal, the third-century
Scottish bard whose work was "discovered" by the controversial
literary figure James MacPherson in the late eighteenth century.
It was also once the home of the MacDonalds of Glencoe, who
suffered an attempted genocide in 1692. The fate of the
Episcopalian/Jacobite cause was sealed when James II/VII went
into exile in 1689, and the Presbyterian/Williamite governors of

Scotland set about suborning the Episcopalian clans, among
them Clan Donald.

King William offered a pardon to those chiefs who would take
the oath of allegiance to him. However, the Campbell faction in the
government – bitter enemies of the MacDonalds – had resolved to
make an example of the MacDonalds of Glencoe. Despite the fact
that their chief took the oath (five days late, owing to bad weather),
two companies of Campbell militia were despatched, led by
Captain Robert Campbell of Glenlyon, with orders to exterminate
the entire tribe of about 400 souls.

The Campbells arrived in February 1692, billeted themselves
upon the MacDonalds for nearly two weeks and were received with
customary Highland hospitality; then, one day they rose up at dawn
and set about slaughtering their hosts as they slept. About forty
men and women were killed in their beds; the rest fled into the
ferocious mountains, where many more perished in the snow.

Of course, massacres and bloody feuds were not uncommon
in the Highlands. The particular horror of the Massacre of Glencoe
lies in the breach of hospitality, traditionally inviolable in the
Highlands whatever the differences between host and guest.
Even today, there are MacDonalds who will not drink with
Campbells, and the pub in Glencoe will not serve anyone who
admits to the name.

Glendarroch

*Category: De Luxe Blend and Vatted Malt Owner: Duncan Taylor &
Co, Glasgow*

Darroch is the Gaelic for an oak tree. I have been unable to elicit
any information about this company.

Glen Dowan

Category: Owner: J&G Grant, Ballindalloch, Speyside

(*see* GLENFARCLAS)

Glendower

Category: Vatted Malt Owner: Burn Stewart Distillers,East Kilbride

An odd name for a whisky, this, since there is no "Glen Dower"
in Scotland, and the name must refer to Owain Glendwr, or Owen
Glendower in English (1359–1415), the last independent prince
of Wales.

Glendower was a national hero who campaigned against
the English, and of whom it has been said that "Wales was never
so close to being united and independent than under Owen's
leadership". At present, the market for the brand which bears
his name is found chiefly in France, Italy, and Japan (*see also*
BURN STEWART).

Glendrostan

*Category: Premium Blend (12 Years Old) Licensee: Longman
Distillers, Glasgow Owner: Whyte & Mackay Ltd, Glasgow*

Longman Distillers was once widely known as the overseas
marketing arm of Invergordon Distillers, selling both bulk and
cased goods. St Drostan, who was a companion of St Columba,
landed at Aberdour near Rosehearty on the Moray Firth around

AD597 and founded Old Deer Abbey. He is also associated with Old Aberdour Church, where the font was said once to have held his miracle-working bones. Alternatively, *see* ABERLOUR.

Glenfairn

Category: Vatted Malt Owner: Co-operative Wholesale Society, Manchester

(*see* HEATHERDALE)

Glen Flagler

Category: Vatted Malt Owner: Inver House Distillers, Airdrie, Lanarkshire

Glen Flagler Lowland Malt Distillery was situated within Moffat Grain Distillers, near Airdrie, and its product was available as a single malt during the 1960s and 1970s. The distillery was closed and dismantled in 1985. Inver House, its owner, still has stocks of Glen Flagler (the malt) but does not sell it as such, preferring to vat it with other malts and sell it as Glen Flagler Pure Malt Special Reserve.

Glenforres

Category: Vatted Malt Owner: Campbell Distillers, Brentford

The Glenforres Glenlivet Distillery Co was once the registered owner of Edradour Distillery under the aegis of William Whiteley & Co; indeed, Edradour malt was once sold as "Glenforres". This brand name now refers to an unusual vatted malt, which is offered for sale mainly in Europe.

Glen Foyle

Category: Standard Blend Licensee: Ewen & Co, Leith
Owner: Whyte & Mackay Ltd, Glasgow

This is another of Invergordon/JBB's off-the-peg secondary brands. Who "Ewen & Co" are is a mystery. There may be a "Glen Foyle" near Aberfoyle in the Trossachs, but I cannot find it.

Glen Garry

Category: Standard Blend Licensee: John Hopkins & Co, Glasgow
Owner: Glen Catrine Bonded Warehouse Ltd

In 1874, John Hopkins acquired the British agency for Otard Cognac, one of the most famous names in the business. He immediately established a company to purvey this and to develop whisky brands, recruiting his brother and cousin to help him. Glen Garry was registered in April 1878, and won "the highest award" at the Chicago Exhibition in 1892. In 1900, the firm's bonded warehouse complex in Glasgow was destroyed by fire (it was rebuilt and reopened the following year). John Hopkins retired from the business in 1911, and five years later the firm became a limited company. In 1916, the entire share capital was acquired by DCL, but it did not become part of the larger company until 1931 (*see also* OBAN, TOBERMORY). Glen Garry is now sold exclusively in Spain. In 2000, the brand was sold to GCBW.

Glen Ghoil

Category: Standard Blend Owner: Hall & Bramley, Liverpool

In 1860, Charlton R. Hall, a prominent Liverpool businessman, set up as a wholesale wine and spirit merchant at 17 Dale Street,

Liverpool. His son, Charlton R. Hall Jr, succeeded his father and went into partnership with J.T. Bramley. In 1892, the firm was referred to as "one of the most noteworthy wine & spirit houses in the city"; by 1900, it was trading under the name Charlton R. Hall & Bramley. The partners had secured the agency for Glen Grant, and were blending their own whisky, which they called Glen Ghoil.

In 1922, two senior members of staff took over, and registered the company under the name of Hall & Bramley. They opened a bonded warehouse at Henry Street, where they blended and bottled Scotch whisky, Irish whiskey, and rum, and acquired the north of England agency for González Byass (sherry) and Charles Heidsieck (Champagne), which expanded the business considerably. In the 1960s, the company diversified into French and German wines, requiring a move to larger premises beside the famous Aintree racecourse.

Today, Hall & Bramley is the only long-established independent shipper in Liverpool and continues to blend and fill its own Scotch whisky. The company also owns Golding Hoptroff, which specializes in transportation for the wine and spirit trade.

Gleniffer

*Category: De Luxe Blend **Owner:** Whyte & Mackay, Glasgow*
(*see* WHYTE & MACKAY)

Glen Lyon

*Category: Standard Blend **Licensee:** Glen Lyon Blending Co, Glasgow **Owner:** Diageo plc*

Originally created as a vatted malt, the blend sells in South Africa. The Glen Lyon Blending Co was a subsidiary of Macleay Duff. Interestingly, I have also seen a "Glen Lyon 100% Blended Scotch Whisky" on the Invergordon/JBB list, sold in export markets.

Glen Nevis

*Category: Standard and De Luxe Blends **Owner:** (home) Safeway (The Argyll Group), Hayes, Middlesex; (export) Gibson Scotch Whisky Distillers, Alexandria, Dumbartonshire*

Glen Nevis Distillery, a subsidiary of Amalgamated Distilled Products (ADP), once produced a vatted malt as well as standard and de luxe blends. ADP bought Barton Distilling (Scotland) in 1982. Following a management buy-out four years later, that part of the business was acquired by The Argyll Group, owner of the Safeway chain of supermarkets.

Glen Nevis was retained by Argyll/Safeway when the company's other brands were bought by Gibson International. Today, Safeway sells Glen Nevis as an own-label in the UK, and Gibson Distillers has responsibility for foreign sales (*see* FRASER MCDONALD, GLEN CATRINE).

Glen Niven

*Category: Standard Blend **Licensee:** Douglas MacNiven & Co, Leith **Owner:** Glenmorangie plc, Broxburn, West Lothian*

(*see* HIGHLAND QUEEN, JAMES MARTIN'S) Glen Niven is available throughout the world in small quantities.

Glen Rosa

*Category: Standard Blend **Owner:** Isle of Arran Distillers, Stirling.*
(*see* ISLE OF ARRAN)

Glen Rossie

*Category: Standard Blend **Licensee:** Glen Rossie Distilleries, Glasgow **Owner:** Victoria Wine Co*

When Stewart & Son of Dundee (*see* STEWART'S CREAM OF THE BARLEY) joined the Allied Breweries Group in 1969, Glen Rossie Distillers was placed under its control. The latter remained responsible for the brand of the same name in export markets, while it was licensed to another Allied subsidiary, the Victoria Wine Co, in the home market.

Glen Salen

*Category: Standard Blend **Owner:** Whyte & Mackay Ltd, Glasgow*
(*see* WHYTE & MACKAY)

Glen Shee

*Category: Standard Blend **Licensee:** Whitmore & Bayley, London **Owner:** The Invergordon Distillers, Leith*

One of the Angus Glens, reaching north from Blairgowrie into the Grampian Mountains, Glen Shee means "the glen of the fairies". More prosaically, it has been a popular ski resort for over twenty years. Until 1993, when it passed to Invergordon, the brand was owned by Findlater Mackie Todd & Co, the well-known firm of London wine and spirits merchants (*see* FINDLATER'S FINEST).

Glen Side

*Category: Standard Blend **Owner:** Thresher, Welwyn Garden City*

In 1911, Glenside, a bay gelding with a pronounced blaze, was ridden to victory in the Grand National by one of the few amateur jockeys in the race, Jack Anthony. Glenside was the only horse to complete the race without mishap, a remarkable achievement as he was marked number thirteen and started at odds of 20–1! This blend is sold exclusively through the UK off-licence chain, Thresher.

Glen Stag

*Category: Standard Blend **Owner:** Whyte & Mackay Ltd, Glasgow*
(*see* WHYTE & MACKAY)

Glen Stuart

*Category: Standard Blend & Vatted Malt **Owner:** W. Brown & Sons, Glasgow*

Both the grandfather and great-grandfather of William Brown had been spirits merchants in Glasgow, and when he set up his own company in 1976, his aim was to concentrate exclusively on export markets. The firm is family owned and controlled (four of Brown's sons currently sit on the board), and as well as exporting Scotch whisky, it imports and bottles Jamaican rum, gin, and vodka.

Several of Brown's brands were bought from The Stuart Whisky Co in the late 1970s, and have been registered for many years (included Glen Stuart, the company's leading brand); none of them is available in the home market.

Glentromie

Category: Vatted Malt **Owner:** *Speyside Distillery Co, Glasgow*

The Speyside Distillery is situated on the banks of the River
Tromie, near Kingussie (*see* SPEYSIDE) – hence the name of its
vatted malt, which is largely composed of Highland malts and
sells mainly in France, Japan, and the USA.

Glenturret Malt Liqueur

Category: Whisky Liqueur **Licensee:** *Glenturret Distillery, Crieff*
Owner: *The Edrington Group, Glasgow*

(*see* FAMOUS GROUSE, GLENTURRET)

Gold Blend

Category: Standard Blend **Owner:** *Kinross Whisky Co, Haywards
Heath, Sussex*

Kinross is a family company, founded in 1970 by John Stoppani,
his wife, and sons, following research into export whisky markets.
Gold Blend and the company's other brands are currently
available in Europe, the Far East, parts of Africa, and Ecuador.

Gold Label

Category: Standard Blend **Owner:** *Red Lion Blending Co,
London*

The main markets for this whisky, the creation of which – like all
the company's products – is personally supervised by the two
owners of the company, are the Far East, South America, Europe,
and Japan (*see* DINER'S).

Golden Cap

Category: Standard Blend **Owner:** *J.C. & R.H. Palmer, Bridport,
Dorset*

The brand is named after the highest point on the south coast of
England, Golden Cap cliff, and was first created in the 1930s by
H.R.C. Palmer. J.C. & R.H. Palmer are brewers in the West Country
and sell their brand through their tenanted public houses, to the
free trade, and through their own off-trade Wine Store, which
is adjacent to the brewery. Golden Cap is available only in west
Dorset, east Devon, and southeast Somerset, in which parts it
has a devoted following.

The Golden Drop

Category: Premium Blend **Owner:** *JW Kerr, The Canny Man's,
Edinburgh*

The Canny Man's public house is an Edinburgh institution. It was
founded in 1871 by the great-great-grandfather of the present
owner, Watson Kerr. This blend was first made and bottled the
same year in the cellars of the bar – known then as "The
Volunteer's Rest" (the original seal from this inn "authenticates
each bottle") – and is "unchanged from father to son".

A letter from The Glenlivet and Glen Grant Agencies in
1970 notes that the bar had taken delivery of three casks of The
Glenlivet 1958 and three from 1959. "If you feel that either or both
of these parcels are surplus to your requirements, we would be
very pleased to offer 62/6d per original proof gallon for the 1958s
and 60/- ppg for the 1959s. Since this is a matter of considerable

importance, we look forward to receiving an early reply. Sgd Ivan Straker (Managing Director)." They were not returned.

Mr Kerr recommends his blend on the rocks with Apollinaris Sparkling Table Water ("a favourite in the bar since the 1950s") as an early evening drink. I would not dare to suggest otherwise.

James Gordon's

*Category: Premium Blend **Licensee:** James Gordon & Co, Elgin* ***Owner:*** *Gordon & MacPhail, Elgin*

(*see* MacPhail's) James Gordon went into partnership with John Alexander MacPhail in 1895 as "Italian warehousemen". Whisky blending and bottling was an important part of their business from early on, and the firm also had a broking side which dealt in mature whiskies. This was named James Gordon & Co.

Grand MacNish

*Category: Standard and De Luxe Blends **Owner:** Macduff International, Glasgow*

The Grand MacNish was created by Robert McNish (the name of the whisky was given an extra letter to make it easier to pronounce), a licensed grocer specializing in tea, tobacco and whisky, who established his business in York Street, Glasgow, in 1863. It was his goal to create a blend that was lighter than usual but which had the appearance of a mature malt. Over 40 different whiskies went into his recipe and the result was a product much lighter-bodied than single Highland malt, but with a full flavour.

Robert McNish died in 1904 and was succeeded by his two sons, John and George, who formed a limited company in 1908, moved to larger premises and laid down a large stock of maturing whisky. John, who had a flair for salesmanship and entertaining, moved to London; George remained in Glasgow to supervise production. He served in the Highland Light Infantry during the First World War, rising to the rank of colonel, and was awarded the CBE in 1919. On his return to civilian life, he resumed his business activities, local government and charity work, becoming Deputy Lord Lieutenant for the City of Glasgow and a JP. He died in 1943, aged seventy-seven. Colonel McNish renamed his brand "Grand" MacNish, simply because so many of his friends referred to it as "grr-and" whisky! He also adopted the motto *Forti Nihil Difficile* ("to the strong, nothing is difficult") which was included when the company's arms were registered in 1945.

In 1927, the company was sold to Canadian Industrial Alcohol of Montreal (which changed its name to Corby Distilleries in 1950), but remained based in Scotland. Export sales of Grand MacNish, in North America and elsewhere, were boosted considerably by the sale.

In 1967, Corby authorized Hiram Walker (Scotland) to manage the brand (*see* Ballantine's). During the reorganization which followed Hiram Walker's merger with Allied Vintners, Grand MacNish was dropped, along with Lauder's. In 1991, both brands were sold to Macduff International, which has relaunched them in export markets. They are especially successful in the

Pacific Rim and India, and widely available in duty-free outlets.
(see MacDUFF)

William Grant's

Category: Standard Blend Owner: William Grant & Sons, Glasgow

William Grant & Sons prospered in family ownership for five
generations, and although the descendants of the eponymous
William Grant recently appointed non-family members to the
board, they still retain a close interest. The appropriately named
Family Reserve (formerly Grants Standfast) is the fourth best-
selling whisky in the world. Over the past decade, sales have
grown by fifty-seven per cent (while total Scotch whisky sales have
declined by twelve per cent). It has been particularly successful
in France, where sales rose from three million bottles in 1988 to
nearly eight million bottles in 1991, and is showing growth in
markets as diverse as Spain, Portugal, Greece, Canada, and
South America.

The brand came about as a result of a crisis. William Grant and
his nine children had established the Glenfiddich and Balvenie
distilleries in the 1880s and 1890s (see GLENFIDDICH). Their principal
customer was Pattison's of Leith, one of the largest blenders and
wholesalers in the country, which unexpectedly collapsed in 1898.
To avoid the same fate, the family decided to blend and market their
own whisky, and named it with the Grant battle-cry, "Standfast".

William Grant's son-in-law, Charles Gordon, became sales
manager; it is said that after 503 visits in Glasgow, he had sold only
a single case! But gradually, his perseverance paid off.

In 1904, an office was opened in Blackburn, Lancashire; in
1905, another member of the family was despatched to Canada
and the USA with instructions to set up distribution networks; and
in 1909, Charles Gordon embarked on a year-long tour of the Far
East. By 1914, William Grant & Sons had established sixty agencies
in thirty countries.

In 1957, the company sought a way to distinguish its product on
the shelf and came up with the now-familiar triangular bottle. There
is a tradition in Sweden that this unusual bottle was designed by
Prince Sigvard Bernadotte, brother of the king, and himself an
eminent designer. This helped fix the brand in customers'
memories, and the move was so successful that William Grant &
Sons built its own grain distillery at Girvan in Ayrshire in 1963 – at
the time, the largest and most technically advanced distillery in
Europe – and another malt distillery on the same site (see
LADYBURN). A fourth malt distillery was opened in 1990 at Kininvie,
within the Glenfiddich/Balvenie complex at Dufftown.

Family Reserve was the fastest-growing blend worldwide in
1996, and stands at number four in the world, selling 4.2 million
equivalent cases (i.e. 8.4 million litres) a year. Superior Strength
sells worldwide but in duty-free only; Classic won "Best Blended
Whisky" and a gold medal at the 1990 International Wine & Spirit
Competition awards, and another gold in 1993. It was repackaged
in 1996 and sells well in South America.

Grierson's No 1

Category: Vatted Malt Owner: Grierson's, London

Grierson's is a well-known company of wine shippers and
merchants, and a major supplier to the hotel and restaurant
trade. The company was established in 1820 with a shop in
the Strand, London.

Haig

Category: Standard and De Luxe Blends **Licensee:** *John Haig &
Co, Clackmannan and London (Haig currently licensed to Whyte &
Mackay in the UK)* **Owner:** *Diageo plc*

(*see also* PINCH, DIMPLE)

With good reason, the Haig family is described as "the oldest name
in Scotch whisky". Connections with whisky distilling go back to at
least 1655, when Robert Haig, a farmer at Throsk in Stirlingshire
(and the younger son of the ancient Bemersyde Haigs), was
summoned before the Kirk Session for distilling on the sabbath. It
is supposed that he had been making whisky for his own domestic
use since 1627, when he arrived at Throsk.

In 1751, Robert's great-great-grandson John married
Margaret Stein, whose family had established successful
distilleries at Kilbagie and Kennetpans in Clackmannanshire. John
Haig died in 1773, leaving Margaret with five sons. All were
trained in their uncle's distilleries, and in time established their
own distilleries in Edinburgh, Leith, Kincardine, Seggie (near
Guardbridge in Fife), and Dublin.

In the 1770s, Kilbagie was the largest distillery in Scotland. By
1784, the Haig and Stein families were exporting 400,000 gallons
(1.8 million litres) of whisky a year – mainly to London (where most
of it was "rectified" into gin) and made mainly from grain imported
from Europe (harvests had been poor in Scotland in the early
1780s, and the distilleries had even been attacked by mobs).

In 1824, a grandson of John Haig (also named John) built a
grain distillery at Cameronbridge in Fife, installing (in 1827) the
recently invented Stein Patent Stills (*see* CAMERON BRIG).
Production was immense, and led to amalgamation with other
grain distillers to form DCL in 1877. John and one of his sons
became directors of the new company; another son became
company secretary.

John Haig & Co had been producing blended whisky since
the 1860s, and by John Haig's death in 1878, the company was
producing over a million gallons (over 4.5 million litres) annually.
The blending side was transferred to Markinch, three miles from
Cameronbridge, and in 1894, John's youngest son, Captain
Douglas Haig, joined the board.

Douglas Haig was to become commander-in-chief of the
British Forces in France in 1916 and a field marshal. He was
created Earl Haig after the war, became chairman of the family
business in the 1920s, died in 1928, and was buried in Dryburgh
Abbey – a privilege that has been enjoyed by the Haig family since
the thirteenth century. Beside him is the tomb of Sir Walter Scott.

In spite of being one of the moving forces behind DCL, John Haig & Co only merged with the larger company in 1919. By 1939, Haig was the best-selling whisky in the UK, supported by its well-known slogan "Don't be vague, ask for Haig". Today, it ranks thirteenth in the UK and twentieth in the world. In 1986, the UK rights to the brand were sold to Whyte & Mackay, the rest of the world being controlled by UDV.

Hamashkeh

Category: Kosher Blend **Owner:** *Whyte & Mackay, Glasgow*

This and Prince London (*see* entry) are the only kosher Scotch whiskies I am aware of, prepared according to Jewish ordinances to make sure it is not tainted with anything which is deemed "impure".

The most important element in the preparation is that the individual malt and grain whiskies which comprise the blend must be drawn only from casks that have not contained wine – so sherry cask maturation is out. A kosher supervisor is in attendance at all stages of blending and bottling. He checks the cask histories and watches while they are disgorged and the blending vat filled. He checks what the blending vat is cleaned with (going back to the supplier of the cleaning agent), checks the composition of any colourant (*i.e.* caramel) which is added, applies his seal across the bung of the casks in which the blend is married, and later unseals them in the bottling hall, when the blend is bottled.

Hankey Bannister

Category: Standard and De Luxe Blends **Licensee:** *Hankey Bannister & Co* **Owner:** *Inver House Distillers, Airdrie, Lanarkshire*

Hankey Bannister (wine and spirit merchants) was established in the fashionable West End of London in 1757. The company enjoyed royal and aristocratic patronage (customers included the Prince Regent, King William IV, and the Dukes of Norfolk and Queensberry), and began marketing its own blended whisky in the 1890s. The old-established wine and spirits company, Saccone & Speed, which bought the company in 1932 and which had long associations with the armed forces, extended the brand's cachet by introducing it into diplomatic circles, army messes, and naval ward rooms. Today, Hankey Bannister is owned by Inver House, which has succeeded in doubling its market in recent years, selling large quantities in South Africa, France, and Holland as well as in the UK (*see* INVER HOUSE).

Hart's

Category: Standard Blend **Owner:** *Donald Hart & Co, Glasgow*

This company was formed after Hart Brothers (Vintners) (established in 1967) went into receivership in 1985. There is also an associate company, Hart Brothers (1988), which is used to market the exclusive 31 Years Old Bowmore Dynasty Decanter.

Harvey's Special

Category: Standard Blend **Licensee:** *John & Robert Harvey, Glasgow* **Owner:** *Diageo plc*

John and Robert Harvey set up first as grocers and wine merchants, then as distillers (at Dundashill) in Glasgow in 1770. The firm began to blend its own whiskies about 100 years later, but was badly hit by the collapse of Pattison's of Leith in 1898, and applied to join DCL. At the time, DCL was engaged in other negotiations, so did not acquire Harvey's share capital until 1902, by which time Dundashill Distillery had closed. DCL did not reopen it, since at that time the industry was suffering from over-production.

Harvey's is blended for the USA (shipped in bulk) and for Israel (bottled in Scotland). Rare bottles can be found in the UK on-trade.

Heatherdale

*Category: Standard Blend **Licensee:** (in UK) Co-operative Wholesale Society (CWS), Manchester **Owner:** (worldwide) Invergordon Distillers, Leith*

A respectable own-label, blended and married for CWS at Invergordon. CWS also has a twelve-year-old vatted malt that is made by Invergordon Distillers (see GLENFAIRN).

Hedges & Butler Royal

*Category: Standard and De Luxe Blends and Vatted Malt **Licensee:** Hedges & Butler **Owner:** Peter J. Russell, Broxburn, Midlothian*

Hedges & Butler was established in 1667 as a firm of wine shippers and blenders and has enjoyed the patronage of the royal household since the reign of Charles II. Its services to royalty extend beyond Europe: the company can boast eleven past royal warrants, including that of the Emperor of Japan. Hedges & Butler began blending and exporting whisky after the First World War, and the Royal range has had a good reputation as premium whisky for some years. The company also produces a vatted malt. Royal Malt is not available in Britain although it is well-established in the European export market.

High Commissioner

*Category: Standard Blend **Licensee:** A Bulloch & Co, Eaglesham, Glasgow **Owner:** Glen Catrine Bonded Warehouse, Catrine, Ayrshire*

This blend is the company's biggest-selling brand in the UK market (see GLEN CATRINE).

Highland Blend

*Category: Premium Blend **Owner:** Avery's of Bristol, Bristol*

Bristol has always been one of England's major ports, and has long had trading links with Europe. The city's records show that in 1726, casks of wine captured from French ships were auctioned at an old coaching-inn close to the harbour, and this inn subsequently became the premises of Avery's (1793). A hundred years later, the firm was described as "having a leading position in the trade of Bristol and a high reputation for quality". Avery's great reputation was, and is, based upon its French wines (principally from Bordeaux and Burgundy), sherries, and madeiras.

The first members of the family mentioned in the records were

Joseph (who had been a customs officer) and his sons, Joseph
Clark and John. In 1923, Ronald Avery, John's grandson, joined
the successful family business and set about expanding it,
building up a tremendous stock of wines and creating the
company's reputation as shippers and blenders. The company's
very considerable wine-blending experience was later turned to
whisky, although its most distinguished brands – Queen
Elizabeth and Highland Blend – are now blended and bottled for
the firm (owing to restrictions being placed upon independent
bottlers in the early 1980s). Each of these blends retains an
unusual, old-fashioned style: the only other blend I have
encountered with this quality is James Gordon's. Ronald Avery
died in 1976 and was succeeded by his son John (one of the
pioneers of New World wines), who has developed the
company's agency side and established the whisky brands in the
export market, especially in Japan.

Highland Clan

Category: Standard Blend Owner: Chivas Bros, Paisley.
(see CHIVAS REGAL)

Highland Fusilier

Category: Vatted Malt Owner: Gordon & MacPhail, Elgin
(see MACPHAIL'S) The Royal Highland Fusiliers regiment was
formed in 1959 by the amalgamation of the Royal Scots Fusiliers
(the 21st Fusiliers) and the Highland Light Infantry (the 71st and
74th Highlanders). Highland Fusilier was first created to mark
the amalgamation.The 21st was the first Infantry Regiment of the
Line to be raised in Scotland (in 1678); the 71st was the first Clan
Regiment, raised in 1777 by John Mackenzie, Lord MacLeod, and
originally mustered in Elgin; the 74th was a Campbell regiment,
raised in Argyll in 1788.

The brand won double gold awards at the International
Wine & Spirits Competition in 1981, and a gold in 1982.

Highland Gathering

*Category: De Luxe Blend Owner: Lombard Scotch Whisky,
Ramsey, Isle of Man*
Highland Gathering was launched in September 1992 for
worldwide distribution. The label features a painting of
the same name by nineteenth-century artist Louis Boswell
Hurt (1856–1929), in the collection of the Lombard-Chibnell
family, the brand-owners. As well as describing the gathering
of Highland cows depicted in the painting, the brand name
is meant to imply the collection of whiskies that goes into
the blend.

Highland Queen

*Category: Standard, Premium, and De Luxe Blends Licensee:
Macdonald & Muir, Leith Owner: Glenmorangie plc, Broxburn,
West Lothian*
Macdonald & Muir, the licensee to this brand, was founded in
1893 at Leith, the port of Edinburgh, by Roderick Macdonald
and Alexander Muir. Until 1995, the founding family was still

represented on the board by Macdonald's grandson, who was chairman. That year, the company underwent radical internal reorganisation, changed its name to that of its best-known brand, Glenmorangie, and moved from Leith to more spacious premises at Broxburn, to the west of Edinburgh, where blending and bottling are also undertaken.

Until the 1980s, Highland Queen was the company's leading product. The brand was named after Mary, Queen of Scots, who landed at Leith in 1561 from France. Recently widowed (she had been married to the king of France), she was about to succeed her father as King of Scots. She was eighteen years old, beautiful and passionate. The labels of all three expressions depict Mary riding a white palfrey.

Highland Queen was one of the early blends to be sold in Mexico, Egypt, Scandinavia, and parts of South America and the Far East. It also enjoyed a high reputation in the critical Scottish market, although it is not as common now as it once was.

Today, it sells in forty-three countries. Majesty and Queen of Scots were lavishly repackaged in 1994 for the Far East Asian markets.

Highland Stag

Category: Standard Blend Licensee: R.N. MacDonald & Co Owner: Red Lion Blending Co, London

R.N. MacDonald & Co was founded in 1970 by Major Andrew MacDonald, the direct descendent of "Long" John MacDonald – one of the best-known characters in the Scotch whisky industry, who established the Ben Nevis Distillery at Fort William. In 1982, the company was acquired by Highland Stag Whiskies. Highland Stag is marketed exclusively through Aldi supermarkets in England and is distributed in France by Champagne Deutz (*see* DINER'S).

Highland Woodcock

Category: Standard Blend Owner: J.T. Davies, Croydon, Surrey

J.T. Davies & Sons is a family business, established in 1875. Its eponymous founder died in 1913, when he was succeeded by his two sons. One of them, Alfred, built up the firm and then became personal private secretary to Lloyd George during the First World War. He was MP for Lincoln from 1918 to 1926, was knighted in 1933, and died in 1942. His sons, John and Anthony, joined the firm before the Second World War; John was killed in 1940 leading a Polish Hurricane squadron.

At the end of the war, Anthony returned to head the company and proceeded to expand the business to eighty wine shops (under the "Davisons" name), a managed and tenanted public-house estate, and a wholesale division serving the Greater London area.

Holy Island Cream Liqueur

Category: Liqueur Whisky Owner: Isle of Arran Distillers, Stirling
(*see* ISLE OF ARRAN)

House of Lords

Category: De Luxe Blends **Licensee:** *William Whiteley & Co,
Pitlochry* **Owner:** *Campbell Distillers, Brentford, Middlesex*

The company was founded in 1922 by William Whiteley, a Leith
whisky blender who had inherited the family firm from his
grandfather (the latter having set up business in the mid-
nineteenth century). Whiteley, known as "the Dean of Distillers",
was one of the characters of the industry in his day. He was
highly respected as a blender and was ahead of his time as a
marketing man (*see* EDRADOUR). One of his ploys was to create
a blend especially for the House of Lords, and then to market
it overseas so successfully that it was soon in demand in ninety-
four countries. He also managed to persuade the College of Arms
to grant his company a coat of arms which uses the griffons
of Westminster as supporters.

Today, these blends are only available in the UK in the
House of Lords. However, they are available in some export
markets and have proved especially popular in the USA, Latin
America, and Paraguay.

House of Peers

Category: De Luxe Blend and Super-de Luxe Blend; Vatted Malt
Owner: *Douglas Laing & Co, Glasgow*

Douglas Laing & Co maintains that it is able to use unusually
old malt fillings in its blends, yet still sell them at a manageable
price, by using young (and therefore cheaper) grain fillings
(*see* KING OF SCOTS). The brand has been marketed since 1947
and is presented in a traditional style of bottle, known as a
"mason's mallet" (Old Parr uses the same style, but it is
dark green).

The whiskies sold under the House of Peers label are similar
in character, with the malt fillings becoming progressively older.
Several of the malts in the twelve-year-old blend are considerably
older than twelve years, and the blend is returned to cask for
marrying. The vatted malt draws constituents from Islay,
Speyside and the Lowlands, each of them aged for at least
twenty-two years.

100 Pipers

Category: Standard Blend **Licensee:** *Joseph E. Seagram & Sons,*
Owner: *Chivas Bros, Paisley*

Until the acquisition of Arthur Bell & Sons by Guinness in 1984
the Seagram Company was the largest producer of alcoholic
beverages in the world.

The Seagrams were farmers and innkeepers from Wiltshire
who emigrated to Canada in the early nineteenth century. The
next generation turned to grain-milling and distilling, and in
1857, Joseph Seagram established the family distilling business in
Waterloo, Ontario. The founder has been described (by P.C.
Newman) as "a pompous and flamboyant man, who modelled
himself on Edward VII", and his company soon became the
largest distiller of Canadian rye whisky.

After Joseph Seagram's death, control of the company was divided between his family, and in 1928, his own shares were acquired by The Distillers Corporation of Canada. This company was headed by one of the great figures of the whisky industry, Samuel Bronfman.

Bronfman's first involvement with wines and spirits was as an interprovincial mail-order distributor: an arrangement whereby he bought quantities of wines and spirits directly from distillers and vintners and sold them by mail order to individual homes. This system ended in the 1920s, when the provincial governments took over the sale of alcohol in their areas, so Bronfman decided to build his own distillery at La Salle, a suburb of Montreal.

During the First World War, Canadian distilleries were closed down and the only whisky available was Scotch. In order to retain this market after the war, Bronfman invited DCL of Scotland to buy shares in The Distillers Corporation, and by this move he secured not only supplies of Scotch, but also the licences to several popular brand names.

By 1928, when he bought Seagram, Bronfman was convinced that Prohibition in the USA would end shortly. He increased production at both La Salle and Waterloo, built warehouses and began to assemble a huge stock of maturing whiskies.

At this time, DCL decided to concentrate its energies on Scottish distilling and exports and sold its shares back to Bronfman. A few years earlier, Bronfman had travelled to Scotland to pursue his interests in Scotch whisky; with the help of his friend James Barclay (see BALLANTINE'S), he purchased the Robert Brown Co and began to lay down stocks of Scotch.

In 1949, he bought Chivas Brothers (see CHIVAS REGAL), and Milton/Strathisla Distillery (see STRATHISLA). He also bought land at Keith, Paisley, and Dalmuir on Clydeside. On these sites he built warehouses and blending and bottling plants. Paisley is now Seagram's headquarters in Scotland, and holds one of the largest stocks of Scotch whisky in the world.

In 1957, the Corporation built Glen Keith Distillery and bond; Braes of Glenlivet followed in 1973 and Alt a'Bhainne in 1975. This portfolio of distinguished distilleries was completed with the acquisition of The Glenlivet Distilleries in 1978 (see THE GLENLIVET).

100 Pipers was first introduced in 1965 as a price-competitive, popular blend, although it includes Glenlivet, Glen Grant, and Longmorn among its fillings. It ranks among the top twenty world brands today. The name derives from the dreadful Scottish song of the same name, which begins:

Wi' a hundred pipers an' a', an' a' . . .

We'll up an' gie 'em a blaw a blaw

100 Pipers is available through Oddbins' outlets (a subsidiary of Seagram). Key export markets include Latin America, Spain, and the Far East.

Huntly

Category: Standard Blend **Licensee:** *Huntly Blending Company, Hurleford* **Owner:** *Diageo plc*

Huntly Blending Company is a subsidiary of Slater, Rodger & Co (*see* RODGER'S). Huntly's markets are Hungary, the former Yugoslavia, and the Lebanon.

Immortal Memory

Category: Premium Blend (8 Years Old) **Owner:** *Gordon & MacPhail, Elgin*

(*see* MACPHAIL'S) Immortal Memory was chosen as the Best Blended Whisky in the 1991 International Wine & Spirit Competition awards.

The name commemorates Robert Burns, who is traditionally toasted on Burns Night (January 25, the poet's birthday) with a speech entitled "The Immortal Memory".

Inverarity

Category: Premium Blend, Single Malt **Owner:** *Inverarity Vaults, Edinburgh*

A small, independent wine and spirits company, established in 1991 by Professor Ronnie Martin, former production director with United Distillers, and his son Hamish. Inverarity was Professor Martin's mother's name.

As well as the blend, the firm bottles Aultmore under its own label and has the Scottish agency for Ruinart Champagne and several wines.

Inver House Green Plaid

Category: Standard Blend **Owner:** *Inver House Distillers, Airdrie, Lanarkshire*

Inver House Distillers was established in 1965 by the American distiller, Publicker Industries of Philadelphia. At the time of its foundation, it was given a new distilling complex, the Moffat Distilleries (originally known as Garnheath), which was situated on the site of a disused paper mill some three miles from Airdrie, in central Scotland.

Equipped with five continuous stills, the new distillery produced plain spirit and grain whisky, and within the complex was a pair of pot stills producing Glen Flagler and Killyloch malt whiskies (*see* entries).

Between 1973 and 1983, Inver House Distillers also owned Bladnoch Distillery, Wigtown (when it was sold to Arthur Bell & Sons). Whisky production at Moffat Distilleries ceased in 1985, but the firm continued to blend and market spirits and to produce gin and vodka. In 1988, the company was purchased by its management, and the following year Inver House, in turn, purchased Knockdhu Distillery, Banffshire. It added to its acquisitions by buying Speyburn Distillery, Rothes, in 1992, followed by Pulteney Distillery, Wick, in 1995, Balblair Distillery, Edderton, in 1996, and the distinguished Balmenach Distillery at Cromdale (Speyside) in 1998.

Ninety-five per cent of Inver House's sales are made overseas, and in 1992 the company was awarded the Queens' Award for Export Achievement.

Iona Royale

Category: Deluxe Blend **Owner:** *J&G Grant, Ballindalloch, Speyside*

Iona Royale is a twenty-five year-old de luxe blend with Glenfarclas at its heart. (*see* GLENFARCLAS).

Islander

Category: Standard Blend **Licensee:** *Arthur Bell & Sons, Perth* **Owner:** *Diageo plc*

(*see* BELL'S) Islander was introduced in the late 1980s, supported by substantial advertising. The blend uses a high proportion of Islay, Skye, and Oban malts, which impart, a slightly smoky flavour.

Islay Legend

Category: Standard Blend **Owner:** *Morrison Bowmore Distillers, Glasgow*

This blend has a high malt content, mainly from the Bowmore Distillery on Islay, and its main market is in France (*see* ROB ROY).

Islay Mist

Category: Vatted Malt **Owner:** *Macduff International, Glasgow*

Laphroaig Distillery on Islay was founded in 1815 by the Johnston family, who retained ownership until 1962 (*see* LAPHROAIG). Islay Mist – a blend of Islay and Highland malt whiskies – was created by them in 1928 to mark the twenty-first birthday of the Laird of Islay House, Lord Margadale. It bears the seal of the Lord of the Isles (whose stronghold was in Islay) on its label, has a distinctive salty/smoky flavour reminiscent of Laphroaig, and was originally blended at that distillery. The brand was acquired by Macduff International in 1991 (*see* MACDUFF).

Isle of Skye

Category: Premium and De Luxe Blends **Licensee:** *Ian MacLeod & Co, Broxburn, East Lothian* **Owner:** *Peter J. Russell & Co, Broxburn, East*

The Isle of Skye is the heartland of Clan MacLeod, and the blend was originally created in Skye by Ian MacLeod (whose grandson is still a consultant to the company) about 100 years ago. The label depicts the entrance to Loch Scavaig on the southwest coast of the island, together with the bull-and-flag crest of the MacLeods. Ian MacLeod & Co was incorporated in 1934.

The blend is made from Island and Speyside malts, and is allowed to marry for at least six months subsequent to blending. The flavour its creator was looking for was "a taste of home" – hence the peaty notes, with oaky overtones in the younger expressions. The Standard Blend is of eight-year-old malts and four-year-old grains. The eighteen-year-old blend has a delicious nutty, oaky aroma and boasts the full-bodied flavour one would expect of an elegant old whisky (*see also* CHIEFTAIN'S CHOICE).

J&B Jet

Category: Premium Blend **Owner:** *Diageo plc*

This is a premium expression of J&B Rare. The company owns

three Speyside distilleries, and over eighty per cent of the malt content in the brand is from that region.

J&B Rare and Reserve

Category: Standard Blend; De Luxe Blend **Licensee:** *Justerini & Brooks, London* **Owner:** *Diageo plc*

Together with Englishman George Johnson, Giacomo Justerini, from Bologna, established his business in 1749 as a wine merchant in London. Eleven years later, the firm was awarded what was to be the first of many royal warrants, and in 1779, it placed the earliest-known advertisement for Scotch whisky (*i.e. uisge beatha*) in the *London Morning Post*. George Johnson was killed by a runaway horse in 1785; he was succeeded by his son, Augustus. In 1831, the company was bought by Alfred Brooks, and it has been known as "Justerini & Brooks" ever since. In the 1880s, it was among the first London firms to buy up stocks of old whisky in Scotland and create a superior blend (*see* CLUB).

J&B Rare was created in the early 1930s specifically to appeal to the US market. From 1937, the agent for the brand was the Buckingham Corporation, which had been established in 1933 (as soon as Prohibition was lifted) by a former Prohibition enforcement officer and an Irish property speculator. It was heavily promoted in and around New York. Market growth was interrupted by the Second World War, but by the late 1950s, the brand had conquered America, where it is still a top-seller. With this secure base, the company appointed distributors and agents throughout the world, and J&B Rare is today the number-two best-seller in the world, available in over 150 markets and still growing. The company received the Queen's Award for Export Achievement in 1972, 1973, 1977, 1985, and 1989.

In the early 1950s, J&B pooled its assets with another company to form United Wine Traders. Ten years later, this company merged with W&A Gilbey to form Independent Distillers & Vintners (IDV) – a merger which facilitated J&B Rare's promotion in export markets. In 1972, IDV was acquired by the hotel and catering giant, Grand Metropolitan. In 1998, Grand Met merged with Guinness to become the world's largest drinks conglomerate, Diageo plc.

J&B Rare is blended from forty-two individual whiskies at Strath-leven (the headquarters of J&B Scotland). The brand has a base of Speysides, including aged products from Knockando, Auchroisk, Glen Spey, and Strathmill, and this accounts for its delicate flavour.

Jackson's Row

Category: Vatted Malt **Owner:** *Diageo plc*

The major whisky companies have been obsessed in recent years by winning the support of a "lost generation" of younger drinkers in the home market. Jackson's Row is one of the ploys to achieve this by the leading player in the industry, UDV. It is a very pale, light-flavoured whisky, designed to be drunk either straight (ice-cold in a shot glass, like vodka) or with mixers. It is said that the heart of the blend is Glenkinchie (*see* entry).

The Jacobite
Category: Standard Blend **Licensee:** *Independent Cellars*
Owner: *Nurdin & Peacock, London*

First created in 1983 to compete in the cut-price marketplace of
British cash-and-carries, The Jacobite has built a strong position
among independent retailers, supported by continual promotions.

The blend was created for Nurdin & Peacock by Invergordon
and employs forty-seven malts. It sets out to be good value for
money, with a distinctive character.

Jamie Stuart
Category: Standard Blend **Owner:** *Whyte & Mackay Ltd, Glasgow*
(*See* WHYTE & MACKAY)

Jock ("The Formidable Jock")
Category: Standard Blend **Licensee:** *The Bennachie Whisky Co,
Inverurie, Aberdeen* **Owner:** *International Multibrand Products,
Keith, Aberdeenshire*

The blurb for this brand, which sells only in export markets, is
worth quoting:

"It is said in Inverurie that of all the Highland cattle in
Scotland, the most famous was the Highland Steer known as
'Black Jock', so called because of his distinctive coat of long
black hair – rare in Highland cattle . . . Black Jock was a gentle
giant, who loved to graze with the new season's calves. Like
Black Jock, 'The Formidable Jock' Scotch Whisky is known for
its rare blend of strength and smooth character . . . A Highlander
with a great pedigree."

Jock Scott
Category: Standard Blend **Owner:** *Whyte & Mackay Ltd, Glasgow*

John o'Groat's
Category: Standard blend **Owner:** *The Drambuie Liqueur Co,
Edinburgh*

John o'Groat's is the northernmost village on mainland Britain.
In 1495, Jan de Groot and his two brothers arrived in Caithness
and were granted lands at Canisbay by James IV. The family, of
which there were eight branches, met annually to celebrate their
arrival in the north of Scotland. At one of these meetings there
was a dispute about which branch was senior, and therefore
who should sit at the head of the table closest to the door. John
de Groat (the name was now Anglicized) solved the problem by
building a house with eight doors in which he placed an octagonal
table. The house later gave its name to the district (*see* DRAMBUIE)
as well as to this brand.

King George IV
Category: Standard Blend **Licensee:** *The Distillers Agency,
Edinburgh* **Owner:** *Diageo plc*

Created by DCL in the early 1880s as an export brand, KG IV, as
it became known, was registered and licensed to Distillers' export
branch, which became the Distillers' Agency in 1924. It is the
best-selling brand in Denmark, thanks largely to the efforts of its
distributor, Hans Just & Co, which was founded in 1867 and has

represented KG IV since 1899. The brand also sells in territories as far flung as French Guiana, South Africa, and Surinam.

George IV's trip to Edinburgh in 1822 was the first visit to Scotland by a British monarch for nearly 200 years. The king was received with all the ceremony and pageantry that Sir Walter Scott (in charge of proceedings) could discover or invent. Much of the mythology of Highland custom and dress accepted today as ancient tradition was invented for the occasion.

The king was handed a glass of whisky as he landed (*see* GLENLIVET) and enjoyed several more during his visit. Walter Scott, who had arranged the visit, begged to be allowed to keep the glass from which the king had his first taste of whisky; he put it in his coat-tail pocket and later sat on it!

It is arguable that the attention drawn to "things Scotch" by "The King's Jaunt" made it easier, the following year, for the Duke of Gordon to persuade Parliament to pass the Excise Act which laid the foundations for the modern whisky industry.

The portrait of King George IV on the label is from a painting by Sir Thomas Lawrence which hangs in the Pinacoteca Vaticana in Rome.

King Henry VIII

Category: Standard Blend **Licensee:** *Highland Blending Co*
Owner: *The Premier Scotch Whisky Co, Glasgow*

This brand and its sister, Queen Mary I, were registered in 1953 by Henry Stenham, who traded from London as a one-man whisky merchant. Upon Mr Stenham's retirement in 1996, his business was bought by Rossendale Blenders (International), a family-owned company, and the name was changed to The Premier Scotch Whisky Company (one of Stenham's trading names). Operations were transferred to Glasgow. The brands sell entirely overseas, mainly in Europe and the Far East.

King James VI

Category: Standard Blend **Licensee:** *Redford Bonding Co*
Owner: *Forth Wines, Milnathort, Kinross*

Forth Wines is an independent wholesaler established in 1963. The company sells wines and spirits throughout the UK. King James VI is the firm's own-label brand; it also markets own-labels in other spirits, including gin and vodka.

James VI was the son of Mary, Queen of Scots, and became King James I of England in 1603. The label bears his portrait.

King of Scots

Category: De Luxe Blends **Owner:** *Douglas Laing & Co, Glasgow*

The brand name King of Scots was first registered in the 1880s and was acquired by Douglas Laing & Co in the 1950s. Its market was once almost exclusively in South America; its owner has now achieved a position for it in the Far East and the Pacific Rim. Each of the expressions sold under the brand name is variously packaged in ceramic and crystal decanters – this is considered to be one of the reasons for their success in these markets, and in the duty-free market, where they also do well.

Another reason is the firm's blending policy. Only younger grain whiskies are used in the blends (which make no age statement) and the associated cost savings enable the firm to purchase some very old malts (up to twenty-five years), and to offer the brands at a competitive price against its major competitors.

Douglas Laing & Co is an independent company, wholly owned and directed by members of the Laing family. Established in 1950, it has grown steadily since and was awarded the Queen's Award for Export Achievement in 1990.

King Robert II

Category: Standard Blend; De Luxe Blend **Licensee:** *William Maxwell (Scotch Whisky)* **Owner:** *Ian MacLeod & Co, Broxburn, West Lothian*

King Robert II is part of a range of competitively priced spirits (including vodka and gin). It is a lighter blend of whiskies at four years old, designed for large volume sales in export markets, principally the Middle East, but also in twenty-five other countries. The blend was first created in the 1950s, and the licensee company is part of the Peter J. Russell Group (*see* CHIEFTAIN'S CHOICE).

King Robert II himself was Scotland's first Stewart king (1371–90) – "tall and handsome, though the beauty of his face was marred by bloodshot eyes" – the founder of the most ill-fated of any royal house. Of thirteen successors (down to Bonnie Prince Charlie in the late eighteenth century), only two died peacefully in their beds in their own kingdom – James VI (and I of England) and Charles II.

King's Legend

Category: Standard Blend **Licensee:** *Ainslie & Heilbron (Distillers), Glasgow* **Owner:** *Diageo plc*

(*see* AINSLIE'S) Currently, King's Legend's only market is Norway, although it used to do well in Dubai and Réunion.

King's Pride

Category: Standard and De Luxe Blend **Owner:** *Morrison Bowmore*

(*see* BOWMORE)

Laird o'Cockpen

Category: De Luxe Blend **Licensee:** *Cockburn & Campbell, London* **Owner:** *Diageo plc*

Cockburn & Campbell was established in Edinburgh in the early nineteenth century by members of the Cockburn family of Leith (*see* THE DOMINIE), and began selling whisky in the 1840s. The bonded warehouse on Duke Street in Leith had vaulted cellars well below street level, which had an earthen floor and maintained an even temperature of 50°F (10°C) – conditions which inhibit the loss of whisky during maturation. Indeed, HM Customs was sometimes surprised to find casks "bung full", rather than reduced by several gallons as would be expected.

Langs

Category: Premium Blend; De Luxe Blend **Licensee:** *Lang Brothers* **Owner:** *Peter J. Russell & Co, Broxburn, West Lothian*

Alexander and Gavin Lang commenced business as whisky merchants and blenders in 1861, and their company remained under the control and direction of their successors until it was acquired by another independent firm, Robertson & Baxter, in 1965.

The brothers Lang bought Glengoyne Distillery in 1876, and this light Highland malt has formed the heart of their blends ever since. Langs Supreme is a blend of some twenty-five whiskies, and is married for nine months in oak casks; Langs Select has a high proportion of Speysides, and the youngest of the whiskies used in the blend is twelve years old. Like its sister, it is married in oak casks for at least nine months. The Langs Supreme main market is in the UK. Lang Brothers and Glengoyne Distillery were bought by Peter Russell & Co in 2002.

Lauder's

Category: Standard Blend Licensee: Archibald Lauder & Co, Glasgow Owner: Macduff International, Glasgow

Lauder's is believed to be a brand with a distinguished pedigree, but its history is obscure; the label maintains that the blend was "established in 1837" and is "a fine reminder of the Scotch Whisky of Old". This date, of course, predates the acknowledged origin of blended whisky as we understand it today (1853).

Be this as it may, Lauder's won gold medals at the Edinburgh International Exhibition in 1886, the Manchester Royal Jubilee Exhibition 1887, the Glasgow International Exhibition 1888, the Paris Exhibition 1889, and the Chicago World Columbian Exhibition 1893. The brand, which was bought from Hiram Walker by Macduff International in 1991 (*see* BALLANTINE'S, GRAND MACNISH), has achieved strong positioning in the Swedish, Canadian, Latin American, and western European markets, and more recently in the Pacific Rim markets.

William Lawson's

Category: Standard and De Luxe Blends Licensee: William Lawson Distillers, Coatbridge, Lanarkshire Owner: John Dewar & Sons, Glasgow

This blend was first created in 1849 by William Lawson, a whisky merchant and blender. Today, it is among the twenty best-selling export brands worldwide.

Lawson's initial business failed and remained in abeyance until after the Second World War, when it was moved to Liverpool from whence direct exports could be made. Subsequently, the company moved back to Scotland, where a blending and bottling complex was set up in Coatbridge, near Glasgow. Connections with the Martini-Rossi group gave the brand outlets all over Europe, and it continues to grow in popularity.

The need to secure malt fillings for blending led the firm to buy Macduff Distillery, near Banff on the Moray Firth (1972). The distillery's product is occasionally found in merchant bottlings under its name but is more generally available as Glen Deveron. In 1988 Bacardi Ltd bought John Dewar & Sons through its subsidiary, William Lawson's (*see* DEWARS).

Lismore

*Category: Standard and De Luxe Blends **Owner:** William Lundie & Co, Glasgow*

This small, family-run company of whisky blenders and brokers was founded in 1932 by Robert Donald Lundie, who had learned his trade under David Sandemans, of the well-known wine and spirits family.

Lundie's original company was sold some years later, and other members of the family launched a new venture. This pattern repeated itself, but the company remained under the control of the family, and is now one of the best-regarded broking houses in Scotland. The company has two directors, Bruce and Alan Lundie, both third generation from the founder. They export their brands chiefly to the Far East, North America, and Europe.

Loch Fyne

*Category: Premium Blend **Owner:** Loch Fyne Whiskies, Inveraray, Argyll*

The brand name was first registered in 1884. In the 1950s, it was assigned to the Glenfyne Distillery Co, which sold it in 1996 to Loch Fyne Whiskies of Inveraray in Argyll. The latter was founded by Richard Joynson and Lindsay Shearer in 1993, and is one of the leading whisky shops in Scotland, with an extensive mail-order business and an excellent newsletter, *The Scotch Whisky Review*.

Guided by Professor Ronnie Martin OBE (former director of production with DCL), a new premium blend was created in 1996, which won a bronze award at the International Wine & Spirit Competition the same year.

Loch Lomond

*Category: Standard Blend **Owner:** Loch Lomond Distillery Co Ltd*

Launched in 2003 and sharing the same design of bottle and label as the single malt of the same name, Loch Lomond claims to be the only "single" blended Scotch, since both grain and malt fillings are produced at Loch Lomond distillery.

Lochranza

*Category: Standard Blend **Owner:** The Isle of Arran Distillery Co, Lochranza, Isle of Arran*

(*see* ISLE OF ARRAN) Lochranza is a picturesque village on a bay with a ruined castle in its midst, in the northwest corner of the Isle of Arran. A new distillery opened just outside the village in 1995. Its product was not available as a single until 2001, so in the meantime, the company is issuing a blended whisky.

Logan's De Luxe

*Category: De Luxe Blend **Licensee:** White Horse Distillers, Edinburgh **Owner:** Diageo plc*

(*see* WHITE HORSE) First created by J.L. Mackie & Co in the 1890s; the "Logan" was James Mackie's middle name. The blend was once very popular in Scotland, but is now difficult to find.

Lombard's Gold Label

*Category: Standard Blend **Owner:** Lombard Brands, Ramsay, Isle of Man*

Lombard Scotch Whisky is a small company of brokers, blenders, and exporters – the only one based on the Isle of Man. The company is currently expanding its range of whiskies, but no detailed information is available.

Long John

Category: Standard Blend Licensee: Long John International Owner: Allied Distillers, Dumbarton

"Long" John Macdonald – so called because of his height – established the first legal distillery in the Fort William area, Ben Nevis, in 1825. He had previously been a small farmer, but could trace his ancestry back to Somerled, King of the Isles, through the Macdonalds of Keppoch. His great-grandfather had fought for the Jacobite cause in the 1715 rising, and had rallied the Macdonalds of Keppoch to Bonnie Prince Charlie's banner in 1745. He was killed at Culloden the following year.

Long John's whisky was named Dew of Ben Nevis, and its reputation was made when Queen Victoria visited the distillery in 1848 on one of her Highland tours. *The Illustrated London News* reported: "Mr Macdonald has presented a cask of whisky to Her Majesty and an order has been sent to the Treasury to permit the spirits to be moved to the cellars of Buckingham Palace free of duty. The cask is not to be opened until His Royal Highness the Prince of Wales attains his majority" (*i.e.* fifteen years later).

By the time he died in 1856, Long John was a famous figure in the Highlands. A contemporary traveller wrote: "When a man goes to Caprera, he, as a matter of course, brings a letter of introduction to Garibaldi. When I went to Fort William, I, equally as a matter of course, brought a letter of introduction to Long John . . . I presented my letter and was received with the hospitality and courteous grace so characteristic of the old Gael" (Alexander Smith).

The distillery passed to Long John's son and later to his grandson, who sold the brand name to the London wine and spirits merchant, W.H. Chaplin & Co, but retained the Ben Nevis Distillery. In 1981, the two happily came together again, when Long John International (at that time a subsidiary of Whitbread & Co) acquired Ben Nevis (Fort William). The current owner is Allied Distillers.

Lowrie's

Category: Standard Blend Licensee: W.P. Lowrie & Co, Glasgow Owner: United Distillers

W.P. Lowrie claimed to be the first to blend pot-still malt whisky with patent-still grain whisky, although this distinction is usually accorded to Andrew Usher (*see* USHER'S).

Lowrie had been manager of Port Ellen Distillery in Islay, and in 1869, started in business on his own account as a whisky broker and agent. His company was apparently the first to be granted permission from the Customs and Excise to bottle in bond, although this had been allowed by Gladstone's Spirit Act of 1860. The company also had its own cooperage (the largest in the world at the time), its own case-making works, its own bottle manufactory, and an extensive transport fleet.

To complete its requirements, W.P. Lowrie bought Convalmore Distillery (1904) and a substantial holding in Glentauchers Distillery. The latter was owned by Lowrie's friend, James Buchanan, and when Lowrie retired he invited Buchanan to chair the company. When Buchanan's joined DCL in 1906, Lowrie & Co went, too.

Lowrie's is not currently being shipped, although the brand is still available in some export markets.

MacAndrew's

*Category: Standard Blend **Licensee:** Alistair Graham, Leith **Owner:** Glenmorangie plc, Broxburn, West Lothian*

The brand was named after Lord Douglas MacAndrew, a colourful character who lived during the nineteenth century near Inverness. The label depicts him riding what appears to be a unicorn (he was a noted horseman) outside his home.

MacArthur's

*Category: Standard Blend **Licensee:** J. MacArthur Jr & Co* *Owner: Inver House Distillers, Airdrie, Lanarkshire*

MacArthur's Select Scotch was first created in 1877, but it became prominent in the 1970s as a secondary brand. It sold principally through supermarkets in the UK at a lower price than was normal, and caused a number of leading blenders to introduce similar "fighting brands". It is now available internationally, and does particularly well in France and Holland.

McCallum's Perfection

*Category: Standard Blend **Licensee:** D&J McCallum, Edinburgh* *Owner: Diageo plc*

The brothers Duncan and John McCallum went into business together in Edinburgh as innkeepers and wine and spirits merchants in 1807. Their base of operations happened to be a pub known as the Tattie Pit, which was soon expanded to include a shop and warehouse. By 1914, the McCallums numbered many members of the Scottish aristocracy among their customers.

Sadly, the pub was utterly demolished in April 1916, during the only zeppelin bombing raid of the First World War that took Edinburgh as its target.

Long before this date, however, the company had passed to the brothers' nephew (they had remained bachelors), Duncan McCallum Stewart, who set about selling his brands overseas rather than in the home market.

McCallum's Perfection was introduced in 1911, and became a favourite in Australia (where the company established an office in Sydney) as well as in New Zealand. It is one of only two brands described as "Scots" whisky (the other is Cutty Sark).

McCallum joined DCL in 1937. Perfection is available in the UK, but its principal market is in Thailand. Secondary markets are in New Zealand, Montserrat, St Kitts, and Nevis.

Time was when every misty glen,
From Cruachan to Cowal Shore,
Saw clans that gathered for the fray,
Their gathering cry "McCallum mhor".

These days are dead and gone now,
But in Auckland, Sydney or Quebec,
Where Scots forgather day by day,
Their gathering cry is "More McCallum".

Sandy Macdonald

Category: Standard Blend Licensee: Macdonald Greenlees, Edinburgh Owner: Diageo plc

(see OLD PARR) Sandy Macdonald has a square, "mallet"-shaped, bottle – reminiscent of its sister blend, Old Parr – with a "cracked" pattern moulded in relief on its surface. This was originally introduced in the 1920s as a means of frustrating counterfeiters. The brand is currently big in Paraguay, Uruguay, and Chile.

McDonald's Special Blend

Category: Standard Blend Licensee: C&J McDonald, Perth Owner: Diageo plc

This company was once a subsidiary of Arthur Bell & Co, and became part of United Distillers following the Guinness takeover of Bell's in 1986.

Today, the brand sells mainly in South Africa.

The (Stewart) Macduff

Category: De Luxe Blend Owner: Macduff International, Glasgow

Macduff International was formed in 1991 by three of the Scotch whisky industry's senior executives. The company has acquired Grand MacNish and Lauder's from Allied Distillers, and has launched several new brands, initially in five export markets (Canada, the USA, Sweden, France, and South Africa). In the past six years this has become fifty markets, with regular orders from twenty of them.

The Macduff's claims to antiquity ("a family product handed down through generations") are based upon the pedigree of the Macduff family – the premier clan in medieval Scotland – the chiefs of which were created Earls of Fife in 1056 and eventually became hereditary crown-bearers to the Scottish monarchy.

In point of fact, the brand is named (as are so many great whisky brands) after its founder, and the company's current managing director, Stewart Macduff.

(The Original) Mackinlay

Category: Standard, Premium and De Luxe Blends
Licensee: Charles Mackinlay & Co Owner: Whyte & Mackay Ltd, Glasgow

Charles Mackinlay set up business as a wine merchant in Leith in 1815. His son James joined the business after serving an apprenticeship with a firm of sherry shippers in London, and became chairman in 1867. James was succeeded in 1926 by his son Charles, grandson Ian (in 1934), and great-grandson Donald, who was chairman until his retirement in 1992. He was one of the leading figures of his generation in the whisky industry and remains World Grand Master of the Confrèrie de l'Ordre des Tastes Whisky Ecossais.

The Mackinlay brand was first introduced in the mid-nineteenth century, named simply Mackinlay's. It was one of the first to be supplied to the Houses of Parliament, and was carried to the South Pole by Sir Ernest Shackleton in 1907. In 1985, it was renamed The Original Mackinlay, and relaunched. Today, it is just outside the top ten most successful brands in the UK, and stands at number thirty in world sales, its major markets being in Scandinavia, France, Portugal, Italy, Holland, Thailand, and Japan.

Succeeding generations of the Mackinlay family have been closely involved in perpetuating the blend and maintaining its quality, although their involvement ceased when the company was acquired by Whyte & Mackay in 1993.

Sandy Macnab

Category: Standard Blend Owner: Macnab Distilleries, Montrose

After the Second World War, Joseph Hobbs bought the Ben Nevis Distillery near Fort William and installed a Coffey still alongside the traditional pot stills in order to secure a reliable supply of both grain and malt whiskies for blending (*see* BEN NEVIS). This had never been done before.

In 1957, he also bought Lochside Brewery, which he converted to a distillery and in which he conducted the same dual-still experiment (*see* LOCHSIDE). The blend produced by the company was named Sandy Macnab – apparently after the distillery manager – and a controlling company named Macnab Distilleries was set up to manage the production and sales of this new blend. (Incidentally, the "loch" referred to in the distillery's name was long ago filled in.)

Sandy MacNab inspired a lengthy poem, which starts:

We are sitting tonight in the fire glow,
Just you and I alone . . .

(and finishes:)

And the woes of the world have vanished
When I've pressed my lips to yours;
And to feel your life-blood flowing
To me is the best of cures.
You have given me inspiration
For many a soulful rhyme –
You're the Finest Old Scotch Whisky
I've had for a long, long time.

In 1973, Lochside was sold to Destillerias y Crianza del Whisky of Madrid, which quickly closed the grain production plant and, in 1992, ceased production altogether. It has since been dismantled and turned into flats.

Mac Na Mara

Category: Standard Blend Owner: Praban na Linne, Isle Ornsay, Isle of Skye

Macnamara joined Sir Iain Noble's stable of Gaelic whiskies in 1992. It is lighter and more grainy than Te Bheag, and, being sold at a competitive price, is now the company's biggest seller. *Macna-Mara* is Gaelic for "son of the sea".

James Martin's

Category: Premium and De Luxe Blends **Licensee:** *James Martin & Co, Leith* **Owner:** *Glenmorangie plc, Broxburn, West Lothian*

James Martin was known as "Sparry" due to his prowess in the boxing ring. He went into business as a whisky merchant in 1878 in Edinburgh, and was a noted philanthropist in his home town. VVO – the initials either stand for "Very Very Old" or "Vatted Very Old" – was originally simply called Martin's VVO, but Martini-Rossi, the vermouth manufacturer, objected. The brand became famous when a shipload went down with the *SS Politician* off the island of Eriskay in the Outer Hebrides (February 4, 1941) – the story was immortalized by Compton Mackenzie in *Whisky Galore* (*see* SS POLITICIAN).

Macdonald & Muir (*see* HIGHLAND QUEEN) acquired James Martin & Co in the 1920s; a holding company, Macdonald Martin Distilleries, was set up in 1948 and changed its name to that of its most famous brand in 1995 (*see* GLENMORANGIE). VVO is one of the most popular whiskies in the USA and is within the top forty in the world. Until recently, it was not available in the home market, but in 1997, it was listed for the first time by Oddbins.

McGibbon's

Category: Standard and De Luxe Blends **Owner:** *Douglas Laing & Co*

The McGibbons range is designed as novelty gifts, closely associated with golf (*see* KING OF SCOTS)

Mitchell's

Category: Deluxe Blend **Owner:** *J&A Mitchell, Cambeltown*

Mitchell's is the house blend of Cadenhead's, the well-known independent bottler. Both are owned by the family firm (founded in the 1820s) which owns Springbank and Glen Gyle distillers (*see* SPRINGBANK).

(Sir Iain's Standard & Special) Moncreiffe

Category: De Luxe Blends **Licensee:** *Moncreiffe plc* **Owner:** *Gibson International*

Sir Iain Moncreiffe, eleventh Baronet and twenty-third Laird of Moncreiffe in Perthshire, died in 1985. He was one of the most colourful Scots of his generation, and was also well known in the south, where he was once described as "the most clubbable man in London . . . And he used them all as a vehicle for his kindness." Moncreiffe "8" was launched by Sir Iain in 1983, supplied by the distinguished London wine and spirits merchants, Dolamore (which was originally available only through such fashionable outlets as Annabel's nightclub, The Ritz, and [of course] in Sir Iain's many London clubs), but it is now available through Peter Dominic's off-sales premises. The brand won a gold award and

was nominated Best Blended Whisky at the International Wine &
Spirit Competition awards in 1989.

Monster's Choice

*Category: Standard Blend **Licensee:** Strathnairn Whisky,
Inverness **Owner:** Gordon & MacPhail, Elgin*

(*see* MacPHAIL'S) This curiously named whisky is in fact of some
antiquity – it was registered at the turn of the century. The
attractive label has recently been redesigned, and states that the
blend is "Nessie's Favourite Dram"!

Muirhead's

*Category: Standard Blend **Licensee:** Charles Muirhead & Son,
Edinburgh **Owner:** Glenmorangie plc, Broxburn, West Lothian*

Charles Muirhead & Son was a well-known Edinburgh wine
and spirit merchant and shipping company, established in
1824 to import wines from France. The firm's interests extended
to whisky after it acquired another wine shipper in the 1920s,
and Muirhead's Blue Seal (to give the brand its full title) was
introduced then, first only in Edinburgh, then in northern
Scotland when Muirhead became a specialist supplier of
wines and spirits to country estates. Today, it sells worldwide.

Murdock's Perfection

*Category: De Luxe Blend **Owner:** Speyside Distillers Co Ltd,
Glasgow* (*see* SPEYSIDE)

Murrayfield

*Category: De Luxe Blend (12 Years Old) **Licensee:** The Bennachie
Whisky Co, Inverurie, Aberdeen **Owner:** International Multibrand
Products, Keith, Aberdeenshire*

Murrayfield is Scotland's international rugby ground, located in
Edinburgh, and the brand celebrates this fact on a label which
depicts struggling players. It is sold in export markets only.
Toffee, even treacle, has been detected on the nose and in the
flavour of this rich blend.

Northern Scot

*Category: Standard Blend **Licensee:** Bruce & Co. Leith
Owner: Whyte & Mackay Ltd, Glasgow*

(*see* INVERGORDON) This is a secondary brand, available only in
export markets.

Old Angus

*Category: Standard Blend **Licensee:** R.H. Thomson & Co,
Edinburgh **Owner:** Diageo plc*

An old-established company that once held the licence for
Teaninich Distillery at Alness on the Cromarty Firth (*see*
TEANINICH), this firm became part of Macdonald Greenlees & Co
in the 1890s (*see* OLD PARR), and of DCL in 1925.

Old Angus, the company's sole surviving brand, sells
principally in Uruguay and South Africa.

Old Bridge

*Category: Premium and De Luxe Blend **Licensee:** Bridge of
Dulnain Blenders, London and Edinburgh **Owner:** London &
Scottish Spirits, Guildford, Surrey*

The River Dulnain rises in the Monadhliath Mountains, in the heart of "Whisky Country", and is a tributary of the Spey. The "Old Bridge" referred to in this brand name is near the village of Dulnain Bridge and was built in 1746 as part of the communications network established to pacify the Highlands following the '45 Rising.

A very elegant stone structure, accessible today only on foot, it once provided a link between Speyside and Loch Ness. The company's brand notes say "it represents a permanent reminder of the beauty man can create, and from this sentiment lies the heritage of Old Bridge Scotch Whisky – 'The Scotch from the Hills.' Currently, Old Bridge is available only in export markets (*see* SCOTTISH REEL).

Old Court

Category: Standard Blend Owner: Gibson International, London

This blend is marketed exclusively in the Far East. The scene on the label derives from a woodcut depicting King James I of Scotland holding court in Edinburgh in 1424, and comes from an early copy of Holinshed's *Chronicles*, now in the British Museum (*see* ROYAL CULROSS).

Old Crofter

Category: Standard Blend Licensee: Smith & Henderson, Edinburgh and London Owner: London & Scottish Spirits, Guildford, Surrey

Crofting is the communal farming method pursued throughout the Highlands & Islands, and crofters were the people worst hit when home distilling was made illegal in 1784.

The brand, which "harks back to this heritage", is available in export markets only (*see* SCOTTISH REEL).

Old Elgin

Category: Vatted Malt Owner: Gordon & MacPhail, Elgin

(*see* MACPHAIL'S, PRIDE OF STRATHSPEY) Elgin, the "capital" of Speyside, was once the main bottling centre for the thirty-odd distilleries in the region. G&M has the largest stocks of old whiskies in the world, and is uniquely able to produce vattings of very aged whiskies. Old Elgin employs Speyside whiskies exclusively.

Old Glomore

Category: Standard Blend Owner: James Williams (Narberth), Dyfed, Wales

Established in 1830, this firm has been blending and bottling its own brand, by hand, since the middle of the nineteenth century. The whisky is found only in Pembrokeshire.

Old Highland Blend

Category: Standard Blend Owner: Eldridge, Pope & Co, Dorchester, Dorset

The company was founded in 1833 and is now one of the largest regional brewers in England. It has been blending and bottling its own whisky since 1907. Old Highland Blend is said to have a higher than usual malt content – a familiar claim, but supported and made credible by the fact that the malt fillings are listed on the label. The current director of wines and spirits, Mr Naughtie, is a Master of Wine and takes personal responsibility for blending.

Old Inverness

Category: Standard Blend Licensee: J.G. Thomson & Co (parent: Bass) Owner: Tennent Caledonian Breweries, Glasgow

This blend first appeared in 1961, in the retail outlets of HD Wines (Inverness). The brand is now owned and distributed by J.G. Thomson, mainly in the north and northeast of Scotland, but increasingly in the central belt. (*see* AS WE GET IT).

Old Macphunn

Category: Vatted Malt Owner: The Creggans Inn

This vatting was supervised by the late Sir Fitzroy Maclean of Dunconnel (1911–96), celebrated author, soldier, diplomat, and politician. At the time of writing, it is available only from the Creggans Inn at Strachur, Argyll, where the public bar is also named after Archibald Macphunn of Dripp.

This character was a local laird of ancient lineage but slender means who was caught stealing sheep. He was tried at Inveraray, on the other side of Loch Fyne, and there hanged. His widow was returning across the loch with the corpse when she noticed some sign of life. Mixing some whisky with her own milk (she was nursing a baby at the time), she forced the liquid between her husband's lips and revived him.

They landed close to Strachur at a spot now marked by a cairn. Since by law you cannot be hanged twice for the same crime, Macphunn, now known as "half-hangit Archie", was a free man. He lived to a ripe old age and is buried in Strachur kirkyard.

This story so appealed to Sir Fitzroy that he named his bar after Macphunn, and honoured his memory by naming a whisky for him.

Old Matured

Category: Standard Blend Licensee: Daniel Crawford & Sons, Leith Owner: Diageo plc

A firm of whisky merchants in Glasgow, Daniel Crawford & Sons came into being in 1850. Its offices were moved to Leith by DCL (1972). Old Matured was once a big name in Europe, New Zealand, Mauritius, and Bahrain; today, its main market is Greece.

Old Mull

Category: Standard Blend Owner: Whyte & Mackay, Glasgow

(*see* WHYTE & MACKAY)

Old Orkney

Category: Premium Blend Owner: Gordon & MacPhail, Elgin

(*see* MACPHAIL'S) "Double O", as this whisky is sometimes known, has the epithet "The Island's Peedie Dram" on its label: "peedie" means "little" in Orkney. The brand name has a distinguished provenance, once being used to describe the product of Stromness Distillery in Orkney (founded 1818, closed 1928).

Old Parr

Category: De Luxe Blends **Licensee:** *Macdonald Greenlees,*
Edinburgh **Owner:** *Diageo plc*

In 1635, John Taylor, known as "The Water Poet", published a
pamphlet entitled *The Olde, Old, Very Olde Man or Thomas Parr,*
the Sonne of John Parr of Winnington in the Parish of Alderbury in
the County of Shropshire, who was borne in 1483 in the Reigne of
King Edward the 4th and is now living in the Strand, being aged
152 yeares and odd monthes, 1635. Old Parr became a celebrity
when he was discovered and brought to London by the Earl
Marshal of England, the Earl of Arundel. He was presented at
Court to Charles I. The king said, "You have lived longer than other
men. What have you done more than other men?" He replied, "I
did penance when I was an hundred years old."

The penance was for an illicit amour! Parr had married in his
eightieth year, and some twenty years later he fell for another, but
was discovered. He was obliged to be "purged by standing in a
sheet" in the parish church. He married again in his 120th year –
"Catharine Milton, his second wife, whom he got with child; and
was, after that era of his life, employed in threshing, and other
husbandry work"! He was painted by Van Dyck and Rubens, and
died in November 1635, to be buried in Westminster Abbey on the
king's order.

Promotional material for the brand makes this connection:
"Just as Thomas Parr lived through the reigns of ten English
monarchs, so Old Parr represents timeless quality in an ever-
changing world . . . Its makers were inspired by a man whose
prestige and enduring quality stood for everything their brand
represents"!

The brand is one of the world's largest-selling de luxe
whiskies, and is number one in the important Japanese market.
Tradition has it that it was introduced to Japan over a hundred
years ago by the foreign minister, Tomoni Iwakura.

Old Parr De Luxe Scotch Whisky was first created in 1871 by
James and Samuel Greenlees, brothers from Ayrshire. It
immediately did well in London, where it was described as having
an almost "total monopoly on supply", but, somewhat surprisingly,
this success did not survive long. The brand soon became an
export whisky, early consignments going to Canada and Brazil.

Greenlees & Co was bought by Sir James Calder and merged
with Alexander & Macdonald (*see* SANDY MACDONALD) about 1900.
It became part of DCL in 1925. Glendullan Distillery was licensed
to the company, but the heart of Old Parr has always been
Cragganmore (*see* GLENDULLAN, CRAGGANMORE).

Old Smuggler

Category: Standard Blend **Licensee:** *J&G Stodart, Dumbarton*
Owner: *Allied Distillers, Dumbarton*

In 1835, James and George Stodart, brothers from a wealthy
Glasgow family, began a whisky-blending business. They named
their leading brand Old Smuggler – a reference to the quality of

the illicit distillers' product which, pre-1823, was generally acknowledged as being better than that which was produced legally. The brothers Stodart are reputed to have been the first to "marry" their blend in sherry butts.

In 1931, J&G Stodart was acquired by Hiram Walker-Gooderham & Worts, the giant Canadian distilling company, in anticipation of the repeal of the Prohibition laws in the USA. In 1936, Hiram Walker also acquired a share in Ballantine's, which had already established good distribution in the United States. In order to secure stocks of malt whisky, the company bought two distilleries – Glenburgie-Glenlivet and Miltonduff-Glenlivet (the former was licensed to Stodart's and the latter to Ballantine's) – and built what was at the time the largest grain distillery in Scotland.

These moves resulted in both Old Smuggler and Ballantine's becoming two of the most popular blends in America, and they remain so to this day. Old Smuggler is also well-established in Europe, with a significant position in the German market.

Glen Parker

Category: Standard & De Luxe and Single Malt **Owner: Angus Dundee Ltd, London**

(*see* ANGUS DUNDEE)

Passport

Category: Standard Blend **Licensee: William Longmore & Co Owner: Chivas Bros, Paisley**

(*see* 100 PIPERS, CHIVAS REGAL) Although unknown in the UK market, Passport is one of the top 20 whisky brands worldwide, well-known in Europe and with key markets in the USA, Mexico, Brazil, Spain, Portugal, and Korea. It was introduced in 1968, and, with Seagram's acquisition of The Glenlivet Group, now makes use of such distinguished malts as The Glenlivet, Glen Grant, Longmorn, and Caperdonich. The malts are vatted in the Highlands and blended with grain whisky at Paisley.

Peatling's

Category: Standard Blend **Licensee: Thos Peatling & Co, Bury St Edmunds, Suffolk Owner: Greene King, Bury St Edmunds, Suffolk**

Thomas Peatling, from Bury St Edmunds, started a wine and spirits business partnership with a Mr Hepplewhite in 1826, at Wisbech, Cambridgeshire. By 1830, Smith, Brown & Peatling had established branches in Bedford and St Ives. Later, Brown dropped out and the company became Thos Peatling & Sons.

At the beginning of this century, the company acquired an old business situated in King's Lynn, and in 1911, it took over the spacious cellars of Aplin Robinson & Percival, which enabled the firm to become the agent for the well-known brewer, Greene King & Sons of Bury St Edmunds, with whom it amalgamated in 1934.

Greene King was founded in Bury St Edmunds by Benjamin Greene in 1799. His descendants and those of the King family are still involved in the company. Peatling's was introduced in 1955,

blended for the company by Macdonald & Muir (*see*
GLENMORANGIE). At this time, the firm was trading as Peatling &
Cawdron, but reverted to Thos Peatling in 1988.

Pig's Nose

*Category: Standard Blend **Licensee:** Sheep Dip Whisky Co,
Oldbury on Severn, Bristol **Owner:** Whyte & Mackay Ltd, Glasgow*

Pig's Nose was introduced in 1977 by M.J. Dowdeswell Esq, the
owner of a free house at Oldbury-on-Severn, as a companion
brand to his remarkably successful Sheep Dip.

It took over two years to come up with a name as memorable
as its running-mate, and the explanation is supplied on the label:
"tis said that our Scotch is as soft and smooth as a pig's nose".
Anyone selling this brand is invited to become a member of the
Pig's Nose Club.

Pinch

*Category: De Luxe Blend **Licensee:** John Haig & Co
Owner: Diageo plc*

This is the name Haig's Dimple has long been sold under in the
United States (*see* HAIG, DIMPLE).

Poit Dhubh

*Category: Vatted Malt **Licensee:** Praban na Linne, Isle Ornsay, Isle
of Skye **Owner:** Sir Iain Noble, Bt, OBE*

Poit Dhubh (pronounced "potch doo") has a high proportion of
Island and Islay malts in its blend, as befits a member of Sir Iain
Noble's "Gaelic Whiskies" stable (*see* TE BHEAG). The 12 Years Old
is bottled at forty per cent (termed "Black Label"; the original
version) and at forty-six per cent (termed "Guagers" – the Scottish
word for an exciseman). The latter is not chill-filtered, so retains
an old-fashioned style and may go slightly cloudy if ice is added
to the glass.

The brand was introduced in 1978 to support the local
economy and promote the Gaelic language. In parallel, Sir Iain
Noble, its owner and inspiration, established a college at Eilean
Iarmain to teach business studies through the medium of Gaelic.
This has been a great success in training people for careers in the
West Highlands and Islands, rather than them having to emigrate.
For his services to the Gaelic language and the people of the
Hebrides, Sir Iain was awarded the OBE in 1979.

Poit Dhubh literally means "black pot", and was the term used
to describe the illicit still of the smuggler. The brand has won a
loyal following in Scotland, especially in the Islands, and also in
France, Switzerland, and Canada. The twenty-one-year-old
expression was introduced in 1993; it has been described as
"heavier in style, rich and aromatic".

John Player Special

*Category: Premium Blend; De Luxe Blends **Licensee:** Douglas
Laing & Co, Glasgow **Owner:** Langside Distillers*

Like the other Douglas Laing brands (*see* MCGIBBONS; KING OF
SCOTS), John Player Special's principal market is in the Far East
and the Pacific Rim – it is among the top ten duty-free brands in

Taiwan. Each of these expressions benefits from the company's policy of including a proportion of very old malt whiskies in the blend. Special Rare includes malts from Islay, Speyside, and the Lowlands of up to twenty-five years old, and employs more than twenty-five different malts in the blend. Each bottle of this blend is numbered to ensure quality control and to remind customers of its rarity.

Pride of Islay, Pride of the Lowlands, Pride of Orkney, Pride of Strathspey

*Category: Vatted Malts **Owner:** Gordon & MacPhail, Elgin*

Gordon & MacPhail opened its shop in Elgin in 1895. John Gordon was a whisky broker, and with his partner, John Alexander MacPhail, they began trading as "Family Grocers, Tea, Wine & Spirit Merchants". Over the years, the company has gained great experience in vatting malts and blending malt and grain whiskies (see MACPHAIL'S).

It has been said of the firm's distinguished range of vatted malts that "all are skilfully put together and combine to give something which is often superior to some of the single malts which go to make them up".

The constituent malts are selected to demonstrate the classic characteristics of each region.

Putachieside

*Category: Standard Blend **Licensee:** Cadenhead's **Owner:** J&A Mitchell, Campbeltown*

(see SPRINGBANK)

Queen Anne

*Category: Standard blend **Licensee:** Hill Thomson & Co, Edinburgh **Owner:** Chivas Bros, Paisley*

William Hill established a grocer's shop in the Georgian New Town of Edinburgh (Rose Street Lane) in 1793 – not long after the New Town had been built – and moved to the much grander Frederick Street six years later. His sons continued to run the business after his death in 1818, and his grandson took William Thomson as a partner in 1857, at which time the firm began to blend and bottle whisky.

The brand was first created in the mid-1870s and was quickly established by William Shaw, a brilliant export salesman, who later became chairman of the company. Queen Anne was the last reigning Stuart monarch.

Shaw's sons joined the firm in 1919, and descendants were still in control of Hill, Thomson when it combined with The Glenlivet & Glen Grant Distilleries in 1970 to form The Glenlivet Distillers. Queen Anne became the group's leading blend, and was able to draw distinguished fillings from The Glenlivet, Glen Grant, and Longmorn distilleries, all of them Top Dressings.

In 1978, The Glenlvet Group was acquired by the Canadian giant Seagram (see 100 PIPERS), and thence to Pernod Ricard in 2003. Hill Thomson's elegant building on Frederick Street is now a café-bar.

R&H Blenders Selection

*Category: Standard Blend **Licensee:** Roderick & Henderson,
Edinburgh & London **Owner:** London & Scottish Spirits,
Guildford, Surrey*

The blurb on this brand states that the blend was created by two
rival blenders from Edinburgh:

> "Mr Roderick had always liked to include a number
> of Islay Malts in his Scotch, which provided a deep
> flavour and a tangy aroma. Mr Henderson, on the other
> hand, favoured the whiskies of Speyside which had a
> smooth, golden flavour and the lighter aroma of
> highland peat [sic].
>
> "In response to a challenge from a successful blender
> in Glasgow, the two rivals joined forces to combine
> their talents and produce one extraordinarily fine blend,
> now known as R&H . . . The Blenders Selection."

(*see* SCOTTISH REEL)

The Real Mackenzie

*Category: Standard Blend **Licensee:** Peter Mackenzie & Co, Perth
Owner: Whyte & Mackay Ltd, Glasgow*

Peter Mackenzie & Co was originally an Edinburgh distilling
company with its roots in the 1820s. The company owned Blair
Athol and Dufftown-Glenlivet distilleries, and its brand, The Real
Mackenzie, was produced in eight-, twelve- and twenty-year-old
expressions; the brand name may be as old as 1826. It sells in
the UK, but its main markets are in Greece and South Africa.

The company was bought by Arthur Bell & Sons (*see* BELL'S) in
1933 – an event which has been described as "Bell's coming of age
as an all-round whisky operation". The brand passed to Whyte &
Mackay in 1986.

Red Hackle

*Category: Standard Blend **Licensee:** Hepburn & Ross
Owner: Robertson & Baxter, Glasgow (part of the Edrington Group)*

Until the 1960s, Red Hackle was a very popular brand, particularly
in Glasgow; today, it sells almost entirely in export markets. It was
acquired by Robertson & Baxter in 1959. The name recalls the
plume of small red feathers worn in the bonnets of members of the
Black Watch – an honour bestowed upon the regiment in
recognition of its valour at the Battle of Gildersmalsen in 1795. The
original Hepburn and Ross served with the regiment.

Regent

*Category: Standard Blend **Owner:** Macduff International, Glasgow*

This is another name for Cumbrae Castle, which is used for the
brand in certain export markets.

Reliance

*Category: Standard Blend **Licensee:** Forbes, Farquharson & Co,
Perth **Owner:** Diageo plc*

This company was a subsidiary of Arthur Bell & Sons, and became
part of United Distillers following the Guinness takeover of that
company in 1986. The brand sells mainly in South Africa.

Robert Burns

*Category: Premium Blend **Owner**: Isle of Arran Distillers, Stirling*

Isle of Arran Distillers secured the right to name their blended whisky after Scotland's national poet from the International Burns Federation in 2001. It is bottled at various ages and is popular with Burns Clubs around the world.

Robertson's

*Category: Premium Blend **Owner**: Robertson's of Pitlochry*

Robertson's "Rare Old" was introduced in the mid-1980s. It is sold exclusively through Robertson's family-owned grocers, wine, and spirits shop on Atholl Road in the centre of the pretty town of Pitlochry, in Highland Perthshire. This family business was established in the early 1960s, and now offers a very wide range of malt and blended whiskies (some 250 malts), which is available by mail order and via the Internet.

Robbie Dhu

*Category: De Luxe Blend (12 Years Old) **Owner**: William Grant & Sons, Dufftown*

Robbie Dhu was launched in Brazil in 1995 and Korea the following year. The name (properly spelt *Dubh*, i.e. "black") is that of the famous spring from which William Grant's distilleries, Glenfiddich and Balvenie, draw their water. Both these malts go into its composition. It is packaged in the same triangular bottle that distinguishes William Grant's and Glenfiddich.

Rob Roy

*Category: Standard and De Luxe Blends **Licensee**: Morrison Bowmore Distillers, Glasgow **Owner**: Suntory Distillers (Japan)*

The firm was incorporated in 1951 as Stanley P. Morrison, Whisky Brokers. Morrison, a well-respected whisky broker in Glasgow, founded the company with James Howat, a young accountant who succeeded Morrison as chairman on the latter's death in 1971.

The business grew steadily, and in the 1960s, it acquired several companies, including the Bowmore Distillery Co on Islay, the Roseburn Bonding Co, and Tannochside Bonding Co. By this time, Morrison's operations embraced distilling, blending, and broking. In the early 1970s, two more distilleries – Auchentoshan and Glengarioch – were purchased.

In 1989, the son of the founder, Brian Morrison, became chairman and the name of the company was changed to reflect the importance of its major malt whisky, Bowmore. In 1994, the company was bought by Suntory, the major Japanese distiller, but it has adopted a hands-off approach to management. In the year to 1997, Morrison Bowmore's sales and marketing team quadrupled in size; the company was pronounced "Distiller of the Year 1995" (the first time this award was made at the International Wine & Spirit Competition awards) and won the Queen's Award For Export Achievement in both 1996 and 1997 (this is most unusual).

Roderick Dhu

*Category: Standard Blend **Licensee**: Wright & Greig Ltd, Glasgow **Owner**: Diageo plc*

Roderick Dhu was a very popular blend in the 1880s and 1890s, especially in India, Australia, and New Zealand, so popular, in fact, that its owner, the Glasgow firm of brokers and blenders Wright and Greig, built Dallas Dhu Distillery to supply fillings. The brand is now only available at the distillery (*see* WRIGHT AND GREIG)

Rodger's

Category: Standard Blend Licensee: Slater, Rodger & Co, Hurleford Owner: Diageo plc

Thomas H. Slater set up as a dealer in tea and groceries in Glasgow in 1834, and as early as 1856, could boast customers in Australia, India, South Africa, the West Indies, Canada, and the USA.

In 1865, he joined forces with George Smeaton Rodger, and by 1888, they were shipping their own whisky brands to seventy different countries. Ten years later, the company formed an association with John Walker & Co (*see* JOHNNIE WALKER), and Alexander Walker, chairman of that company, joined the board. Slater Walker was taken over by Walkers in 1911, and it became part of DCL.

Rodger's Old Scots (sic; see *also* CUTTY SARK) now sells in Israel and the Middle East, and Rodger's Special is well-established in Paraguay.

Rory

Category: Standard Blend Licensee: Rory McMorran Blenders, Edinburgh Owner: London & Scottish Spirits, Guildford, Surrey

Rory McMullen apparently came from the Island of Colonsay, one of the Southern Inner Hebrides, and learned the craft of home distilling there. The blend that bears his name is only available in export markets (*see* SCOTTISH REEL).

Royal & Ancient

Category: Premium Blend Licensee: Cockburn & Campbell, London Owner: Diageo plc

The brand was originally made for the Royal & Ancient Golf Club in St Andrews, the world's premier golf club (although not, in fact, the most "ancient"). Its precursor, the Society of St Andrew's Golfers, was established in 1754 by twenty-two "noblemen and gentlemen being admirers of the ancient and healthful exercise of golf". Their successors are still the ruling arbiters on the game.

Royal Blend

Category: Standard Blend Licensee: William Sanderson & Son, South Queensferry Owner: Diageo plc

In 1925, William Sanderson & Son dropped all its brands except the leader, VAT 69. In recent years, the company's tradition of tailoring blends to individual customers or markets has been imitated by United Distillers (*see* SANDERSON'S GOLD). Royal Blend, made especially for Israel, is a case in point.

Royal Challice

Category: De Luxe Blend Owner: The Vintage Malt Whisky Company, Glasgow

(*see* FINLAGGAN)

Royal Club
*Category: Standard Blend **Owner:** Charles H. Julian and Co.*
(*see* CARLTON BLEND)

Royal Culross
*Category: Vatted Malt **Licensee:** Glen Scotia Distillery*
***Owner:** Gibson Scotch Whisky Distillers, Alexandria, Dumbartonshire*

So pretty is Culross, in Fife, that it was the first village to be taken on for wholesale preservation by the Historic Buildings Division of the Scottish Office (in the 1950s). It is a charming, if a little over-preserved, sixteenth- to seventeenth-century port, and was a merchant community whose wealth was founded on salt and coal. It is also the birthplace of St Kentigern, the sixth-century founder of Glasgow Cathedral, who, according to tradition, was born on the beach there. Culross was made a Royal Burgh by James VI in about 1590.

The Royal Culross label bears the "royal warrant of the Hammermen of Culross", and a certificate from the "Provost, Magistrates and Councillors" of the tiny town, granted in 1972. (*see* FRASER MCDONALD)

Royal Edinburgh
*Category: Standard Blend **Owner:** Diageo plc*

Royal Edinburgh was invented by the distilling company, Ainslie & Heilbron (*see* AINSLIE'S), and became its most famous brand. It sold especially well in Australia (where it was imported in bulk) and in Belgium, where its name has now been changed simply to Ainslie's. The brand is now sold exclusively in the UK. It reputedly has Clynelish at its heart – a most distinguished malt.

Royal Escort
*Category: Vatted Malt **Owner:** Gibson Scotch Whisky Distillers, Alexandria, Dumbartonshire*

The Third Jacobite Rising, known as "The Forty-five", began with several victories for the Highland army led by Bonnie Prince Charlie. The most notable was at the battle of Prestonpans, which was fought outside Edinburgh on September 21, 1745, when the superior Hanoverian army under General Sir John Cope was routed. The Jacobites had entered Edinburgh four days earlier, but after so convincing a victory, nobody could resist them, and the label of this whisky depicts the prince's triumphant entry into Edinburgh after the battle, surrounded by his "royal escort".

Royal Findhorn
*Category: Standard Blend **Owner:** Gordon & MacPhail, Elgin*

(*see* MACPHAIL'S) The River Findhorn rises south of Inverness, not far from the ancient homelands of Clan MacPhail. Like the Spey, it is renowned for its salmon fishing.

Royal Game
*Category: Standard Blend **Owner:** Winerite, Leeds*

Winerite was started in 1973 by Gerry Atkinson, who owned a small licensed grocery in Leeds. Today, it is the largest independent importer and distributor in the UK, with an annual turnover in excess of £150 million. The end of retail price maintenance in the early 1970s allowed the business to expand into the wholesale market. The company's policy has always been to offer "value for money": products are bought in bulk, and a range of own-brand wines and spirits is continually being enlarged. Royal Game is the company's main whisky brand and is available to its retail customers.

Royal Heritage

Category: De Luxe Owner: William Lundie and Co, Glasgow

This blend is sold in Continental Europe (*see* LISMORE).

Royal Salute

Category: Premium and De Luxe Blend Owner: Chivas Brothers, Paisley

A royal salute is a twenty-one-gun tribute to a member of the Royal Family on a special occasion, such as the Queen's birthday. Royal Salute was introduced in 1953 to commemorate the coronation in the same year. It won a gold medal at the 1996 International Wine & Spirit Competition awards.

Originally, it was made available only in the American market – presented in a ceramic decanter made from Royal Doulton china and wrapped in a velvet bag. Today, the flagon is supplied by the Wade potteries, and the brand is available in over 100 countries (*see* 100 PIPERS, CHIVAS REGAL).

Sainsbury's

Category: Standard and Premium Blends; Vatted and Single Malts Owner: J, Sainsbury, London

J Sainsbury was established in 1869, and today owns 369 supermarkets throughout the UK, as well as thirteen Savacentre hypermarkets. The company has been offering price-competitive, own-label whiskies for at least thirty years, and their consistency and high quality make them worthy of inclusion in a book such as this. Sainsbury's whiskies are supplied by the Peter J. Russell Group (*see* CHIEFTAIN'S CHOICE).

St James's

Category: De Luxe Blend Owner: Berry Brothers & Rudd, London

(*see* CUTTY SARK) The Berry family, or their relatives and close associates, have occupied the same premises in the fashionable St James's district of London since the seventeenth century. The label of St James's depicts St James's Palace, built by Henry VIII for Anne Boleyn, now occupied by the Lord Chamberlain's department.

Sanderson's Gold

Category: Standard Blend Licensee: William Sanderson & Sons, South Queensferry Owner: Diageo plc

Sanderson's Gold was first introduced in 1991, and is blended specifically for the West African market. It continues Sanderson's tradition of tailoring brands to individual tastes (*see* VAT 69): in this case, a light whisky appropriate to a tropical climate.

Scotia Royale

Category: De Luxe Blend **Licensee:** *A. Gillies & Co (Distillers)*
Owner: *Loch Lomond Distillery Co Ltd, Alexandria*

A. Gillies & Co bought Glen Scotia Distillery in 1955, and was itself
acquired by Amalgamated Distilled Products in 1970. Scotia
Royale "12 Years Old Bottled in Scotland Blended Rare Scotch
Whisky" (to give its full title) used to be produced by Glen Scotia
Distillery in Campbeltown (*see* entry).

Ancient legend maintains that the Scots were originally
Greeks who sailed via Egypt and Spain to Ireland, and thence
came to Kintyre. Before they arrived in Ireland, their leader
married an Egyptian princess, Scotia, from whom the race took its
name. Scotia Royale has been prominent in the Far East for some
years, particularly in Japan, South Korea, and Taiwan. The brand is
now making good progress in Europe.

Scottish Leader

Category: Standard Blend, De Luxe Blend **Owner:** *Burn Stewart
Distillers, Glasgow*

(*see* BURN STEWART) Scottish Leader is targeted at the supermarket
customer, and is the company's fastest-growing brand. A de
luxe expression at fifteen years old won "Best Blended Whisky"
and a gold medal at the 1996 International Wine & Spirit
Competition awards.

Scottish National Tartan

Category: Vatted Malt **Licensee:** *The Benachie Scotch Whisky Co,
Inverurie, Aberdeenshire* **Owner:** *International Multibrand Products,
Keith, Aberdeenshire*

(*see* BENNACHIE) This brand was launched to coincide with the
creation of a Scottish national tartan in 1995, and is presented in an
engraved decanter, packed in a velvet box, which is lined with the
new tartan and accompanied by a kilt pin.

Scottish Reel

Category: Standard Blend **Licensee:** *Balerno & Currie, Edinburgh
& London* **Owner:** *London & Scottish International, Guildford,
Surrey*

London & Scottish is an independent company, wholly owned by
the Parker family, who hail from Edinburgh but run their business
from Surrey in order to be within easy access of their (entirely)
international customer base. As well as several whisky brands, the
company purveys gin and vodka and works hard to establish close
relations with the overseas importers appointed to manage its
business, which is currently in Western and Eastern Europe, the
Far East, and the Americas.

Scottish Reel is the company's leading brand. Balerno and
Currie (the name of the licensee for this brand) are both small
villages on the outskirts of Edinburgh. (*see also* OLD BRIDGE, OLD
CROFTER, GLEN TORRAN, R&H, RORY).

Scots' Club

Category: Standard Blend **Owner:** *Whyte & Mackay Ltd, Glasgow*
(*See* WHYTE & MACKAY)

Scots' Earl
Category: Standard Blend **Owner:** *Glen Catrine Bonded Warehouse*
(*see* LOCH LOMOND)

Scots Grey
Category: De Luxe Blend **Licensee:** *Grey & Rodgers*
Owner: *Whyte & Mackay Ltd, Glasgow*

The Scots Greys, also known for a time as the "North British Dragoons", is probably Scotland's most famous cavalry regiment, celebrated most notably for a charge at the Battle of Waterloo. This blend was once well-known in the home market, having been acquired by Invergordon in 1979 when the company bought Grey Rodgers from Pedro Domecq, the sherry shipper. Also available in a 15-year-old expression.

Scots Poet
Category: Standard Blend **Licensee:** *H. Stoddart and Taylor, London* **Owner:** *The Invergordon Distillers (subsidiary of Whyte & Mackay)*

This was a Findlater, Mackie, Todd brand until 1993, when it passed to Invergordon (*see* FINDLATER'S FINEST). It goes without saying that the poet referred to and depicted on the label is Robert Burns.

Jock Scott
Category: Standard and De Luxe Blends **Licensee:** *Whitmore & Bayley* **Owner:** *The Invergordon Distillers (subsidiary of Whyte & Mackay)*

Jock Scott was introduced in the 1930s and is named after the well-known salmon fly, which was especially popular on the River Tweed before the war. The labels of all expressions except the 12 Years Old depict salmon fishermen.

The brand was owned by the well-known London firm of wine and spirits merchants Findlater, Mackie, Todd & Co until 1993, when it passed to The Invergordon Distillers (*see* FINDLATER'S FINEST). The latter company is now owned by Whyte & Mackay.

Sheep Dip
Category: Vatted Malt **Licensee:** *Sheep Dip Whisky Co, Oldbury on Severn, Bristol* **Owner:** *The Invergordon Distillers (subsidiary of Whyte & Mackay)*

M.J. Dowdeswell, a Gloucestershire gentleman farmer and owner of a free house in Oldbury-on-Severn, introduced this blend in 1974 for his customers, mainly local farmers; indeed, the label even proclaims: "This whisky is much enjoyed by the villagers of Oldbury on Severn". Its popularity and availability has grown steadily ever since, however, following early orders from major stores such as Harrod's.

According to local sources, Sheep Dip (pronounced "ship dip") has always been the name given to whisky in this part of England, although one cannot help but wonder about the possible tax advantages to a farmer putting several gallons of Sheep Dip through his books . . . Sheep Dip and its sister brand, Pig's Nose,

were bought by The Invergordon Distillers. It is available in
Canada, Italy, New Zealand, Australia, the UK, and Ireland.

Slaintheva

*Category: De Luxe Blend Owner: Alexander Dunn & Co,
Bracknell, Berks*

Slaintheva (the name derives from the Gaelic toast, more usually
spelled *slainte mha* – "good health") was first created in 1959. It
won a gold medal for quality and excellence at the nineteenth
World Selection of Wines, Spirits and Liqueurs in Amsterdam,
1981. It is sold in the UK, Japan, and Europe as an "executive gift",
each bottle being individually inscribed with the recipient's name.
As well as the standard size, it is bottled as a "kingnum" (the
company's registered name for a 1.75 litre flagon) (*see also*
ALEXANDER DUNN.)

Something Special

Category: Premium Blend Owner: Chivas Bros., Paisley

This was once blended specially for the directors of The Glenlivet
Distilleries in the early 1970s (*see* 100 PIPERS).

Spey Cast

*Category: De Luxe Blend Licensee: James Gordon & Co, Elgin
Owner: Gordon & MacPhail, Elgin*

(*see* MACPHAIL'S) Spey Cast was first created by the distinguished
blender John Urquhart, whose sons and grandchildren still own
and manage Gordon & MacPhail. Its name derives from that most
elegant of all methods of casting a salmon fly, evolved to cope with
the Spey's steep banks and overhanging trees. The label, which
was designed in the 1920s, depicts a be-tweeded angler
nonchalantly casting; the decorative loops and arabesques make
the cast look impossibly difficult! Spey Cast won a double Gold
Award at the International Wine & Spirit Competition in 1982.

Spey Royal

*Category: Standard and Premium Blends Licensee: W&A Gilbey,
Harlow, Essex Owner: Diageo plc*

Walter and Alfred Gilbey founded their firm of wine merchants in
London in 1857, upon returning from the Crimean War. Starting
with a single half-inch advertisement for South African port and
sherry, within ten years they had moved into opulent premises in
the Pantheon, Oxford Street. Within twenty they had their own
vineyards in the Médoc, and were able to invest a million pounds
in brandy alone in one year!

In 1887, seeing the growing taste for Scotch whisky, they
bought Glen Spey Distillery and began bottling it as Castle Grand
(selling at 3/6d the bottle). Strathmill Distillery was bought in 1895,
and Knockando in 1904. Originally, the Gilbeys bottled only pure
malt, but from 1905, they were blending Spey Royal.

Alfred Gilbey died of pneumonia aged forty-six in 1879; Walter
was created a baronet in 1893. Their sons and grandsons
continued to control the business until 1962, when the company
merged with United Wine Traders to form IDV. In 1997, IDV
merged with Guinness to form Diageo plc.

In 1968, a new subsidiary, Glen Spey, was formed to market Spey Royal and Strathspey, a vatted malt. The former's principal market is the Pacific Rim, to which it is exported in bulk to be bottled and labelled in Hong Kong.

Speyside

Category: Premium and De Luxe Blends **Owner: Speyside Distillery Co, Glasgow**

The company was incorporated in 1955 by the Christie family with the aim of marketing a range of blended whiskies, a vatted malt (*see* GLENTROMIE) and a single malt (*see* DRUMGUISH). In 1990, the company opened the "new" Speyside Distillery, near Kingussie, close to the site of a distillery of the same name which had been established in 1895 and which has long been out of production.

The company has high hopes for its product (the first batch of which was bottled in 1995), and in keeping with quality policy, it has built the new distillery entirely in stone. It is almost entirely the work of one man: dry-stone dyker Alex Fairlie of Reswallie. Somewhat confusingly, the brand name "Speyside" is used for a range of old blended whiskies and for the single malt make of the distillery.

SS Politician

Category: De Luxe Blend (limited edition) **Owner: SS Politician** *Licensee: Douglas Laing & Co, Glasgow*

In February 1941, the SS *Politician* sank off the island of Eriskay in the Outer Hebrides. Her principal cargo was whisky – some 50,000 cases, it is estimated – and the tale was immortalized by Sir Compton Mackenzie in his (much-filmed and much-loved) book, *Whisky Galore*.

In 1989, a company was established to salvage what remained of the cargo, and in 1990, a small number of intact bottles were raised from the wreck. The whisky they contained was distilled in 1938 and bottled at proof strength. Its years on the sea bed had done it no harm at all. Rather than offer the small stock of bottles for sale individually at huge prices, it was decided to blend the whisky with appropriately aged malts and grains and make it available to a wider, though still extremely limited, market.

Before the Second World War, it was usual for whisky to be more richly coloured than it is today. This fact, combined with the age of the malt fillings that have gone into this individual and unique blend, has created an unusually dark whisky (*see* KING OF SCOTS).

Stag's Breath Liqueur

Category: Whisky Liqueur **Owner: Meikle's of Scotland, Newtonmore, Baddenoch**

"Then he went to a locker and produced a bottle of Stag's Breath, a brand which had been particularly favoured by the inhabitants of the two Toddays in the good old days of plenty. 'Stack's Press,' murmured Jockey, transfixed by the beauty of the sight before his eyes . . . " (from *Whisky Galore* by Compton Mackenzie [*see* SS POLITICIAN]).

The Meikle family of Newtonmore, in the ancient Lordship of Baddenoch in Upper Speyside, first created their whisky liqueur in the early 1980s, and introduced it to the market in 1989 after careful refinement.

The liqueur is a clever commingling of Speyside whiskies and fermented heather honeycomb, blended to be lighter and drier than traditional whisky liqueurs.

Stewart's Cream of the Barley

*Category: Standard Blend **Licensee:** Alexander Stewart & Son of Dundee **Owner:** Allied Distillers, Dumbarton*

Alexander Stewart founded his company in 1831 at the Glengarry Inn in Castle Street, Dundee, and quickly won a reputation for his whisky, first locally, then throughout Scotland. Until relatively recently, the blend went under the name Century Hyatt Cream of the Barley.

Stewart's became part of the Allied Lyons Group in 1969, and the brand was repackaged in an unusual bottle (somewhere between a cut-glass decanter and an aftershave flask) in 1989. It is currently placed number four in Scotland and is winning ground in the UK mid-price sector. It is also available in Ireland, France, Italy, the Netherlands, Norway, and Canada.

Stewart's Finest Old

*Category: Standard Blend **Owner:** Whyte & Mackay, Glasgow*
(*see* WHYTE & MACKAY)

Strathbeag 17/20

*Category: Standard Blend **Owner:** Macduff International, Glasgow*
Strathbeg is a loch, about two and a half miles long, in northeast Aberdeenshire. It lies parallel to the coast and is separated from the sea by a ridge of sand about half a mile broad. It formerly had a tidal communication with the sea, but in 1720, a strong east wind blew a mass of sand into the channel, stopping the communication and forming a lagoon – hence the "17/20" in the brand name! Apparently, there was once a hamlet here named Cox Haven, a community of half a dozen families all bearing the name "Cox". History does not relate where they came from. One source maintains, curiously, that their true name was "Kuchs", that they were refugees from religious persecution in the Low Countries, and that they held ritualistic ceremonies connected with "fresh-water" dolphins that had been stranded in Loch Strathbeg at the time it was cut off from the sea.

Strathbeg is a new blend created by Macduff International to complement its range of Scotch whiskies (*see* MacDUFF). It does well in parts of Europe and in Kenya.

Strathfillan

*Category: Standard Blend **Owner:** Forth Wines, Milnathort, Kinross*
(*see* KING JAMES VI) This brand is found mainly in the UK market although a foothold has been achieved in markets abroad.

Strathfillan is near Killin in Perthshire. Fillan was a Celtic saint, whose relics (notably his staff and arm-bone) were very influential

in the Highlands, before the rites of the Celtic Church were
superseded by Roman ways.

Strathspey

*Category: Vatted Malt Licensee: W&A Gilbey, Harlow, Essex
Owner: Diageo, plc*

This is a vatted malt and the sister brand to Gilbey's Spey Royal.
Strathspey was also the original name for Dalwhinnie Distillery.

(JM & Co) Superior Mountain Dew

Category: Standard Blend Owner: Malpas Stallard, Worcester

Josiah Stallard of Worcester is one of the oldest wine merchants
in Britain, having records dating back to 1642. Josiah Malpas &
Co now purveys the blend.

Swing

*Category: De Luxe Blend Licensee: John Walker & Sons,
Kilmarnock Owner: Diageo plc*

Sir Alexander Walker, grandson of the eponymous Johnnie
Walker, was one of the great blenders of all time, as well as being
among the ablest of businessmen. He created Swing in 1932, a
rich-flavoured blend originally designed to appeal to transatlantic
travellers and the North American market.

The bottle shape was unusual. Just as the square bottle
had been pioneered by Walker in the 1870s (*see* JOHNNIE
WALKER), so Swing's bottle was designed with a convex base, so that it
could rock (or "swing") as the ocean liner negotiated the swell
of the Atlantic.

In recent years, the company's sales effort has focused on the
Far Eastern markets and the original has been joined by even
more deluxe expressions: Superior and Premier (which has an
individually numbered neck-tag). In Taiwan, Japan, Southeast
Asia, and the Pacific region, the brand is the epitome of a
generous gift.

Swords

*Category: Standard Blend Licensee: James Sword & Son
Owner: Morrison Bowmore Distillers, Glasgow*

Sword & Son was formed in 1814 as a traditional small blending
house in Glasgow. It was acquired by Stanley P. Morrison & Co in
1983. At present, its main markets are Spain and Portugal (*see*
ROB ROY).

Syndicate 58/6

Category: De Luxe Blend Owner: Whyte & Mackay, Glasgow

(*see* WHYTE & MACKAY)

The Tallisman

*Category: Standard Blend Owner: J&W Hardie (a subsidiary of
Tomatin Distillers Ltd)*

(*see* THE ANTIQUARY)

Tambowie

*Category: Vatted Malt Owner: Vintage Malt Whisky
Company, Glasgow*

In 1885, Tambowie Distillery, Milngavie, Dumbartonshire,
produced 48,000 gallons of malt whisky, according to Alfred

Barnard. The distillery was destroyed by fire in 1920. The brand name has now been revived by the Vintage Malt Whisky Company and sells principally in export markets.

Tayside

Category: Vatted Malt Licensee: Glen Talla, Edinburgh
Owner: Whyte & Mackay, Glasgow

Following the reorganisation of Scotland's county boundaries, Tayside became the region which incorporated Angus, Forfar, and part of Perthshire. The label depicts Blair Castle, seat of the Duke of Atholl and headquarters of the Keepers of the Quaich, the world's most distinguished whisky club.

Teacher's

Category: Premium and De Luxe Blends Licensee: William Teacher & Sons Owner: Allied Distillers, Dumbarton

In 1830, William Teacher was employed in a small grocery business in Anderston, Glasgow. He married the owner's daughter, and persuaded the firm to take out a liquor licence. By 1851, he was listed as a wholesale wine and spirits merchant, and had expanded into take-home retail shops and "dram shops": basic public houses, where customers could drink on the premises. By the time he was joined in the business by his sons, Adam and William, he was the single largest licence-holder in Glasgow, with eighteen shops.

The art of creating blends of consistent quality was still in its infancy. The Teacher sons showed great aptitude in this field, and the quality of their blends not only made their dram shops popular, it led to requests from other retailers for supplies of blended whisky. Bulk sales developed throughout the 1870s, with the firm – by now named William Teacher & Sons – offering a range of its own blends as well as blending to individual specifications. The blend which was to make the family fortunes, Teacher's Highland Cream, was registered in 1884; today, it is the third most successful brand in Britain and among the top twenty best-sellers worldwide, with annual sales in excess of two million cases. The de luxe expression, Royal Highland, was first created in 1968.

The need to secure adequate supplies of malt fillings led the company to build its own distillery, Ardmore, at Kennethmont in Aberdeenshire, in 1897–8. In 1960, Teacher acquired Glendronach Distillery, the other main component in the blend. Highland Cream is guaranteed to contain at least forty-five per cent malt whisky, and is credited with being the first brand to position itself as a "premium" blend, falling between "standard" and "de luxe".

In 1913, William Manera Bergius, a nephew of Adam Teacher, devised and patented the now-familiar stopper cork (*i.e.* a cork with a wooden cap which did not require a corkscrew). Highland Cream was thus described as "the self-opening bottle", and it was advertised with the slogan "Bury the Corkscrew".

Until it became part of Allied Lyons in 1976, Teacher was the largest independent Scotch whisky company still under the control of its founder's descendants, and members of the family continue to be involved. An earlier attempt by DCL to acquire the

company in 1921 – principally to obtain the firm's considerable
stocks of whisky, husbanded during the Great War by a self-
rationing scheme – had failed.

Even in the 1920s, Teacher advertised Highland Cream as "The
Whisky of the Good Old Days": its distinctive flavour is rich and
well-rounded, it has good depth of body, a smooth mouth-feel and
a clean finish. Its makers describe it as appealing to the
experienced whisky drinker.

Tears of Scotland

Category: Standard Blend **Owner:** *Charles H. Julian and Co,
London*

(*see* CARLTON BLEND)

Te Bheag

Category: Premium Blend **Licensee:** *Praban na Linne, Isle Ornsay,
Isle of Skye* **Owner:** *Sir Iain Noble, Bt, OBE*

Te Bheag nan Eilean (pronounced "chay vek nan eelan") to give the
brand its full name – is Gaelic for "the little lady of the islands". *Te
bheag* – "the wee one" – is a familiar term of affection among
Gaelic speakers, and it also puns on the Gaelic for a large Scotch:
te mhor ("a big one"). The brand was first created in 1976, with the
label partly in English, but a local bard remarked that "this whisky
is greatly improved in flavour by having Gaelic on the label", so
now the packaging is written entirely in Gaelic.

Praban na Linne is based at Isle Ornsay on the Isle of Skye, the
home of its owner, Sir Iain Noble. Isle Ornsay (*Eilean Iarmain*, to
give the place its correct Gaelic name) was an important fishing
harbour until the railway reached Mallaig on the mainland, and it
is still a popular anchorage. A fishing boat is depicted on Te
Bheag's label.

The brand was launched by Sir Iain Noble expressly to
strengthen the local economy and to promote the Gaelic language.
It has been most successful, and is highly regarded in Scotland,
especially in its natural marketplace, the Western Isles. It is also
becoming popular in France (half the output now goes to Paris)
and Nova Scotia, Canada, where there is still a sizeable Gaelic-
speaking community. It is also supplied to the British embassies in
both Washington and Paris (*see also* POIT DHUBH).

Tobermory

Category: Vatted Malt **Owner:** *Burn Stewart Distillers, East Kilbride*

Tobermory often appears on stock lists as a single malt, and the
confusion is understandable (*see* LEDAIG [malt]). In fact, it has been
a vatted malt since 1979, although the current owners of the
distillery now issue it as a single, produced from unpeated malt.

Tribute

Category: Standard and De Luxe Blend **Owner:** *William Lundie and
Co, Glasgow*

This blend is sold in the Far East (*see* LISMORE).

Ultima

Category: Super-De Luxe Blend **Licensee:** *Justerini & Brooks,
London* **Owner:** *Diageo plc*

Launched in 1994 to commemorate the 500th anniversary of the first mention of whisky, Ultima is a blend of every available Scotch whisky, both malt and grain – 128 in all! Even in 1994, there were only ninety-eight operating distilleries; the remaining thirty are either mothballed or dismantled. So some of the fillings in this blend are extremely rare.

Union Glen
Category: Secondary Blend **Licensee:** *The Bennachie Whisky Co, Inverurie, Aberdeen* **Owner:** *International Multibrand Products, Keith, Aberdeenshire*

(*see* BENNACHIE) Popular in pubs and clubs in northern Aberdeenshire, this is a low-priced blend designed for mixing. Its label is decorated with an old photograph of the top of Union Street, the principal street in Aberdeen.

Usher's Green Stripe
Category: Standard Blend **Licensee:** *Andrew Usher & Co, Edinburgh* **Owner:** *Diageo plc*

Andrew Usher II is generally credited with being the first blender of malt and grain whiskies. His father, Andrew Usher I, was born in the Borders in 1782, and set up as a wine and spirits merchant in Edinburgh in 1813. By the early 1820s, he was the agent for The Glenlivet, the best-known whisky at that time, and by 1840, it was recorded that "Messrs Usher controlled the whole output of the famous Glenlivet Distillery". His principal market remained local until the middle of the century, although he was selling Glenlivet in London by 1844. In 1845, he took his sons, Andrew II and John, into the business.

Andrew Usher II turned his hand to vatting together malt whiskies of different ages in 1853, in response to an Act which allowed vatting under bond (*i.e.* before tax was paid). Family tradition maintains that it was Andrew's mother, Margaret Balmer, who taught him the art of blending whiskies; she had developed an expertise in making and mixing cordials. The result was Usher's Old Vatted Glenlivet (OVG). Later on, this became an extremely popular blend, and remained available until the 1920s.

Gladstone's Spirits Act of 1860 extended the provisions of 1853 to allow the blending of malt and grain whiskies before duty was paid, and thus made it possible to produce blended whisky in quantity.

The Ushers had purchased Glen Sciennes Lowland Malt Distillery in 1859 (they renamed it Edinburgh Distillery); before long, the firm built extensive warehousing nearby at St Leonard's, including the largest maturation warehouse in the world at that time, some 150 yards long. So when blended whisky began to supersede brandy in popularity in the early 1880s, the Ushers were ready to take the initiative. They rapidly developed their export trade, which had been growing steadily since the mid-1850s, and by 1910, the *Illustrated London News* recorded that "They are represented by leading firms all over the world, and their organisation is so complete that in every important centre in practically every country, the foremost houses are closely identified with Messrs Ushers' interests."

Both the Usher brothers were great benefactors of the City of Edinburgh. Andrew endowed "the finest concert hall in Great Britain", the Usher Hall, with £100,000 in 1896. Meanwhile, John built the Usher Institute for Public Health – a medical research laboratory – for the university, and was created a baronet in 1900.

In 1919, Andrew Usher & Co was acquired by DCL through its subsidiary, the distinguished firm of J&G Stewart (*see* As We Get It). Green Stripe's main market today is in South America, and it is the leading brand in Venezuela (which imports it in bulk). It also goes to the USA, (in bulk), to Canada, France, and South Africa.

VAT 69

Category: Standard Blend Licensee: William Sanderson & Son, South Queensferry Owner: Diageo plc

Leith-born William Sanderson set up as a "manufacturer [*i.e.* blender] of wines and cordials" in 1863, aged twenty-four. He was one of the first to sell his own blends of malt and grain whiskies. VAT 69 is not the Pope's telephone number, as is often suggested by dullards: the true story is that Sanderson created 100 different blends, and in July 1882, he invited a group of knowledgeable friends and colleagues from the whisky trade to sample them and name their favourite. The unanimous choice was sample ("vatting") number 69; as no one suggested anything else, the name stuck.

In 1914, quantities of the blend accompanied Sir Ernest Shackleton on the Imperial Trans-Antarctic Expedition – Sir Ernest promising that it would be "used for medicinal emergencies and for feast days in the Antarctic". Again in 1921, stocks accompanied Shackleton's third expedition, and this time he wrote: "It has been used on the trip on Saturday nights when the naval toast of 'sweethearts and wives' is drunk, and has been greatly appreciated by the members of the expedition."

The business was run by the founder's son and grandson until 1935, when it merged with Booth's, the London gin distiller. This partnership was short-lived, however, since both companies joined DCL two years later. For the past ten years, VAT 69 has remained about tenth in the list of best-selling whiskies in the world. It deserves a revival in the UK.

Johnnie Walker

Category: Standard, Premium, De Luxe Blends; Vatted Malt Licensee: John Walker & Sons, Kilmarnock, Ayrshire Owner: Diageo plc

Perhaps no whisky company has such a distinguished record as Johnnie Walker. The company which is now a household name across the world was established in Kilmarnock, Ayrshire, in 1820, as a general grocer.

John Walker was born in 1805, the son of a dairy farmer, outside Kilmarnock. His father died in 1819; the farm was sold and yielded the handsome sum of £417. The executors invested the money in a grocer's shop in Kilmarnock – a small industrial town which had nearly doubled its population between 1801 and 1820 – and the shop sold teas, spices, dried fruits, household goods, wine, and whisky.

The business was nearly ruined in 1852 by a terrible flood, and four years later, John's son, Alexander (aged twenty) joined the firm. John Walker himself died in 1857.

Alexander immediately expanded into wholesale trading and focused on whisky; by the time of his death in 1889, he had transformed the small shop into an international whisky business. His principal vehicle was Walker's Old Highland Whisky, copyrighted in 1867 and trademarked (when the laws changed) in 1876. This became known as "Walker's Kilmarnock Whisky". From early on, he attached his label at a slant – now a characteristic of the Johnnie Walker brands – and from the late 1870s he was using the (at the time, innovative) square rectangular bottle, another of the brand's characteristics that has remained.

During the 1880s, Alexander brought his three sons, Jack, George Paterson, and Alexander II, into the business. Jack died young in Australia, which had already been established as a major market for the brand; it won top awards at Sydney (1880), Melbourne (1881), Adelaide (1887), and Dunedin (1890). George Paterson Walker succeeded him in Australia, and then took over the running of the London office (which had been opened in 1880). Meanwhile, Alexander II concentrated on the blending side in Kilmarnock. His work still influences the company's blending practice today. In 1894, the company acquired Cardhu Distillery (*see* CARDHU).

In 1909, the brothers introduced the now-famous Black and Red Label brands. Black Label was the original Walker's Old Highland Whisky, and was one of the first to carry an age statement on the label (12 Years Old). At the same time, the familiar striding figure of a pawky Regency buck was drawn by a well-known cartoonist named Tom Browne; it recalled the 1820s, when the firm was founded.

Around the same time, James Stevenson, a director of the company, suggested the slogan "Born 1820 – Still Going Strong". Over the years, the figure has been reinterpreted by several leading artists, most recently in 1996 by Michael Peters OBE.

Stevenson was a superb administrator. During the First World War, he and Alec Walker showed great ability in the Ministry of Munitions, where they supervised the production of ammunition. Walker was knighted for his services and Stevenson was made a baronet, and later, a peer.

By this time, John Walker & Sons was one of the "Big Three" whisky companies (the others being Dewars and Buchanans). The company went public in 1923 and joined DCL after protracted negotiations two years later.

The brand continued to grow worldwide, and the facilities at Kilmarnock were dramatically expanded during the 1930s. Johnnie Walker was Winston Churchill's favourite whisky, and no doubt inspired his famous memo at the end of the Second World War, warning against depriving the Scotch whisky industry of its supplies of barley. Shortly after the war, Red Label emerged as the world's leading whisky brand, and sales increased fivefold by 1955. Johnnie Walker & Co was awarded one of the first Queen's Awards for Export Achievement in 1966. In 1977, Red Label had to be withdrawn from the UK market due to EC rules (see JOHN BARR), but it is now available again.

The Johnnie Walker expressions have done uniquely well in recent International Wine & Spirit Competition awards; both Red and Black Labels won gold medals in 1996 (Black Label had won "Best Blended Whisky" in 1993) and Blue Label won "Best Blend" in 1993.

Wallace

Category: Malt Whisky Liqueur Licensee: The Wallace Malt Liqueur Co, Deanston, Perthshire Owner: Burn Stewart Distillers, East Kilbride

William Wallace of Elderslie began the Scottish War of Independence when he killed the English sheriff of Clydesdale in May 1297. In the previous year, King Edward of England had seized the Scottish throne and installed a governor. Discontent was widespread. Wallace's significance is that he marshalled the opposition to the English king, and in doing so, became a legend.

In September 1297, with a raggle-taggle army, he defeated the mailed chivalry of England at the Battle of Stirling Bridge. For eight months he was "Guardian" of Scotland, and his leadership and infectious courage inspired love, unity, and sacrifice in the Scottish people. Alas, he was betrayed in August 1305, and taken to London, where he was hanged, drawn, and quartered.

Wallace Liqueur first appeared in 1995, shortly after the phenomenally successful film about William Wallace, *Braveheart*. Unlike some other whisky liqueurs, its base is pure malt whisky, from Deanston Distillery, which is located only a few miles from Stirling Bridge.

White & Gold

Category: Standard Blend Licensee: Alistair Graham, Leith Owner: Glenmorangie plc, Broxburn, West Lothian

(see HIGHLAND QUEEN, JAMES MARTIN'S) Alistair Graham was an early blender. He was also reputed to be an obsessive experimenter who travelled the length and breadth of Scotland visiting distilleries and buying fillings.

White Heather

Category: Standard Blend Licensee: White Heather Distillers Owner: Chivas Bros Campbell Distillers, Brentford, Middlesex

This brand is a running-mate to Campbell Distillers' successful Clan Campbell brands and, like the latter, does especially well in France, where it is distributed by Campbell's owner, Pernod Ricard. It also sells well in Australia and Uruguay.

White Horse

Category: Standard Blend **Licensee:** *White Horse Distillers, Edinburgh* **Owner:** *Diageo plc*

White Horse was first created in 1890, on Islay, by the owner of Lagavulin Distillery, J.L. Mackie & Co. The distillery is now licensed to its famous creature. J.L. Mackie was one of the few heads of whisky firms in the 1880s to have learned distilling (at Lagavulin), and he named his brand after a tavern in Edinburgh's Canongate. The inn had served as an informal officers' mess during Bonnie Prince Charlie's occupation of Edinburgh in 1745; twenty years on, Dr Johnson arrived there off the London stagecoach to be met by James Boswell, who hurried him away.

The name is interesting. A white horse was the heraldic crest of the House of Hanover, so the pub sign may well have been adopted to display political loyalty. Tradition has it, however, that the hostelry was named for a real horse, owned by the publican, which won a race on Leith Sands, saving its owner from bankruptcy.

J.L. Mackie brought his nephew, Peter, into the business in 1878, and was succeeded by him as senior partner in 1890. Peter Mackie was one of the leading characters of his day in the whisky trade. He was described as "one-third genius, one-third megalomaniac and one third eccentric". He was known as "restless Peter" and met all counsels of caution with the words "nothing is impossible" – the phrase became a by-word within the company. He was an acknowledged authority on shooting, and wrote *The Keeper's Book*, a seminal work on the subject. Mackie was also an ardent Conservative (although he was made a baronet by a Liberal Prime Minister in 1920), and he was the outspoken champion of several good causes, not least that of allowing whisky to mature.

By the outbreak of the Great War, White Horse was the favourite of many army messes and had achieved a strong position in both the home and export markets. In 1926, the firm was the first to introduce the screw-cap, an innovation which took the marketplace by storm and doubled sales of the brand in six months.

Today, White Horse sells about two million cases per annum in 100 countries throughout the world, and rates within the top ten best-sellers. It is currently rated number one in the important Japanese market, and its other main markets are South Africa (where it was formerly number one), Chile, and Portugal. It is rated number two in the UK mid-market, but its sales are almost all through the off-trade.

Whyte & Mackay

Category: Standard & De Luxe Blends **Owner:** *Whyte & Mackay Ltd, Glasgow*

Charles Whyte & James Mackay joined the firm of Allan & Poynter (General Merchants and Warehousemen, founded in Glasgow in 1844) in 1875, and in 1881 successfully bid for the wine and spirits division of this business, naming it Whyte & Mackay. They began to blend whisky in 1896, and by the following year were advertising Whyte & Mackay whisky in Western Australia.

The firm became a private limited company at the end of the First World War, and the founding partners died in 1919 and 1921. In 1926, the company was reconstructed with their sons, Hartley Whyte and William Mackay, as directors. In 1935, when William Mackay left the board, the Whytes took full control of the company.

During the 1930s the company developed a strong export market, particularly in North America, South Africa, and New Zealand. After the war, it concentrated on the UK market with considerable success.

In 1960, Whyte & Mackay merged with Mackenzie Brothers, owners of Dalmore Distillery, and three years later acquired its English distributor, Jarvis Halliday & Co. The same year, Whyte & Mackay pioneered a plastic screw-cap which doubled as a measure or small cup; in 1963, the firm introduced the forty-ounce bottle size, which has since become standard in bars. Such moves have combined with soccer and golf promotions and widespread advertising to make it the best-selling brand in the massive Glasgow market – a position it holds today.

In 1972, the company was taken over by Sir Hugh Fraser's Scottish & Universal Investments, which bought Fettercairn and Tomintoul Distilleries the following year. Following rulings against DCL in 1986, Whyte & Mackay acquired worldwide ownership of The Claymore, John Barr, Stewart's Finest Old, Jamie Stuart, and Old Mull, and UK domestic rights to Haig, The Real Mackenzie, The Buchanan Blend, and Crawford's 3 and 5 Star. In 1988, the established bottling and blending company, William Muir (Bond 9) of Leith, was also acquired by Whyte & Mackay.

In 1990, Whyte & Mackay was bought by Gallaher, a wholly owned subsidiary of American Brands, which had long been the company's US agent through another subsidiary, Jim Beam Brands (JBB). The following year, the company attempted to take over the Invergordon Distillers. The bid succeeded in 1993, with the result that the two companies merged. In 1995, American Brands changed its name to that of its most famous product, and ownership of Whyte & Mackay/Invergordon came under JBB (Northern Europe). Following a management buy-out in 2002 (for £209 million), the company became Kyndal Ltd, but reverted to "Whyte & Mackay" again the following year.

Whyte & Mackay Special Reserve incorporates about thirty-five malts and employs the admirable but uncommon practice of vatting the malts and grains separately in sherry butts for some months before they are blended. The blend itself is then returned to cask for a second period of marrying – a fact that the company's advertising made much of for almost two decades, and which it maintains contributes to the whisky's "smooth taste and texture". The company's master blender, Richard Paterson, is an acknowledged expert in this field. Among the world's top fifteen best-selling brands, it consistently ranks number five in export markets.

William & Mary

Category: Premium Blend Owner: Edwin Cheshire, Stansted, Essex

This brand was first produced in 1988 to mark the tercentenary of the accession to the throne of William of Orange and his queen, Mary Stuart. The label depicts the Dutch and British flags (*see also* FIRST LORD).

Wright and Greig

*Category: Standard Blend **Licensee:** Wright and Greig*
***Owner:** Diageo plc*

In the late nineteenth century Wright and Greig was one of the leading whisky houses in Glasgow. They were brokers, blenders, and owners of Dallas Dhu Distillery, which they built in 1899–1900. The firm joined the DCL in 1927. The blend which perpetuates the firm's name is sold only in export markets.

Yellow Label

*Category: Standard Blend **Licensee:** John Robertson & Son*
***Owner:** Diageo plc*

The firm originated in Dundee in 1827, and moved to Leith upon joining DCL in 1915. Yellow Label is available in small quantities in the UK, and is exported to Spain.

Ye Monks

*Category: Standard Blend **Licensee:** Donald Fisher & Co,*
*Edinburgh **Owner:** Diageo plc*

Ye Whisky of Ye Monks was registered in 1898. The name makes reference to the belief that whisky was introduced to Scotland by Irish monks (in Ireland, it is believed that the art of distilling was brought by St Patrick after his sojourn in southern Scotland!). As we have seen, the first written reference to whisky was in an Exchequer Roll of 1494, in which King James IV ordered eight bolls of malt (just over 500 kilograms) from Friar John Corr, "wherewith to make *aqua vitae*".

According to a history of the firm, Ye Monks owes its origin to the Anglo-Indian president of the wine committee of an exclusive club in India, who had been deputed to select a whisky which would satisfy the discerning tastes of the members. The vatting selected "embraced the makes of nearly a score of distilleries, and the components and ages have been strictly adhered to ever since".

Donald Fisher, who died in 1915, has been described as "one of the pioneers of the Scotch whisky trade". His success was based upon his understanding of the value of using mature whisky in blending long before the Immature Spirits Act required a minimum three years, maturation. It was said that his whiskies were "contained in sherry casks imported direct from the bodegas in Spain, where they have contained fine old soleras and which give exceeding mellowness which is characteristic of Donald Fisher's whiskies".

His company was purchased by DCL in 1936. Ye Monks was packaged in handmade stone jars, and this became its trademark. It was originally a de luxe blend, known throughout the world, and sold for export only (mainly in South and Central America, where it is still a major brand). The company was awarded the Queen's Award for Export Achievement in 1982.

Appendices

Tasting notes

Tasting notes should follow the tasting procedure outlined in the introduction (pages 29–33), *i.e.:*

Whisky (age, strength, bottler)
Date (time and location of tasting)
Appearance (colour, clarity)
Aroma (natural strength)
Intensity of aroma
Complexity of aroma
Nose-feel (prickle, warming, drying, etc).
Notes on aroma*
Aroma (reduced strength)
Notes on aroma*
Development of aroma after ten, twenty minutes
Flavour
Mouth-feel (astringent, viscous, smooth, cloying, etc).
Primary taste (sweet, sour, salty, bitter)
Notes on flavour
Development
Finish
Score 1–10

* There is no fixed vocabulary for describing smell, and the memories and associations triggered by smell are born of personal experience. However, I would suggest that there are eight cardinal aromatic groups to be found in Scotch whisky. These can each be expanded into sub-groups, called "second-tier terms", and each of the sub-groups further expanded into "third-tier terms". There is not room to list the latter, but, for example, the third-tier terms for "cooked mash" include porridge, draff (lees), cooked maize, and hen's mash; those for "fragrant" include perfume, fabric softener, barber's shop, carnations, coconut, lavender. Many of the descriptors that you will use to describe the scent of a whisky are found within the third tier.

It goes without saying that not all the cardinal aromatic groups will be represented in every sample of Scotch whisky.

Cereal – cooked mash, cooked vegetables, malty, husky, yeasty
Fruity (estery) – citrus/fresh fruit, cooked fruit, dried fruit, solvent
Floral (aldehydic) – fragrant, greenhouses, leafy, hay-like
Peaty (phenolic) – medicinal, smoky, kippery, mossy
Feinty – honey, leather, tobacco, sweat, plastic
Sulphury – vegetative, coal-gas, rubbery, sandy
Woody – new wood, old wood, vanilla, toasted
Winey – sherried, nutty, chocolatey

Visiting distilleries

Just as a touring holiday in France would be incomplete without a visit to a vineyard or château, visits to distilleries have become an essential part of a holiday in Scotland. They are rewarding experiences: the distilleries are often picturesque and their situations delightful; the tours are often free of charge and conclude with a free tasting. And, since every distillery is different, the comparisons are fascinating. Visiting distilleries is a relatively recent phenomenon, associated with the massive growth in interest in malt whisky during the last decade. Many distilleries are now equipped with extensive facilities for visitors: often with a bar, coffee shop and gift shop; several with lecture theatres, video presentations, and full-blown restaurants. Others have no formal facilities, but all of the distilleries listed below welcome visitors and are happy to provide guided tours. Most are open between 10am and 4pm, but there are sometimes variations between summer and winter opening times, and some visits are by appointment only. It is wise to telephone in advance.

Aberfeldy Distillery *("Dewar's World of Whisky") Aberfeldy, Perthshire, tel: 44 (0)1887 820330*
Aberlour Distillery *Aberlour, Banffshire, tel: 44 (0)1340 871204*
Ardbeg Distillery *Port Ellen, Isle of Islay, tel: 44 (0)1496 302244*
Auchentoshan Distillery *Dalmuir, Clydebank, Dunbartonshire, tel: 44 (0)1389 878561*
Balblair Distillery *Edderton, Ross-shire, tel: 44 (0)1862 821273*
Ben Nevis Distillery *Lochy Bridge, Fort William, tel: 44 (0)1397 700200*
Benromach Distillery *Forres, Morayshire tel: 44 (0) 1309 675968*
Bladnoch Distillers *Wigtown, Wigtownshire 1988, tel: 44 (0)1888 402200*
Blair Athol Distillery *Pitlochry, Perthshire, tel: 44 (0)1796 472234*
Bowmore Distillery *Bowmore, Isle of Islay, Argyll, tel: 44 (0)1496 810671*
Bunnahabhain Distillery *Bunnahabhain, Isle of Islay, Argyll, tel: 44 (0)1496 840646*
Caol Ila Distillery *Port Askaig, Isle of Islay, Argyll, tel: 44 (0)1469 840207*
Cardhu Distillery *Knockando, Aberlour, Banffshire, tel: 44 (0)1340 810204*
Clynelish Distillery *Brora, Sutherland, tel: 44 (0)1408 621444*
Dallas Dhu Distillery *(preserved by Historic Scotland as a museum) Forres, Morayshire tel: 44 (0)1309 676548*
Dalwhinnie Distillery *Dalwhinnie, Inverness-shire, tel: 44 (0)1528 522208*

Edradour Distillery *Pitlochry, Perthshire,*
tel: 44 (0)1796 472095
Fettercairn Distillery *Distillery Road, Fettercairn,*
Kincardineshire, tel: 44 (0)1561 340205
Glendronach Distillery *Forgue, by Huntly, Aberdeenshire,*
tel: 44 (0)1466 730202
Glenfarclas Distillery *Ballindalloch, Banffshire,*
tel: 44 (0)1807 500257
Glenfiddich Distillery *Dufftown, Keith, Banffshire,*
tel: 44 (0)1340 820373
Glengoyne Distillery *Dumgoyne, Stirlingshire,*
tel: 44 (0)1360 550254
Glen Grant Distillery *Rothes, by Aberlour, Banffshire,*
tel: 44 (0)1340 831413
Glen Keith Distillery *Station Road, Keith, Banffshire,*
tel: 44 (0)154 278 3044
Glenkinchie Distillery *Pencaitland, Nr Tranent, East Lothian,*
tel: 44 (0)1875 340451
The Glenlivet Distillery *Glenlivet, Ballindalloch, Banffshire,*
tel: 44 (0)1542 783220
Glenmorangie Distillery *Tain, Ross-shire,*
tel: 44 (0)1862 892477
Glen Ord Distillery *Muir of Ord, Ross-shire,*
tel: 44 (0)1463 870421
Glenturret Distillery *("The Famous Grouse Experience") The*
Hosh, Crieff, Perthshire, tel: 44 (0)1764 656565
Highland Park Distillery *Holm Road, Kirkwall, Orkney,*
tel: 44 (0)1856 874619
Isle of Arran Distillery *Lochranza, Isle of Arran,*
tel: 44 (0)1770 830264
Isle of Jura Distillery *Craighouse, Isle of Jura, Argyll,*
tel: 44 (0)1496 820240
Lagavulin Distillery *Port Ellen, Isle of Islay, Argyll,*
tel: 44 (0)1496 302400
Laphroaig Distillery *Port Ellen, Isle of Islay, Argyll,*
tel: 44 (0)1496 302418
The Macallan Distillery *Craigellachie, Aberlour, Banffshire,*
tel: 44 (0)1340 871471
Oban Distillery *Stafford Street, Oban, Argyll,*
tel: 44 (0)1631 564262
Pulteney Distillery *Huddart Street, Wick, Caithness,*
tel: 44 (0)1955 602371
Royal Lochnagar Distillery *Crathie, Ballater, Aberdeenshire,*
tel: 44 (0)1339 742273
The Speyside Cooperage *Craigellachie, Banffshire*
tel: 44 (0)1340 871108
The largest independent cooperage in the country; displays on
cask history; video presentation; viewing gallery overlooking the
coopers at work; shop; tea room.

Strathisla Distillery *Seafield Avenue, Keith, Banffshire,*
tel: 44 (0)154 278 3044
Talisker Distillery *Carbost, Isle of Skye, tel: 44 (0)1478 640203*
Tobermory Distillery *Main Street, Tobermory, Isle of Mull,*
tel: 44 (0) 1688 302647
Tullibardine Distillery *(extensive visitor facilities will open*
2004) Blackford, Perthshire PH4 1QG tel: 44(0)1764 682252

VISITOR CENTRES
The Scotch Whisky Heritage Centre
Castlehill, Royal Mile, Edinburgh, tel: 44 (0)131 220 0441
The Centre is close to Edinburgh Castle, and the "experience"
includes time-travel in a motoried half-barrel past various tableaux
depicting key events in the history of Scotch whisky (commentary
in English, Dutch, French, German, Italian, Japanese, and Spanish).

There is also an A/V presentation, a model of Tormore
Distillery and lectures on making whisky and blending. A shop
sells a variety of malts.

THE MALT WHISKY TRAIL
A signposted tour on Speyside guides the visitor to seven
distilleries, all with visitor facilities. The trail is about seventy miles
long and its member distilleries include: Glenfarclas, Glenfiddich,
Glen Grant, The Glenlivet, Strathisla, Tamdhu, and Tamnavulin.

Whisky societies

The Scotch Whisky Association (SWA)
20 Atholl Crescent, Edinburgh EH3 8HF, tel: 44 (0)131 229 4383
Established in 1942 by the leading companies in the industry to
protect and promote the interests of the Scotch whisky industry
worldwide.

The SWA has a secretariat of full-time staff, operating from
offices in Edinburgh and London, headed by the director general
Hugh Morison. It is governed and its activities are determined by a
council of eighteen, drawn from the member companies; all the
leading companies in the industry are represented. The council is
supported by several committees and working parties which
examine and progress specific areas and issues.

The Keepers of the Quaich
Burke Lodge, 20 London End, Beaconsfield, Bucks HP9 2JH,
tel: 44 (0)1494 670 035
Although it is of relatively recent foundation (1988), The Keepers of
the Quaich is the most prestigious and exclusive whisky society in
the world. It was established by some of the Scotch whisky
industry's leading companies (including United Distillers, Allied

Distillers, Justerini & Brooks, Highland Distilleries, and Chivas/Glenlivet) to honour those who have contributed significantly to the prestige and success of Scotch whisky worldwide, as well as to advance the standing and reputation of the Scotch whisky industry and the hospitable traditions of Scotland.

The society has just over 500 members in thirty-eight countries (only about half the membership is British). Its current grand master is Lord Macfarlane of Bearsden, and its patrons include the Dukes of Atholl and Argyll, and the Earls of Erroll, Elgin & Kincardine, and Mansfield. Its headquarters are at Blair Castle, the magnificent seat of the Duke of Atholl, where splendid banquets are held biannually.

The Scotch Malt Whisky Society (SMWS)

The Vaults, 87 St Giles Street, Leith, Edinburgh EH6 6BZ, tel: 44 (0)131 554 3451 and 19 Greville Street, London EC1N 8SQ, tel: 44 (0)171 831 4447

SMWS grew out of the enthusiasm for cask-strength malt whisky of a handful of connoisseurs in Edinburgh. It was established in 1983, and now has a worldwide membership of over 20,000. The society selects casks and bottles their contents without chill-filtering or reduction, so that the individual characteristics of the cask and the whisky can be appreciated. Although available bottlings vary, the society has bottled a range of ages from over 100 distilleries. Members have the use of splendid accommodation at the Vaults, Leith (the old port of Edinburgh), and, since 1999, in the City of London. There is a quarterly newsletter and seasonal "Bottlings" catalogue, listing whiskies currently available (usually twenty to thirty at a time).

Independent bottlers and specialist shops

The following firms offer mail-order services, worldwide – or wherever they are allowed to export. Export and import regulations, excise duties, and taxes are complex and change from time to time, so customers wishing to order by post should check their local regulations and speak to the individual merchant.

The Adelphi Distillery

3 Gloucester Lane, Edinburgh, tel: 44 (0)131 226 6670

The original Adelphi was one of the largest distilleries in Scotland, and stood in the heart of Glasgow. It closed down in 1902, but the name was revived in 1993 by the great-grandson of its last owner, James Walker, to select and bottle a small number of individual casks of fine malt whisky at full strength.

William Cadenhead

172 Canongate, Royal Mile, Edinburgh, tel: 44 (0)131 556 5864

Established in Aberdeen in 1842 and now based in Campbeltown (with a shop in Edinburgh's old town, and one in Covent Garden, London), Cadenhead is Scotland's oldest firm of independent bottlers. The business is owned by J&A Mitchell, who also own Springbank Distillery. Under their own-label, they bottle a range of malts at cask and reduced strength.

Gordon & MacPhail

George House, Boroughbriggs Road, Elgin, Morayshire, tel: 44 (0)1343 545 111

Founded in 1896, and still family owned and managed, Gordon & MacPhail offers the largest selection of whiskies in the world for sale in its shop in Elgin (about 500 brands and expressions). The company has also been buying casks of malt whisky direct from distilleries, and warehousing and bottling these itself since the turn of the century. In 1992, Gordon & Macphail purchased Benromach Distillery, which resumed production in 1999. The Connoisseur's Choice range of about 50 single malts, some more than 30 years old, is exemplary.

Loch Fyne Whiskies

Inveraray, Argyll, tel: 44 (0)1499 302219

Founded in 1992 by Richard Joynson, a local fish farmer, and Lyndsay Shearer, Loch Fyne is now among the largest UK mail-order firms for whisky. It offers almost as many whiskies as Gordon & MacPhail, including vintage and miniature bottlings, books and whisky paraphernalia, and publishes an entertaining newsletter, *The Scotch Whisky Record*.

Murray McDavid Limited

56 Walton Street, London SW3 1RB tel: 44 (0) 171 823 7717

Established in 1995 by three men who can number nine generations of whisky expertise in their antecedents, Murray McDavid lists around ten single-cask bottlings at any time, with the list changing every couple of months. The casks selected tend to reflect the partners' fondness for coastal malts. Murray McDavid owns Bruichladdich Distillery.

Signatory Vintage Scotch Whisky Company

Elizafield, Bonnington Industrial Estate, Newhaven Road, Edinburgh, tel: 44 (0)131 555 4988

Founded in 1988 by Andrew and Brian Symington, the Signatory Vintage Scotch Whisky Company offers a changing list of about fifty single malts from currently operating, mothballed and silent distilleries. They are bottled both at cask strength and at forty-three per cent. Signatory owns Edradour Distillery.

Blackadder International

Logie Green, Larkhall ML9 1DA, tel: 44 (0)1435 883309

Established in 1995 by John Lamond and Robin Tucek (the authors of the *Malt Whisky File*), following their resignation from the Malt Whisky Association, Blackadder selects and bottles about fifty casks of malt whisky per annum, as well as offering other independent bottlings on its list. The company operates an extensive mail-order business as well as selling through agents in Europe.

The Master of Malt

96a Calverley Road, Tunbridge Wells, Kent, tel: 44 (0)1892 513295

The Master of Malt is both a specialist whisky shop – stocking over 200 malt whiskies, together with some blends, some Irish whiskeys, books, maps, and whisky paraphernalia – and an independent bottler, selecting and bottling some ten to fifteen casks per annum and operating a worldwide mail-order service.

The Vintage Malt Whisky Company

2 Stewart Street, Milngavie, Glasgow G62 6BW,
tel: 44 (0)1419 551700

Founded in 1992 by Brian Crook, a former sales executive with Morrison Bowmore, The Vintage Malt Whisky Company bottles a range of its own single and vatted malts mainly for overseas markets (*see* TANTALLAN, FINLAGGAN), and also offers a number of single-cask bottlings under the Cooper's Choice label.

The Whisky Shop

1 Fife Street, Dufftown, Speyside AB55 4AL,
tel: 44 (0)1340 821097

Fiona Murdoch's family have been in the wine and spirit trade for generations. She was brought up in Glenlivet, so it seemed logical to open a whisky shop in "The Capital of Distilling". This she did in 1997. It now stocks over 300 single malts, books, maps, and memorabilia, and provides visitors not only with regular in-store tastings but with detailed information about where to go and what to see locally. Mail-order service; also a fine selection of real ales from the growing number of small Scottish breweries.

World sales

The following tables are compiled from information supplied by HM Customs and Excise and from individual whisky companies. I am also indebted to analysis which has been carried out by The Scotch Whisky Association (*Statistical Report 2002*), Sutherland's Limited (*The Scotch Whisky Industry Review 2003* by Alan S. Gray), and *Impact International*. At the time of going to press, the most up-to-date figures are for 2002/3.

WORLD CONSUMPTION OF SCOTCH WHISKY

(millions of litres of pure alcohol [LPA])

	Exports	UK	*Misc	Total
1980	249.92	50.16	3.70	303.78
1981	244.24	47.71	3.88	295.83
1982	251.28	44.75	4.20	300.23
1983	227.84	44.48	4.50	276.82
1984	231.29	43.36	4.89	279.54
1985	225.89	46.15	5.15	277.19
1986	236.19	45.64	5.50	287.33
1987	240.17	44.60	5.98	290.75
1988	245.94	45.18	5.00	296.12
1989	242.49	3.03	5.00	290.52
1990	238.30	41.34	5.00	285.29
1991	227.75	38.26	n/a	270.01
1992	231.27	35.79	n/a	267.06
1993	242.80	37.55	n/a	282.25
1994	254.23	38.34	n/a	292.57
1995	261.86	31.01	n/a	292.87
1996	256.81	32.06	n/a	288.87
1997	276.13	31.93	n/a	307.33
1998	254.04	29.89	n/a	282.16
1999	266.63	30.36	n/a	296.99
2000	277.09	32.15	n/a	309.24
2001	283.63	31.73	n/a	315.36
2002	263.77	32.06	n/a	295.83

*Misc=miscellaneous; *i.e.* ships' stores, Channel Islands, etc.

SCOTCH WHISKY PRODUCTION

(millions of litres of pure alcohol [LPA])

31 Dec	Malt	Grain	Total
1990	192.82	235.94	428.76
1991	186.26	230.53	416.80
1992	166.50	216.98	383.50
1993	140.94	210.23	351.17
1994	146.42	208.49	354.91
1995	158.08	236.16	394.24
1996	170.13	258.96	429.10
1997	192.98	277.89	470.87
1998	184.61	257.53	442.15

TOP 20 MARKETS, 2002

(millions of litres of pure alcohol [LPA])

Volume		1997	1998	2002
1	France	34.38	35.48	41.47
2	UK	30.12	28.86	32.06
3	Spain	28.78	32.64	30.58
4	USA	37.96	33.79	30.3
5	S Korea	11.23	3.73	14.06
6	Japan	12.52	16.16	13.04
7	Germany	11.98	11.48	11.95
8	Greece	9.36	8.97	9.79
9	Thailand	10.42	3.42	9.05
10	Australia	7.71	6.89	8.83
11	Venezuela	7	8.5	8.29
12	Portugal	5.78	5.96	6.91
13	South Africa	8.04	6.5	6.29
14	Italy	6.28	6.4	6.19
15	Brazil	5.78	4.88	4.21
16	Canada	3.34	3.15	3.58
17	Netherlands	4.59	4.37	2.96
18	Taiwan	-	-	2.85
19	Turkey	-	-	2.33
20	Sweden	-	-	2.32

TOP 20 MARKETS, 2002
(value of whisky sold in pounds sterling)

Value		£m
1	USA	302.48
2	Spain	256.01
3	France	236.01
4	South Korea	195.83
5	Japan	115.35
6	German	96.18
7	Greece	91.86
8	Venezuela	75.09
9	Portugal	74.5
10	Taiwan	57.8
11	South Africa	51.23
12	Italy	45.19
13	Mexico	45.06
14	Australia	44.86
15	Thailand	37.59
16	Canada	34.39
17	Panama	31.47
18	Singapore	26.8
19	Sweden	25.1
20	Aruba	24.9

TOP SIX MALT WHISKIES IN 2002

	World sales	UK sales	Export sales
1	Glenfiddich	Glenfiddich	Glenfiddich
2	Glen Grant	Glenmorangie	Glen Grant
3	The Glenlivet	The Macallan	Cardhu
4	The Macallan	The Glenlivet	The Glenlivet
5	Glenmorangie	Laphroaig	The Macallan
6	Cardhu	Bowmore	Glenmorangie

TOP SIX BLENDED WHISKIES IN 2002

	World sales	UK sales	Export sales
1	Johnnie Walker Red Label	Bell's	JW or Johnnie Walker
2	J&B Rare	Famous Grouse	J&B Rare
3	Ballantine's	Teacher's	Ballantines
4	Grant's	Grant's	Dewar's
5	Dewar's	High Commissioner	Grant's
6	Johnnie Walker Black Label	Whyte & Mackay	JW or Johnnie Walker Black

Notes:

1 In 1997 more Scotch whisky was exported, and at higher value, than ever before in history.

2 In 1998, Johnnie Walker Red Label sold 7.4 million nine-litre cases; Johnnie Walker Black Label sold three million cases.
3 In the UK, Bell's sold 1.34 million cases, compared to The Famous Grouse's 995,000.

Collecting whiskies

Most of the "classic" whisky writers of the 1930s, 1940s, and 1950s recount stories of the occasional very old whiskies they have been privileged to sample, some of which were bottled in the nineteenth century. In more prosaic times, these old whiskies are rarely drunk, but they are more avidly collected today than ever before, and proudly displayed by their owners.

Which is not to say they are not drinkable. On the contrary. Michael Jackson, the contemporary whisky writer, pronounced samples salvaged from the wartime wreck *SS Politician* (*see* entry) to be excellent. I have tasted a Macallan that was distilled in 1887 and bottled in 1892 that was absolutely divine – fresh and complex with no undue woody notes – and blended whisky that was bottled during the war that was like old brandy.

It is said that, unlike wine, whisky does not continue to mature in bottle; however, it does change – and I believe for the better. There is something miraculous about a comestible surviving from another age.

Strange as it may seem, all the best collections of Scotch whisky are found abroad. Both the largest and best collections are in Italy, and the second largest is in Brazil. Some of the best collections in the UK are, of course, owned by the distilleries and brand-owners themselves, and they are always keen to acquire bottles for their archives.

Why collect older whiskies at all? To the discerning collector the attraction of old bottles of whisky depends upon: a) rarity, b) originality of bottle-shape and design, and c) the attractiveness of the label. The following are just a few of the features collectors look for with regard to age.

STOPPERS

These give one of the clearest indications of age. The earliest form of seal was melted wax, applied after the cork had been driven in. Often the wax was embossed with the producer or brand-name or badge. By the 1890s, lead or alloy capsules were used to protect the cork, and these, too, were often embossed. Some early bottles were fitted with a glass stopper rather than a cork: a slight indentation around the neck, beneath the capsule, shows where the edge of the stopper meets the neck of the bottle. The replaceable cork (one fitted with a wooden rim) was invented by William Manera Bergius in 1913, and first used by

Teacher for its Highland Cream brand, with the slogan "Bury the Corkscrew". In the early 1920s, spring-caps made of metal were adopted by some companies. The metal screw-cap was first introduced in 1926 by White Horse Distillers; the spring cap in 1928 by DCL; the Roll-on-Pilfer-Proof cap (which is standard today) in 1960.

BOTTLES

Early bottles were hand-blown or made in three pieces and formed while the glass was molten. Look for tiny bubbles and imperfections in the glass, which is usually clear, dark blue, or dark green in colour. Often these handmade bottles are not conventionally shaped, and some will not stand completely upright.

LABELS

The condition and legibility of the label is highly important from the collectors' point of view. Look for date, name of bottler, company name, crest, and logo, as well as brand-name. Some labels are very colourful, and exquisitely designed, sometimes with fanciful (often Highland) subjects; others, including many nineteenth-century malt bottlings are plain and restrained. Where the bottle is a single malt, look for the name of the distillery. "Liqueur Scotch Whisky", "Rare Old Scotch Whisky", etc. indicate that the whisky was moderately mature when bottled. Where blends are concerned, look for the words "Rare" or "Fine Old Blended": some of the malts used in such blends may have spent between five and twenty-five years in cask prior to blending.

AUCTION PRICES

Christie's held dedicated whisky sales in Glasgow between 1989 and 1998. Prior to this date, whisky was attached to wine sales. When they ceased this, their whisky consultant, Martin Green, moved to McTears auctioneers in Glasgow, and since 2000 McTears have held at least two whisky sales a year. Bonhams International Auctioneers also hold occasional whisky sales; I am their consultant. Some of the prices achieved have been impressive, and they have tended to increase over the past few years. Much depends upon the quality of the item, however.

Collections of whisky bottles are generally for display, not consumption, although some buy old and rare malts with a view to sharing them with friends or offering them for sale by the glass.

"Museum" collectors look for rarity, both in terms of age and "limited" or "commemorative" bottlings. Well-known brands tend to do better than obscure distilleries. The Macallan, for example, has consistently done well at auction, as have Springbank and the Islay malts. Connoisseurs look for original bottles, securely stoppered, with attractive labels in good condition. Miniatures, ceramic and commemorative bottlings have long been highly collectable.

"Consumer" collectors are concerned more with the age of the whisky itself, and consider a recent bottling of a very old whisky to be more "reliable" than a very old bottling. Where the latter is being sought, they will check the condition of capsule (cork, stopper, and leading) and the level of the contents, which indicates how much liquor has evaporated.

Selected bibliography

(* indicates leading titles)

Barnard, Alfred, *The Whisky Distilleries of the United Kingdom* (London, 1887; repr Newton Abbot, 1969; Edinburgh, 1987)*

Birnie, William, *The Distillation of Highland Malt Whisky* (Private, 1937 and 1964)

Brander, Michael, *The Original Scotch* (London, 1974)
— *A Guide to Scotch Whisky* (Edinburgh, 1975)
— *The Essential Guide to Scotch Whisky* (Edinburgh, 1990)

Bronfman, Samuel, *From Little Acorns, The Story of the Distillers Corporation – Seagram Limited* (Private, 1970)

Broom, David, *Whisky – A Connoisseur's Guide* (London, 1998)*

Brown, Gordon, *Classic Spirits of the World* (London, 1995)

Checkland, Olive, *Japanese Whisky, Scotch Blend* (Edinburgh,1998)

Bruce-Lockhart, Sir Robert, *Scotch* (London, 1951)*

Cooper, Derek, *A Taste of Scotch* (London, 1989)
— *The Little Book of Malt Whiskies* (Belfast, 1992)

Craig, Charles, *The Scotch Whisky Industry Record*, Dumbarton, 1994) *

Cribb, Stephen and Julie, *Whisky on the Rocks* (London, 1998)

Daiches, David, *Scotch Whisky* (London, 1969)*
— *A Wee Dram; Drinking Scenes from Scottish Literature* (London, 1990)

Distillers Company Limited, *DCL and Scotch Whisky* (London, 1961; numerous editions)

Dunnet, Alastair, *The Land of Scotch* (Edinburgh, 1953)

Gabanyi, Stefan, *Whisk(e)y* (New York, 1997)

Grey, Allan S., *The Scotch Whisky Industry Review*
    (Edinburgh; published annually)

Grindal, Richard, *The Spirit of Whisky* (London, 1992)

Gunn, Neil, *Whisky and Scotland* (London, 1935, repr 1990)*

Hills, Philip et al. *Scots on Scotch* (Edinburgh, 1991)

House, Jack, *Pride of Perth: The Story of Arthur Bell & Co*
    (London, 1976)

Jackson, Michael, *The World Guide to Whisky* (London, 1987)*
    — *The Malt Whisky Companion* (London, 1989; 4th Edition
    1999)*

Lamond, John and Tucek, Robin, *The Malt Whisky File*
    (Edinburgh, 1995)*

Laver, James, *The House of Haig* (Perth, 1958)

Macdonald, Aeneas, *Whisky* (Edinburgh, 1930)

McDowall, R.J.S., *The Whiskies of Scotland* (London, 1967)*

MacLean, Charles, *Malt Whisky* (London, 1997)
    — *Whisky: A Liquid History* (London, 2003)

MacNeill, F. Marian, *The Scots Cellar, Its Traditions and Lore*
    (Edinburgh, 1956)

Mantle, Jonathan, *The Ballantine's Story* (London, 1991)

Milroy, Wallace, *The Malt Whisky Almanac* (Moffat, 1986; 7th
    Edition, Glasgow, 1998)*

Milstead, David, *Bluff Your Way in Whisky* (London, 1991)*

Morrice, Philip, *Scotch, The Schweppes Guide to* (London,
    1983)*
    — *The Whisky Distilleries of Scotland and Ireland*
    (London, 1987)

Moss, Michael S. and Hume, John R. *The Making of Scotch
    Whisky – A History of the Scotch Whisky Distilling
    Industry* (Edinburgh, 1981)*

Murray, Jim, *Classic Blended Scotch* (London, 1999)

Nettleton, J.A., *The Manufacture of Scotch Whisky and Plain*
    (Aberdeen, 1913)*

Nown, Graham, *Malt Whisky* (London, 1997)

Pacult, F. Paul, *Kindred Spirits* (New York, 1997) *

Robb, J. Marshall, *Scotch Whisky, A Guide* (Edinburgh,
    1950)*

Ross, James, *Whisky* (London, 1970)

Scotch Whisky Association, *Scotch Whisky, Questions and
    Answers* (Edinburgh 1957, numerous reprints)

Skipworth, Mark, *The Scotch Whisky Book* (London, 1987)

Sillet, S.W., *Illicit Scotch* (Aberdeen, 1965)

Smith-Grant, Captain W., *Glenlivet: The Annals of the
    Distillery* (Private, 1924, repr 1959)

Spiller, Brian, *Cardhu, The World of Malt Whisky*
    (London, 1985)
    — DCL *Distillery Histories* (London, 1981)*

Steadman, Ralph, *Still Life with Bottle* (London, 1994)

Townsend, Brian, *Scotch Missed, The Lost Distilleries of Scotland* (Edinburgh, 1993)

Weir, Ronald B., *The History of the Distillers Company 1874–1926* (Oxford, 1995)

Wilson, Neil, *Scotch and Water: Islay, Jura, Mull, Skye* (Lockerbie, 1985; 3rd Edition, Glasgow 1998)*

Wilson, Ross, *Scotch Made Easy* (London, 1959)

— Scotch, *The Formative Years* (London, 1970)*

— Scotch, *Its History and Romance* (Newton Abbot, 1973)